Guide Library

Hillwood Museum
Washington, D.C.

THE NORDIC WAY

A Path to Baltic Equilibrium

THE NORDIC WAY

A Path to Baltic Equilibrium

by
Edward L. Killham

Foreword by
Max M. Kampelman

THE COMPASS PRESS
WASHINGTON, DC

This book was written with the support of a grant from the United States Institute of Peace. The opinions, findings, and conclusions or recommendations expressed herein are those of the author and do not necessarily reflect the views of the United States Institute of Peace.

Edited by Mellen Candage

Cover and illustrations designed by Anne Meagher-Cook

Typesetting and page design by Gary Roush

Printed (alk paper) and bound by Edwards Brothers, Ann Arbor, Michigan, USA

Library of Congress Cataloguing-in-Publication Data

Killham, Edward L., 1926-
    The Nordic Way: A Path to Baltic Equilibrium /
Edward L. Killham;
foreword by Max M. Kampelman.
    p. cm.
    Includes bibliographical references and index.
    ISBN 0-929590-12-0.—ISBN 0-929590-13-9 (pbk.)
    1. Scandinavia—Foreign Relations.
    2. Baltic Sea Region—Politics and Government.
    3. Neutrality—Scandinavia—History.
    4. Neutrality—Baltic Sea Region—History. I. Title.
    DL55.K54 1993
    327.48—dc20   92-46316
                                                 CIP

The Compass Press is an imprint of Howells House
Box 9546, Washington, DC 20016

"The world looks with admiration ... to Scandinavia where ... countries, without sacrificing their sovereignty, live united in their thought, in their economic practice and in their healthy way of life. From such fountains, new and brighter opportunities may come to all mankind."

— Winston S. Churchill,
accepting the 1953 Nobel Peace Prize for Literature.

Edward L. Killham, a career Foreign Service Officer with rank of Minister-Counselor, has had numerous diplomatic assignments in Eastern and Western Europe, in NATO Headquarters, and in arms control negotiations, including SALT, MBFR, and CSCE, where he served as Deputy Chairman of the U.S. Delegation in Madrid in 1982-83. A former jazz musician, he holds degrees from Northwestern, Harvard, and Columbia Universities and studied at the London School of Economics; he speaks French, Russian, and Danish. He is a member of the International Institute of Strategic Studies, the American Association for the Advancement of Slavic Studies and is a Councillor of The Atlantic Council. Since his retirement from the Foreign Service in 1987, he has served as an advisor to the United States Information Service, the Department of State, the Department of Defense, the Naval War College, and the U.S. Institute of Peace. He has published numerous articles in professional and news journals.

Scandinavia and the Baltic

Table of Contents

List of Maps

Foreword

Ed Killham's analysis of the delicate Nordic Balance and the role it has played in recent history is an excellent introduction to the study of Russian and Soviet policy in Scandinavia. The book focuses on the long history of mutual entanglement among the Slavs, Germans, and Nordic peoples in peace as well as in war and, in stimulating fashion, projects the likely course of future developments. Although not unfamiliar with the subject, I certainly learned a great deal from reading it. The book will fill an important need, and I am pleased to be part of it.

I noted with particular pleasure the importance the author has ascribed to the Conference on Security and Cooperation in Europe (CSCE) in shaping the remarkable developments in East-West relations over the past two decades. My own extensive experience with the process confirms the enormous importance all of the Nordic countries have given to the CSCE process. Collectively and individually, they have contributed in a major way to the task of improving security and human rights in Eastern Europe and in the former USSR. Mr. Killham served ably for a year as my chief deputy on the U.S. Delegation to the Madrid CSCE Review Conference. He has had ample exposure to the special demands and opportunities of the CSCE forum and speaks with authority.

The emergence of a new political and strategic balance in Northern Europe seems to me to be a logical consequence of an increasing awareness everywhere of how interdependent nations have become in the modern world. I have pointed out on a number of occasions that not only is necessity the mother of invention, but invention is in fact the mother of necessity. As a result, the enormous technological advances we have seen during the twentieth century demand that we human beings develop new ways to deal with one another politically. The world of politics must catch up with the integrated new world of science and technology.

Mankind's universal search for human dignity cannot be stopped by our too frequent failures to restrain the darker sides of our nature, but it can be delayed and even diverted from that high task. The Scandinavians profoundly share our commitment to the cause of human dignity and, for more than a century, have been more effective than most other people in working together in peace and harmony. It is altogether fitting, therefore, that we learn what we can from them in this field.

My own conviction is strong that open and free societies are essential for the preservation of international peace. The Nordic countries, among others, have given us good examples of how such societies can be developed. One can hope, therefore, that the obvious admiration of most Russians for their Scandinavian neighbors will assist the new Russia, which is now taking shape, to follow the Nordic example.

As for our own nation, although Americans and their leaders have made mistakes in their pursuit of a free and just world, we can be proud of what this nation has accomplished. By and large, American might has been on the side of right in the many conflicts the world has seen in the past 200 years.

In this context, Mr. Killham's book illuminates some of the less recognized features of today's strategic landscape. His study points the way to new opportunities as well as to new dangers for all of the nations involved in the evolving Nordic Balance, including the United States.

As a former senior U.S. diplomat, Mr. Killham served at the American Embassies in Moscow and Copenhagen, and he participated in a number of successful negotiations involving the former USSR. He also worked on the international staff of NATO in Brussels and served as the State Department Adviser at the U.S. Naval War College from 1983 to 1985. His extensive dealings with the principal players in the Nordic Balance would be difficult to match. Furthermore, Ed Killham has not relied solely on his own experience but has carefully studied the relevant literature and has conducted interviews with experts on the subject in the former USSR, in the Scandinavian countries, and in the United States. This book, the product of his endeavors, proves to be a most useful one, which I commend to all readers interested in European affairs.

— Max M. Kampelman

Preface

This book is the product of many influences, individual and institutional. Its genesis goes back to 1957 and my experiences as a young Foreign Service Officer in Moscow where, in the depths of the Cold War, I had an opportunity to study the Soviet Union first hand and to meet a number of Scandinavian diplomats assigned there. Further stimulating my interest in Northern Europe during the same period were brief but memorable visits to Finland and Denmark, highlighting the contrast between the Nordic and Slavic approaches to coping with the challenges of the post-war era.

That original stimulus was strengthened during the 1970s by an assignment to Copenhagen as chief of the political section in the American Embassy. There, three thoughtful and articulate Danes, Niels Jørgen Haagerup, Henning Gottlieb, and Peter Dyvig, share the responsibility for explaining to me the concept of the "Nordic Balance," a staple of political discussion throughout Scandinavia at that time, and a term widely used to refer to the special kind of equilibrium which developed in Scandinavia in the aftermath of World War II.

The "Nordic Balance" meant, essentially, that the North Atlantic Treaty Organization (NATO) membership of Norway, Denmark, and Iceland was balanced by Finland's special security relationship with the USSR, while Sweden's armed neutrality acted as a buffer between the Eastern and Western spheres of influence. Further, the concept embodied a tacit recognition by all parties concerned that this "Nordic Balance," if not the ideal situation for everyone, was at least stable and that any attempt to tilt the "balance" would be likely to meet a corresponding reaction from the other side. Ever since the foundation of the North Atlantic

Alliance in the late 1940s, that "balance" had been a constant concern of Scandinavians, whether they accepted the characterization or rejected it, as Finns regularly did. Strategic planners in the Soviet Union and the United States, as well as in Western Europe, also recognized the concept.

However, the term "Nordic Balance" was always to some extent a misnomer; it was neither exclusively Nordic nor really a balance, and it was resented by the Finns, who felt it implied that they were close to the Soviet camp. Nor does the phrase convey the relationships and decision-making process among the Nordic nations on security issues, which may have been more relevant to the Nordic equilibrium than the mere power equation. In this book, I have tried to accommodate these considerations with the phrase "the Nordic way," which I think conveys better the Nordic experience since World War II and the essence of the lessons to be learned.

When I finally had time to study the political and strategic situation in Scandinavia and the Baltic area in some depth, the United States Institute of Peace provided the financial support without which the work probably not have been undertaken. My wife, Lucy Killham, supplied the moral support and encouragement without which it would not have been completed.

Among the other individuals who were instrumental in guiding the work, none of whom should be held to account for its shortcomings, were a number of present and former officials of the U.S. Department of State: Max M. Kampelman; Richard Schifter; Herbert Capps; Ambassadors Charles Redman, James Goodby, and Richard T. Davies; and William Kushlis, Dennis Sandberg, Ward Thompson, and Robert Rinehart. Two former Foreign Service Officers, now on the staff of the Atlantic Institute, John A. Baker and Peter Swiers, offered helpful comments on the manuscript.

My former colleagues on the faculty of the U.S. Naval War College, John Hattendorf and George Bunn, provided timely counsel, as did Danish Ambassadors Peter Dyvig, now Denmark's Chief of Mission in Washington, and Rudolph Thorning-Peterson in Moscow. The view from Moscow was rounded out by Yuriy Davydov and Anatoliy Utkin of the Institute of the USA and Canada there.

The Washington correspondent for Oslo's *Aftenposten,* Per Egil Hegge, one of Scandinavia's best-informed Kremlin watchers, added insights into Russian diplomacy in the North, while Dr. John Rackauskas of the Lithuanian Research and Studies Center in Chicago helped toward a better understanding of the situation in the Baltic states.

In Helsinki, additional insight was offered by Jyrki Iivonen of the Finnish Institute of International Affairs; Jaako Iloniemi, a former Finnish Ambassador to the United States; Professor Raimo Väyrynen; and Pauli Järvenpää, who is currently Counselor of the Finnish Embassy in Washington. In Stockholm, my understanding of the Swedish view was improved considerably by discussions with Nils Gyldén at the Ministry of Defense, Hans Olsson at the Foreign Ministry, and Wilhelm Agrell of the University of Lund. Similar benefits were realized in Copenhagen in talks with Henning Gottlieb, now chairman of Denmark's Commission on Security and Disarmament, Hans Henrik Bruun and Christian Hoppe at the Foreign Ministry, and Klaus Carsten Pedersen of Det Udenrigspolitiske Selskab.

I am grateful to Gregory Flynn and Harley Balzer of Georgetown University, David Yost and Mikhail Tsypkin of the Naval Postgraduate School, and Robert Nurick of Rand Corporation for their comments on various drafts of the final study. I am also indebted to Trevor Gunn for permission to examine his April 1992 Ph.D. thesis on Swedish and Norwegian policies toward the USSR.

One final note: The terms "Nordic" and "Scandinavian" are, of course, not entirely synonymous. Nordic is the broader term, denoting a particular racial type associated with Northern Europe. Such people typically are tall and long-headed, with light skin and eyes. Scandinavian is a geographic and linguistic term, applied in the first instance to the Scandinavian peninsula and to the languages spoken there. However, all of the Nordic countries except Finland speak a Scandinavian tongue, and a good many Finns speak Swedish. In this book, accordingly, I have followed modern American usage, which rarely makes a distinction between the two words.

I

The Nordic Balance and the Nordic Way

As Bismarck pointed out, geography is the only permanent element of international relations. This fact of life can be fully appreciated in Scandinavia, which has been a strategic crossroads between East and West since the days of the Vikings. Until the twentieth century, conflicts in the Nordic area centered on rival claims in and around the Baltic, known in Scandinavian languages as the Eastern Sea (Østsoen). During World War I, the struggle between the British and Imperial German navies focused on the German effort to break out of its Baltic redoubt. That question was decided off the Danish peninsula of Jutland, leaving the vestiges of the German surface fleet which remained outside of the confined waters of the Baltic virtually impotent.

What has been called the High North came into its own during World War II, when Nazi control of the Baltic forced Russia's Western allies to support the Soviet military effort by shipping supplies to Murmansk via the Norwegian Sea. Western losses in shipping, equipment, and seamen were horrendous, but the U.S. and Britain persevered, landing significant quantities of materiel on the Arctic coast of the beleaguered Russian homeland.

The rapid disintegration of the wartime alliance between the Western Allies and the Soviet Union, already anticipated by American strategists in August 1944,[1] drew the attention of military planners to the significance of the trans-Arctic vector. The United States Army Air Corps and the American Embassy in Oslo recognized as early as the spring of 1945 the potentials and the pitfalls, respectively, of a military role in the High North: the Army saw the possible benefits of Allied bases there while the Embassy

1

foresaw, as would others later, the potentially damaging reactions to a U.S. military intrusion in the area.[2] Fortunately for the West, the Soviet Union, which had not fielded a strategic bomber force in World War II, was still tied to its traditional thinking, emphasizing the importance of land frontiers and massive ground forces rather than sea and air lines of communication.

The strategic importance of the Nordic area to the United States was formally recognized in a National Security Council report approved by President Truman on September 8, 1948:

> *The Scandinavian nations are strategically important both to the United States and the USSR. They lie astride the great circle air route between North America and the strategic heart of Western Russia, are midway on the air route between London and Moscow, and are in a position to control the exits from the Baltic and Barents seas. Domination of Scandinavia would provide the Soviets with advanced air, guided-missile and submarine bases, thus enabling them to advance their bomb line to the west, to threaten allied operations in the North Atlantic, and to form a protective shield against allied sea or air attack from the Northwest ...[3]*

As ballistic missile submarines joined bombers and land based missiles in the U.S. and Soviet strategic arsenals, the waters surrounding the High North also gained in significance. The geostrategic relevance to the West of the Danish presence on Greenland and the Faroe Islands, as well as Norway's sovereignty over Jan Mayen Island and the Svalbard archipelago, were underlined by the Soviet Union's military and naval concentrations on the Kola Peninsula. The United Kingdom, also concerned about security in the North, worked with the United States to include Denmark, Norway, and Iceland in the North Atlantic Treaty, signed in April 1949.

The growing appreciation of the military significance of the area over the next twenty years of the Cold War was accompanied by a growing awareness of the delicate political equilibrium in the area and of the sensitivities of the Nordic countries themselves. By the 1970s, Scandinavian scholars had begun to recognize and define the process by which Nordic countries were able to maintain stability and security in their strategically sensitive neighborhood during an era of international tensions and recurring crises. This process was reflected in the concept of a "Nordic Balance." This was usually defined as a tacit understanding among all concerned that the membership in NATO of Norway, Denmark, and Iceland was balanced by Finland's special security relationship with the USSR, while Sweden's armed neutrality served as a buffer between the Eastern and Western spheres of influence.

Arne Brundtland of Norway was apparently the first to use the term "Nordic Balance," but many others, such as Sweden's Nils Andrén, were quick to adopt it. The Finns firmly resisted the term (while not denying the equilibrium to which it referred) because it seemed to disparage their independence and relegate them to the status of a semi-satellite of the Soviet Union. Nor does the term translate easily into Russian. As the American scholar and diplomat Raymond Garthoff pointed out in an article which appeared in *World Politics* more than thirty years ago, the phrase "balance of power" is not normally found in the Russian lexicon. Moscow favors instead the concept "relationship of forces," which usually signifies an imbalance.[4]

Even in the 1970s, some skeptics cast doubt on the validity of the Nordic Balance concept, questioning whether it had any utility in predicting the likely behavior of its various components or even in analyzing that behavior after the event. In recent years, Brundtland himself has stepped back somewhat from his original highly structured vision of the Nordic Balance to suggest a much simplified, almost tautological, formulation. In this modernized version, he says, "The basic question is whether any of the Nordic countries, while pursuing their respective national policies, are influenced by the national security policy of another Nordic nation."[5]

Whatever the terminology, whether a balance, equilibrium, process, or merely the Nordic "way," it is quite obvious that all of the Nordic states have, in fact, paid careful attention to the impact their actions in national security matters might have on their neighbors. In 1977, for example, the Norwegian Government, in spite of domestic opposition, was contemplating the elimination of its ban against West German military exercises in Norway. During a visit to Oslo, Finland's President Urho Kekkonen stated that "it is not a matter of indifference to Finland who Norway will cooperate with militarily,"[6] and Finnish objections evidently tipped the balance against change. Similar, if less dramatic, instances have occurred with regularity. As Erling Bjøl expressed it, "That there is something called the 'Nordic Balance', slippery though its definition may be, seems to be a fact."[7]

In at least one case, the somewhat contrived "note crisis" of 1961, even the Soviet leadership recognized and accepted the prevailing balance in Scandinavia as a reality. At the time, President Kekkonen claimed to have persuaded Nikita Khrushchev that continued Soviet pressure on his country could, if it stimulated American counter-pressures on Norway and Denmark, reduce rather than improve the USSR's security.

Throughout the Cold War, the leaders of NATO's Scandinavian partners frequently invoked the Nordic Balance to resist NATO requests for increased military contributions to the Alliance. In addition, Denmark and Norway conditioned their membership in NATO on excluding nuclear weapons and the stationing of Allied troops on their territories in time of peace. Denmark was also careful to limit its naval operations in the Baltic to "defensive" or "non-threatening" activities, while Norway voluntarily limited its force deployments in the far North, where they might be considered provocative because of their proximity to the Kola Peninsula. Moreover, the Norwegian Government severely restricted the participation of West German forces in NATO maneuvers on Norwegian territory. Both Denmark and Norway, however, stipulated that they reserved the right to reverse their self-denying policies unilaterally, leaving the Soviet Union with no say in the matter.

Iceland, with its dependence on the fishing industry for its economic well-being and the distance which separates it from its fellow Scandinavians, may be regarded as more of an Atlantic than a Nordic country. However, it shares a common culture with its Scandinavian brethren as well as their general reluctance to take sides any more than is absolutely necessary in struggles between the superpowers. Only Iceland, among the three Nordic members of NATO, has had a Communist movement with serious pretensions to political influence.

For its part, Sweden invoked the Nordic Balance to justify a vigorous interpretation of Swedish neutrality. Swedish spokesmen were sometimes uncomfortable with the description of their international posture as neutral, which, they argued, applied only in case of war. Some of them were even more uncomfortable with the label "non-aligned" because the term had been associated in the past with such Third World "neutralists" as Nehru and Nkrumah. Accordingly, the Swedish scholar Nils Andrén suggested the term "not-aligned" to describe a policy designed to permit maintenance of the nation's neutrality in the future, if war should come. The "not-aligned" position was an expensive option for Sweden because it required this former "great power on the Baltic" to maintain a significant defense establishment as a base for eventual mobilization. The economic strains resulting from this defense posture led to domestic rumblings even before the Soviet collapse eroded the previously widespread domestic support for Sweden's go-it-alone policies.

Finland is, of course, a special case because of its proximity to Russia, its history as a part of Romanov holdings before the 1917 revolutions, its conflict with the Soviet Union in the "Winter War" of 1939-40, and its subsequent association with Nazi Germany during World War II. A series of postwar Finnish leaders, beginning with former Prime Minister and President J.K. Paasikivi, drew the necessary conclusions from their circumscribed position and observed a marked degree of deference toward Soviet wishes on foreign policy and military security issues. At the same time, Finland nimbly juggled its obligations under the Soviet-Finnish Treaty of Friendship, Cooperation, and Mutual Assistance (FCMA) and its economic and cultural ties with the West to maximize its political independence. It was not until January 1992 that Russia recognized, via an exchange of notes, that the treaty imposed on Finland in 1948 had ceased to exist.

Without explicitly accepting the notion of a Nordic Balance, the USSR attempted often during the postwar period to exploit the issue in order to limit the participation of the western Scandinavians in NATO as well as to constrain Sweden's freedom of action. Soviet policy makers evidently concluded early on that, while it was not entirely satisfactory, the *status quo* was acceptable as long as it did not shift farther toward the West. Much of their diplomatic and political activity over the years was therefore devoted to preventing such a shift from occurring.

During the 1960s, the Soviet Union's clear disapproval of Finnish membership in Nordek, a proposed Nordic economic union, did much to block Finland's participation and thus to sink the entire project. Soviet propagandists were active in the 1950s and 1960s in pushing the idea of the Baltic Sea as a "Zone of Peace." They were also the fervent supporters, if not the actual authors, of Finnish President Kekkonen's proposal to establish a Nordic Nuclear-Free Zone. Their definition of this zone did not, of course, include the Soviet Union's extensive military installations on the Kola Peninsula.

In addition to the geostrategic equilibrium which supported postwar Nordic stability, a common history and compatible social systems enhanced the distinctive Nordic way of dealing with security issues. The countries of Scandinavia are sometimes regarded as almost identical, and they do have a great many things in common, including their preference for a neutral stance in the world's power politics. Their languages, except for Finnish, are closely related, and they share a Lutheran religious heritage. Echoes of old disagreements give rise to occasional squabbles, but these rarely become serious and tend to be shelved in the face of challenges from outside Scandinavia.

The Nordic nations enjoy the benefits and frustrations of vigorous parliamentary democracy, with a large number of parties qualifying for seats in the legislatures. Representation extends from the far left (left of the orthodox Communists) to the quixotic right, but the overwhelming majority of parliamentarians fall into either a Social Democratic or a center-to-moderate right grouping. The Nordic people share, in addition, an inclination toward political compromise and an aversion to policies that will not command consensus. Scandinavian leaders may sometimes be hampered by the strong public preference for the broadest common denominator. The success of the Nordic people during this century in transforming themselves from poor peasant countries to sophisticated post-industrial societies has encouraged the preference for consensus.

Although three of the Nordic countries have reigning (but not ruling) monarchs, egalitarianism is the most characteristic element of political thought throughout Scandinavia. Closely linked with egalitarianism is a belief that violence, especially military violence, is a vestige of more primitive times and that civilized nations do not settle their differences on the battlefield. The Scandinavian preference for a non-confrontational approach at home goes hand in hand with their proclivity for seeking pacific resolutions to foreign policy and security problems. Their own experience as remarkably homogeneous societies makes it difficult for them to appreciate the national and racial passions which have driven other peoples to violence.

Cooperation, conciliation, and mutual accommodation are the primary virtues in Nordic political discourse. Given this underlying "ideology," it is not surprising that neutral and pacifist tendencies are very strong throughout Scandinavia, ranging from the muscular neutrality introduced by France's Marshal, Jean Bernadotte, who ruled Sweden as King Karl Johan XIV, to postures suggesting to others an inclination to turn the other cheek too willingly to aggressors.

Against the backdrop of the dramatic developments in Europe and the former Soviet Union in the last few years, the Nordic scene has received comparatively little attention recently outside the immediate area. The strategic landscape on which the Nordic countries established their postwar military and political postures has changed dramatically. It may be time, therefore, for scholars and diplomats with a view of the past and an eye to the future to review the roles of the Nordic players and their approach to regional stability and to consider the lessons that can be learned from their experience and example.

Notes — Chapter I

1. John Lewis Gaddis, "The United States and the Question of a Sphere of Influence in Europe, 1945-1949," in *Western Security: The Formative Years.* Olav Riste ed.(New York: Columbia University Press, 1985), 61.

2. Olav Riste, "Was 1949 a Turning Point? Norway and The Western Powers 1947-50," in Riste, *Western Security,* 142-43.

3. ibid., 144.

4. Raymond Garthoff, "The Concept of the Balance of Power in Soviet Policy Making", *World Politics* (October 1951) 88.

5. Arne Brundtland, in *Northern Europe: Security Issues for the 1990s* (Boulder, Westview, 1986), 15-16.

6. Per Egil Hegge, "The Soviet View of the Nordic Balance," *The Washington Quarterly* (Summer 1979).

7. Erling Bjøl, "Nordic Security" (London, IISS Adelphi Paper 181, Spring 1983), 44.

II

What's Past Is Paradigm

Abraham Lincoln remarked in the first speech of his campaign for the American presidency, "If we could know where we are, and whither we are tending, we could know better what to do and how to do it."[1] A similar desire to know "where" and "whither" has inspired this study of the Nordic area, its inhabitants, and their neighbors. This chapter constitutes a brief view of how the region approached the modern era.

The "where" question is relatively easy to address, determined as it is by the twin coordinates of history and geography. "Whither" is more difficult because, for centuries, the nations involved seemed to move in circles, invading and conquering one another in turn, leaving the impression of eddies and swirls rather than a strong current in one direction. Russians fought Swedes, Poles fought Russians, Swedes fought Danes, Lithuanians fought Russians, almost *ad infinitum*. But, like a classic paradigm, surface changes in the pattern do not conceal the roots of continuing conflict.

Now, after exposure to nearly 150 years of pacifist sentiment in Scandinavia, the modern observer may have the impression that peace and goodwill constitute the normal state of affairs in that area. But these same Nordic peoples are descendants of the fierce Viking raiders who entered the historical scene when they attacked the monastery at Lindisfarne on the English coast on June 8, 793, and terrorized much of Europe, East and West, for centuries thereafter. Their forefathers had ranged across the North Atlantic to the New World as early as 1000 A.D., founding a Norse colony at what is now L'Anse aux Meadows, on the north coast of Newfoundland.

Geography has played as critical a role as genes in determining the thrust of Nordic development. The southernmost areas of

Scandinavia — Jutland, the island of Zealand, and the Scania portion of modern Sweden — constitute the great junction of Northern Europe, athwart the transit routes between North and South, East and West. Many countries, both near and far from Scandinavian shores, have sought control of those routes.

During the long period of Danish ascendancy, it was Copenhagen's policy to control those transit routes, both to the West and toward the Slav and Arab worlds to the East. When their ascendancy ended, about 1600, the Danes were reduced to warring with Sweden over Scania and with Germany over southern Jutland. The other countries of Scandinavia and along the southern shore of the Baltic Sea are comparatively recent nation states, having attained independence only during the twentieth century.

Norway admittedly had its "Golden Age" under Haakon IV in the early thirteenth century. When Greenland and Iceland agreed voluntarily to a personal union under the Norwegian King in 1261 and 1262, respectively, a huge Norwegian empire was created, its sway extending as far East as Archangelsk. Norway at that time also included the Faeroes as well as the Orkney and Shetland Islands, none of which were pried away from Norse control until 1469.

Haakon's son, Magnus, formed another personal union with Sweden, which lasted from 1319 to 1355, but this union was rent by a power struggle between his sons, and one of them seized control of Sweden for himself. By the end of the fourteenth century, Norway had become part of Denmark and remained so until 1814, when it was ceded to Sweden as part of the settlement resulting from the last of the many Danish-Swedish wars. Norway did not become independent again until 1905.

Finland belonged to Sweden from 1154 to 1809, when it became an autonomous Grand Duchy under the rule of the Russian Tsar. The Finns successfully declared their independence in December 1917, in the aftermath of the Bolshevik Revolution. As for Iceland, a very early period of independence ended in 1262 with its absorption by Norway; it was later taken, along with Norway, by Denmark.

In 1918, Iceland relaxed its close association with Denmark to one of only personal union under the king; even this was terminated during the period of separation imposed by World War II, and Iceland became an independent republic in 1943. Although

Norse Colonial Empires

1000 A.D.

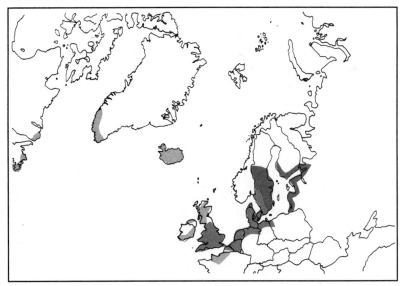

1262

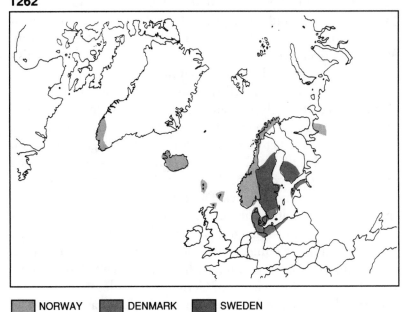

NORWAY   DENMARK   SWEDEN

the Icelanders took advantage of Denmark's enfeebled position under the Nazi boot to liberate themselves unilaterally, there can be little doubt that the Danish preference for a negotiated settlement would have led to the same result without much delay. King Christian limited the official Danish reaction to a telegram of hearty congratulations to his former subjects.

The two long-lived nations of Scandinavia, Denmark and Sweden, are also much reduced from their former imperial territory and ambition. Not so long ago, however, they fought for pre-eminence in the Baltic, took turns at dominating one another, and were briefly united, together with Norway, when Sweden opted for personal union (the Union of Kalmar, 1397) under Queen Margareta Valdemarsdotter in the common struggle against the Germans.

Denmark's leading role in the resulting united Scandinavian state reflected its larger population as well as Queen Margareta's political and diplomatic talents. Denmark's population at the end of the fourteenth century was about 750,000; Sweden had 500,000 and Norway only 250,000. United, they constituted the largest realm in Europe, stretching from Greenland to Karelia and from the North Cape to the Elbe.

The Union of Kalmar broke down by the middle of the fifteenth century, and Denmark and Sweden found themselves at war with one another for much of the next half-millennium. Vilhelm Moberg counts no fewer than eleven Swedish-Danish wars between the break-up of the Union of Kalmar and 1814.[2]

After the Swedes rebelled against the Danes in 1434 and re-established themselves as an independent nation, their power and influence grew impressively. As the larger of the two, Sweden was the most consistent contender for the title of "great power on the Baltic." Under King Gustavus Adolphus (1611–1632), Sweden extended its holdings on the east shore of the Baltic to encompass Finland, Karelia, and Livonia. The King also waged war brilliantly in Germany, revolutionizing earlier concepts of military organization in the process, although his country's total population at the time, including the Finnish territories, was still less than a million.

In the view of British military historian Liddell Hart, the final duel between Gustavus and Germany's Wallenstein and the former's death in the battle of Lützen (1632) was "decisive in quenching the possibility of a great Protestant confederation under Swedish leadership."[3]

A few years later, under the Peace of Westphalia (1648), the Swedish crown acquired a good portion of the German coast, including western Pomerania with the city of Stettin (now Szczecin, Poland) as well as some territories on the North Sea, such as Bremen. Then, in a series of wars with Poland, during which the Polish king claimed the throne of Sweden while a Swedish king claimed to be the king of Poland, the Swedes gained control of virtually all land fronting on the Baltic, except for Denmark and the Prussian province of Brandenburg. Consequently, the Baltic became a Swedish lake, with not only the Russians and Poles excluded, but even the Germans, who had access to it solely on Sweden's terms.

A generation later, a new Swedish king appeared, Charles XII, who was driven to the edge of madness, and perhaps over it, by military ambition. Charles pursued his dream of conquest deep into Poland and Russia. In 1700, at Narva, in Estonia, Charles routed the 40,000-man army of Peter the Great with a force of only 8,000 men. Soon preoccupied with the affairs of Poland, where he succeeded in placing his own candidate on the Polish throne, Charles failed to follow up on this notable victory, not turning against Russia again until almost a decade later.

Peter the Great, in the meantime, had taken advantage of the respite to reorganize his forces, bringing in a multitude of foreign officers and technicians to train and direct them. In a maneuver which would become the classic Russian response to invasion, Peter drew Charles and his attacking army ever deeper onto the Russian steppes, where they were exposed to an exceptionally severe winter. Finally, in 1709, at Poltava in the Ukraine, nearly 200 miles southeast of Kiev, he was able to vanquish what remained of Charles's exhausted army.

It was then Peter's turn to play the role of attacker, and he proceeded to roll back the Swedish advance, while Charles took refuge in Turkey. (King Charles died in 1718, not at the hands of the Russians, but during another war with the Danes.) The Tsar soon took over the Baltic province of Livonia as well as part of eastern Finland and landed troops in the vicinity of Stockholm itself.

When the Great Northern War finally concluded after two decades with the Treaty of Nystadt (1721), Sweden was obliged to

Scandinavia Borders

1660

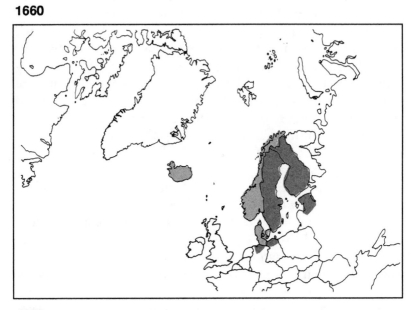

1850

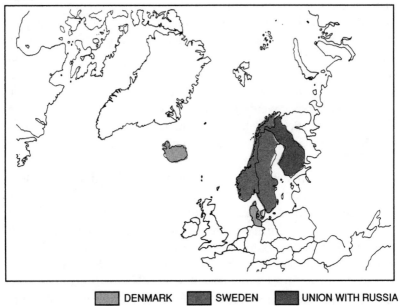

DENMARK   SWEDEN   UNION WITH RUSSIA

convey to the Tsar the provinces of Livonia, Estonia, and Ingria, along with parts of Karelia and some islands off the coast. This victory eliminated the Swedish threat to Russia and made possible the consolidation of Peter's long-sought "window on the West," the city he dubbed "St. Petersburg" in his own honor.

In 1715, Peter had dispatched Heinrich Fick, a former civil servant in the Danish-controlled Duchy of Holstein, to Sweden to study its governmental system. Three years later, the Tsar ordered that Russia's municipal governments be patterned after those of Riga and Reval (now Tallinn). About the same time, he invited Baron Luberas of Silesia to Moscow. The Baron, in turn, brought in more than 100 foreign experts to staff the "colleges," or ministries, which the Tsar had just established to govern his empire. These foreign specialists were later joined by large numbers of Baltic Germans, as well as by many prisoners captured during the victorious war against Sweden.

These were not the first occasions on which Scandinavians and the eastern Slavs came to know one another. Norse (Varangian) warriors evidently played an important role in early Russian history, although some historians have recently raised questions about the precise nature of their exploits. It seems clear that the legendary Riurik did in fact establish himself in Novgorod in 862, founding a dynasty which ruled Russia for more than 700 years.

The Varangians were probably first attracted to the Russian lands because of the important trade route along the waterway of the Western Dvina and the Volga, which linked the Baltic to the Caspian Sea and beyond. Population centers later sprang up along all the trade routes connecting European centers with the East. By the early eleventh century, merchant towns were prospering from northern Italy to Flanders, along the principal rivers, the Rhine and the Danube, and on the shores of the Baltic.

Some of these towns eventually formed alliances for protection against both princes and bandits. The most successful of these was the Hanseatic League, which included Hamburg, Bremen, Bergen, Riga, and Tallinn, and which dominated commerce on the North Sea and the Baltic, spreading its influence as far as Pskov and Novgorod.

The struggle for dominance on the southern side of the Baltic was not only for commercial or economic advantages but also for broader political or imperial purposes. Thus, early in the thirteenth century, King Valdemar of Denmark, supported by Wendic forces, conquered Estonia and gave the town of Reval or Tallinn (meaning "Danish-town") the three Danish lions which are still in its coat of arms.[4] But Valdemar's empire collapsed after only a few years, defeated by an alliance of North German princes. Shortly thereafter, the Teutonic Order, which merged with the Livonian Knights in 1237, relaunched the attempt to impose Latin Christianity on the remaining pagans in the Baltic lands as well as on the Orthodox Russians.

The Teutonic "crusade" and Russian resistance to it, led by the celebrated Alexander Nevski, contributed much to an early sense of nationhood among the Slavs. But Alexander, then Prince of Novgorod, was not unique in struggling against invaders from the West and North. Between 1142 and 1446, Novgorod fought the Swedes twenty-six times, the Teutonic Knights eleven times, the Lithuanians fourteen times, and the Norwegians five times. War and pillage became the established order of things along the Baltic during that period.

In 1307, Lithuanians under the leadership of Mindowh began to absorb some of the Russian principalities, beginning with Polotsk and continuing with other ancient Russian areas such as Smolensk, Chernigov, Kiev, and Volynia. The conquerors, however, failed to impose their language and political culture on their new subjects. "The Lithuanian army, administration, legal system, and finance were organized on the Russian pattern, and Russian became the official language of the new state."[5]

The resulting Russian-Lithuanian state challenged Moscow for supremacy, and by the late fourteenth century, its sway extended from the Baltic to the Black Sea. Dynastic ties created a close link between Poland and Lithuania, and in 1410, the Grand Prince of Lithuania, Vitovt, led a joint Polish-Lithuanian army to a crushing victory over the Teutonic Order and its Livonian allies at Grunwald.

Later, as Vitovt's successors gradually became weaker, Lithuania was effectively swallowed up by Poland. Its vast territory stretched from the Baltic to the Black Sea and included large sections of today's Poland and extensive portions of what are now Belarus and Ukraine. But under Moscovite princes like Ivan the Terrible, Moscovy rather than Poland gradually established itself as the successor to Kiev and the ruler of all the Russias.

Meanwhile, in Scandinavia, it was not until the middle of the nineteenth century that the situation ripened sufficiently to permit the kind of neutrality which has now characterized that area for more than a century. Curiously, one of the most influential advocates of neutrality in the Northland had once been a warrior and was also a foreigner. Jean Bernadotte of France, who had distinguished himself in the wars of the French Revolution and was made a Marshal of France and Prince of Pontecorvo by Napoléon, was elected heir to the Swedish throne in 1810, became king in 1818, and ruled as King Karl XIV Johan.

Before his coronation, however, Bernadotte had mastered the arts of war and become a skilled practitioner of nineteenth-century *Realpolitik*. In the confusion of the Napoléonic wars, the French Emperor had agreed with the Russian Tsar at Tilsit in 1807 on a broad division of responsibilities in Europe. The following year, at Erfurt, Napoléon acquiesced in Alexander I's conquest of Finland. When the Danes then blocked Sweden's attempted invasion of Norway, discontented Swedish nobles, civil servants, and military officers conspired to depose King Gustavus IV, replacing him with his uncle, who assumed the throne as Charles XIII. In their diplomatic isolation, the Swedes then sought to win French support by nominating one of Napoléon's marshals to succeed their childless new monarch. In 1810, they proclaimed Bernadotte, an ex-Jacobin who bore an anti-monarchical tattoo on his arm, as heir apparent.

Bernadotte at first aligned himself with France and, in the name of the senile Charles XIII, declared war on England. But he failed to prosecute hostilities vigorously and reportedly connived at promoting contraband trade with that country, Napoléon's principal enemy. The Emperor retaliated by seizing Swedish Pomerania in 1812; shortly thereafter, Bernadotte sided with the Russians, who promised him Norway in return. In 1813, as Crown Prince, he agreed to send 30,000 men to fight with the allies against Napoléon and personally took command of the expeditionary forces.

Bernadotte later became Tsar Alexander's candidate to replace Napoléon in the French capital but met with Austrian and British opposition and had to content himself with the less temperate climes of Stockholm.[6] There, however, the émigré Frenchman established the intellectual basis for Sweden's eventual policy of neutrality. On January 4, 1834, inspired by the threat of war between Russia and Great Britain over their rivalry in the Middle East, Karl Johan put his views on paper. The King sent a confidential memorandum to both of the contending governments, seeking to give them "a formal explanation of my system of strict and independent neutrality." His memorandum reminded both the British and the Russians that, because of the loss of Finland in 1809 and Sweden's union with Norway in 1814, his country had become virtually an insular power. The Swedish peninsula was separated from Europe by sea in the West, South, and East. His country, the King continued, had abandoned all illusions which might endanger its domestic peace or its existence as a state. Sweden's geographical position, together with its internal conditions, would henceforth dictate its foreign policy. Karl Johan stressed that his countrymen wanted to stand aside from any conflict between Russia and England, the two powers which were most important to them. Sweden wished instead to reciprocate the friendship both countries had shown to her.[7]

The King informed the "secret committee" of Parliament of his memorandum and added a detailed account of how he viewed the development of Swedish foreign policy. In phrases which are pertinent even today, he declared, "In the case of Russia, we must take into account her close proximity to us, her greatly superior strength and certain trading interests. We are linked to Britain through our whole industrial and commercial system and also by naval considerations."[8]

Bernadotte modestly noted his own participation in the war against Napoléon when the French Emperor had threatened Sweden's honor and independence. He reminded the committee about the need to secure the country against sudden attack and set forth what had to be done to bolster Sweden's coastal defenses. A declaration of neutrality was not adequate, he observed, without the will and means to enforce it. "I have the necessary *will*, but only the nation can provide me with the *means*."[9]

Karl Johan pursued his policy of well-armed neutrality until his death in 1844, leaving a legacy which continues to this day. He was not the first to implement a policy of neutrality for Sweden, of course, because the country had been an active member of various "leagues of armed neutrality" before his time. But he was the first to articulate the need for an enduring policy of neutrality for his adopted country, even though he rarely spoke explicitly of "neutrality." Neither a pacifist nor a passive bystander in European politics, Karl Johan preferred to characterize his foreign policy in peacetime as one of "balance between the great powers and non-involvement in continental disputes."[10]

Driven by Swedish public opinion and a resurgence of national ambition, Karl Johan's successors, Oscar I (1844–1859) and Karl XV (1859–1872), were not as successful as he in holding to a policy of non-involvement. They proved unable to maintain a foreign policy balance between the more liberal states such as France and Britain and the reactionary regimes in Russia, Prussia, and Austria.

Poland's plight under the heel of Russia and Prussia was regarded sympathetically by Swedish public opinion, and liberal "Scandinavianists" took Denmark's side in its struggle with Prussia and Austria over Schleswig-Holstein. Liberal Swedes were also favorable to the idea of regaining Finland from Russia if the occasion arose. Some of them, echoing the national unification movements in Germany and Italy in the mid-1800s, hoped eventually to forge a united Nordic state. At that time, however, this romantic Scandinavianism appears to have been largely a literary and academic movement, with few roots in the general population.

Oscar I succeeded in playing a significant role during the war of 1848–49 over the tangled question of Schleswig-Holstein, two duchies separating the Danes from the much more numerous Germans to the South. The Danes had just recently won an important concession from their King, Frederick VII, in the form of a liberal constitution with a wide suffrage, when a nationalist uprising broke out in Holstein. The Holstein rebels, in Palle Lauring's astringent phrase, "were not interested in Danish liberty, merely their own."[11]

The northern duchy, Schleswig, was an ancient Danish borderland. Holstein, in contrast, had always been ethnically German but had gradually become subject to the Danish king. When nationalist enthusiasms seized both Germans and Danes in the mid-nineteenth century, tensions between them grew rapidly. Holsteiners demanded a free and united Schleswig-Holstein as part of the German Confederation. Their liberal Danish opponents, in order to save Schleswig, insisted on a free and united Denmark, including Schleswig, although they were prepared to see Holstein become a member of the German Confederation.

That was a solution that the Danish King and government were not prepared to accept, and the waters were further muddied by the impending international struggle between Prussia and Russia for control of the Baltic, over which the Scandinavian lands had lost their predominance.

Civil war broke out in Denmark in 1848 in the aftermath of the February revolution in France. Prussia, coming to the assistance of the German faction, then invaded Jutland. Under pressure from other countries, particularly Russia, Prussia was obliged to withdraw, but the Danes had to promise they would make no changes in the status of Denmark, Schleswig, or Holstein or link any of them more closely to one another.

During the brief conflict, Sweden had supported Denmark diplomatically, and Swedish troops were sent to the Danish island of Fyn, permitting the Danes to concentrate their troops against the Prussian threat. In addition, many Swedish and Norwegian volunteers fought on the Danish side against the Germans. Sweden's King Oscar later presided over the signing in Malmö of the armistice between Denmark and Prussia. Sweden was also invited to join the great powers in signing the agreements which were negotiated in London during 1850 and 1852 on the future of Denmark and the duchies, which promised to "uphold the integrity of the Danish Monarchy."

Although the unity of the Danish realm appeared to be assured, steady erosion of its territory and prerogatives soon made itself felt. The Danish flag was taken down at Tranquebar in India in 1847 when the installation there was sold to a British company, and by 1850, Denmark had turned over its three colonial outposts on the coast of Guinea to the British government. The only overseas possessions remaining in Danish hands were the Virgin Islands in the West Indies (sold to the United States in 1916), Greenland, the Faeroe Islands, and Iceland.

Denmark's most striking geographic feature is its position astride the outlets from the Baltic to the Kattegat and the Skagerrak and thence into the open sea. The Great Belt, between the islands of Sjaelland and Fyn, and the Little Belt, between Fyn and Jutland, lie entirely within Danish territory. The Øresund, or Sound, divides Denmark from Sweden, and control over that channel is now shared between the two nations. From 1429 until it lost the southern Swedish provinces to Stockholm's rule in the mid-seventeenth century, however, Denmark was able to take advantage of its position to impose dues on all the vessels transiting the straits. The substantial income gained thereby was a key factor in the economic health of the kingdom.

It was not until a treaty of March 14, 1857, that Denmark gave up its Sound and Belt dues and promised in future "never under any pretext whatsoever" to hinder the passage of a foreign vessel on its way through the Øresund or the Belts. In recompense, Sweden (and Norway), Belgium, France, the Netherlands, Prussia and six other German states, Russia, Great Britain, and Austria agreed to pay a once-for-all indemnity of 30,476,000 rix-dollars.[1] A number of other maritime nations, including the United States, separately agreed to pay indemnities also. Not all of the high contracting powers paid their assessments, but Denmark did reap a significant financial harvest from abandoning the system of dues.[12]

Meanwhile, the London peace settlement of the Schleswig-Holstein problem proved to be only transitory. In 1863, the Danish government responded to provocative behavior by the German Confederation by foolishly promulgating a joint constitution for Denmark and Schleswig, thus violating the treaty provisions which forbade it to change the situation in southern Jutland. The Diet of the German Confederation, following in the footsteps of the Frankfurt Assembly fifteen years earlier, called for an all-German war against the Danes. Otto von Bismarck-Schönhausen, Prussia's Iron Chancellor, would have preferred a Prusso-Danish war instead, not wishing to encourage the German Confederation, but he acted jointly with Austria in 1864 to crush the Danes after a brief military campaign.

Bismarck subsequently quarreled with and discredited his Austrian allies by adroit diplomacy. Soon thereafter, Prussia was waging war against Austria and most of the other German states. In 1866, at the conclusion of what became known as the Seven Weeks' War, Prussia was able to annex not only Schleswig-Holstein but the Kingdom of Hanover, the duchies of Nassau and

---

1. A rix-dollar was a silver coin and money of account used in various European countries up until the mid-nineteenth century. It was valued at about three English shillings.

Hesse-Cassel, and the free city of Frankfurt. On this basis, he organized the North German Confederation, joining together twenty-two states, among which Prussia was clearly predominant.

In its war with the Prussians and Austrians, the Danish army suffered great losses, estimated at four times those of the attackers. The defeat also cost Denmark a third of the national territory and two-fifths of its population. Stunned by such losses, the Danes began a drastic revision of their political thinking, domestically as well as in foreign affairs.

At home, men like Kristen Kold built on the pioneering work of the poet-clergyman Nikolai Grundtvig to establish a nation-wide system of folk high schools. The new schools, together with the rejuvenated cooperative movements, constituted a kind of popular renaissance. Under the slogan of "what is outwardly lost is inwardly won" and working with the Danish Heath Society of Colonel Enrico Dalgas to clear and reclaim the moors, they succeeded in transforming the nation from a collection of largely rural and fishing communities into an agricultural, and eventually a modern agro-industrial, state.

In its foreign policy, Denmark after the loss of Schleswig and Holstein was obliged to maintain its neutrality, but its stance tilted increasingly in favor of the surging military and industrial power of Germany. Many Danes questioned the feasibility of defending their kingdom, and there were increasing calls for disarmament.

Norway was naturally influenced by the development of a reasoned pacifism in Sweden, with which it was joined for most of the nineteenth century. But independence was even more of an issue.

Even before it was incorporated by Sweden, Norway had found the Napoléonic conflicts a source of grief because the continental blockade of England had cost it dearly in economic terms. In an effort to escape from the domination of their more powerful Scandinavian neighbors, leading citizens of Norway promulgated a national constitution on May 17, 1814, at Eidsvoll Manor and elected young Prince Christian Frederick, a cousin of Denmark's King Frederick, as their king. Bernadotte insisted on his spoils, however, and Christian Frederick was obliged to yield his throne to Sweden's vastly greater power.

Bernadotte, in turn, accommodated popular sentiment to the extent of accepting the Eidsvoll Constitution and acknowledging a Norwegian self-governing parliament, the Storting. Even so, Norwegians remained uncomfortable in their subordinate position within the Swedish kingdom. Political discontent spread, gaining momentum during the second half of the nineteenth century. Norway actually became the first Scandinavian nation to be governed by parliamentary means as the Storting grew in power, gradually becoming a dominant political force.

Among the pressing issues before the Storting in the last quarter of the nineteenth century was the demand for a foreign minister independent of Sweden. The Venstre (Liberal) Party won an impressive majority in the Parliament in 1891, partly on this issue. There was also a drive for an independent consular service to serve Norway's flourishing merchant fleet. Finally, on June 7, 1905, the Storting declared the union with Sweden dissolved. When the Swedish Parliament refused to accept the dissolution, there were threats of military action and partial mobilization in both countries.

In the end, Norway was obliged to negotiate an end to the union rather than merely declare its demise. In a settlement reached in Karlsbad in September 1905, both sides had to make significant concessions, but the Union of Sweden and Norway was officially dissolved. Prince Charles of Denmark was elected King of Norway and ruled as Haakon VII.

By the early twentieth century, therefore, three of Scandinavia's major subdivisions, Denmark, Sweden, and Norway, had solidified their national independence and were developing into modern constitutional monarchies. Iceland, however, remained under Danish tutelage, and Finland had yet to emerge from Tsarist rule.

Notes — Chapter II

1. Charnwood Lord, *Abraham Lincoln* (New York: Henry Holt, 1917), 158.
2. Vilhelm Moberg, *A History of the Swedish People* vol. 2 (New York: Dorset Press, 1989), 61.
3. B.H. Liddel Hart, *Strategy* (New York: Frederick A. Praeger, 1954), 83.
4. Palle Lauring, *A History of Denmark* (Copenhagen: Høst and Son, 1960), 84.
5. Nicholas V. Riasanovsky, *A History of Russia* (New York: Oxford University Press, 1984), 134.
6. Steven T. Ross, *European Diplomatic History 1789–1815* (Malabar, Florida: Robert E. Krieger, 1981), 341.
7. Krister Wahlbäck, *The Roots of Swedish Neutrality* (Stockholm: The Swedish Institute, 1986), 8.
8. Ibid., 10.
9. Ibid.
10. Ibid., 11.
11. Lauring, *History of Denmark*, 211.
12. Ibid., 220.

III

Finland's Way

Severed from Sweden at the outset of the Napoléonic wars, Finland was annexed to Alexander I's Russia in 1808. Sensing the approach of another war in Central Europe, however, the Tsar convoked the Finnish Diet in March 1809, permitting the establishment of an autonomous state in Finland under his rule as Grand Duke. Alexander would no doubt have found it psychologically difficult to accept a new liberal constitutional order in his newly conquered lands. However, by pledging merely to respect the limited rights the Finns had enjoyed under Sweden's suzerainty, he could avoid setting a dangerous precedent for the rest of his realm, where he remained autocrat of all the Russias.

Accordingly, when the Diet pledged the fealty of the Finnish people to the Tsar, he was able to ratify "the religion and fundamental Laws of the Land, as well as the privileges and rights which each estate in the said Grand Duchy, in particular, and all the inhabitants, in general, be their position high or low, have otherwise enjoyed."[1] Furthermore, in 1816, after the allied victory over Napoléon, Alexander extended the guarantee of Finnish autonomy to posterity by pledging to uphold the fundamental laws of Finland "forevermore under Our scepter and that of Our Successors."[2]

Finnish nationalism was not stilled by the Tsar's gestures; rather, it gained considerable inspiration from the romantic nationalism so popular in Germany and Sweden during the mid-1800s. Swedish nationalism was naturally most influential among the substantial Swedish-speaking minority in Finland, but such sentiments opened the way for the growth of pan-Scandinavian thought throughout the country.

The feeling of an overarching Nordic identity associated with pan-Scandinavianism never brought forth in Finland the enthusiasm generated by Bishop Gruntvig and his followers in Denmark, but it did register some gains, particularly in the aftermath of the Russian defeat in the Crimean War (1854–56). Finnish attention was naturally drawn more to the efforts of the new Tsar, Alexander II, to modernize his empire, most notably his emancipation of Russia's serfs and reform of the lackluster army. The fading of pan-Scandinavian thought accelerated in 1864, when Sweden-Norway refused to come to the military aid of Denmark after it had been attacked by Prussia and Austria.

Although the Tsar-liberator failed to follow through on some initial concessions to his Polish and Lithuanian subjects, the Finns found themselves in a more favored position. In 1869, a reconvened Finnish Diet laid down the principle that the fundamental laws of Finland could be altered only with its consent; to the surprise of many, the Tsar agreed. This converted the unilateral pledge of Alexander I in 1816 into constitutional law, and the autocrat of Russia became simultaneously a constitutional monarch in his capacity as Grand Duke of Finland.

St. Petersburg's concerns in the Balkans and its pursuit of Russia's manifest destiny in Eurasia fortunately provided the independent-minded Finns with a measure of elbow room throughout the remaining years of the nineteenth century. As evidence of this, Finns could point to the fact that they had their own laws, their own Diet, their own administrative system, and their own agency for bringing matters to the attention of the Tsar. Moreover, Russian subjects enjoyed no civil rights in Finland, which maintained a customs boundary against the rest of the empire.[3]

One consequence of Tsar Alexander's acceptance of the existing social and legal structure in Finland when he became its Grand Duke in 1809 was the absence of any attempt to impose the Russian language on its inhabitants. At the time, however, the language of Finland's educated class, and hence the official language, was Swedish. Among educated people, only the clergy were likely to be fluent in Finnish.

Moreover, less educated Finns tended to adopt Swedish as their "mother tongue" as soon as they perceived the opportunity for upward mobility. In 1870, although 85 percent of the population spoke Finnish at home, only 8 percent of students admitted to the university were enrolled as Finnish speakers. The social gap between Swedish and Finnish speakers accordingly remained and was the source of considerable discontent.

Not surprisingly, most of the early literature stimulating the rise of Finnish nationalism was written in Swedish. Both Swedish and Finnish speakers in Finland shared a common nightmare, the imposition of the Russian language by the bureaucrats in St. Petersburg. Encouraged by Tsar Alexander II's proclaimed beneficence, Finnish nationalists pushed for greater acceptance of their native tongue, and in 1855 it was decreed the language of local self-government in the communes where its speakers were in the majority. Even a decade later, however, most public functionaries were unable to express themselves effectively in Finnish; hence, it was impossible to insist on its adoption as the language of administration and justice, and Swedish remained the internal government language.

Russian was, of course, the language of the government offices in St. Petersburg, and many functionaries there were uneasy about the relative political freedoms enjoyed by inhabitants of the Grand Duchy. There were repeated attempts to restrict those freedoms, notably the Tsar's April Manifesto of 1861, which called for the establishment of a forty-eight-man committee to enact provisional laws "until circumstances permitted" the Diet to meet. Alexander II, like his Swedish predecessor, Gustavus III, saw the Diet as a purely advisory body. If he felt no need for advice, there was no need to convene the Diet.

A popular petition was drafted for submission to the Tsar, in which some members of the senate argued that the manifesto could be interpreted as being contrary to the Finnish constitution. The Tsar then obligingly issued an explanation, which amounted to a substantial revision of the original document, stipulating that the resolutions of the proposed committee could not be ratified into laws but were merely recommendations to the sovereign about possible legislation. Alexander's gesture of reasonableness on this occasion was probably stimulated by his concern over Western perceptions of his stern policy in Poland. By his unwillingness to make the April Manifesto a matter of prestige, he was evidently trying to show his Western critics that he was prepared to rule over law-abiding subjects in a constitutional manner.

This link between the situation in Finland and that in Russia's holdings in Eastern Europe was not a contrived one. The Baltic states had been incorporated in the Russian Empire even earlier than Finland, and they too had been permitted to retain some of their former institutions. When the Congress of Vienna agreed to the formation of a "Kingdom of Poland," it provided that the Poles were to maintain a modicum of internal autonomy under Russian sovereignty. This could be interpreted to legitimize some kind of international role over the Tsar's conduct in that area, something St. Petersburg preferred to avoid.

In his early, liberal period, Alexander I evidently did conceive of a multi-national empire grouping a number of semi-autonomous national units under his scepter. After the abortive Polish revolution of 1863, however, the Kingdom of Poland, which constituted only a fraction of Polish lands, was considered occupied territory and, shortly thereafter, the Baltic states were fully incorporated in the empire's closely confined system. Only Finland, therefore, was able to maintain a degree of cultural and political autonomy to serve as a basis for its eventual transition to national independence.

Finland's relatively favored position was the result of considerable pulling and hauling from both sides. In the aftermath of the Polish uprising, the Tsar moved quickly to avoid the likelihood of unpleasant echoes on the other shore of the Baltic. The Diet was convened in Helsinki in September 1863, for the first time in more than half a century, and Alexander II himself opened the proceedings, emphasizing the principles of constitutional law and promising to enlarge the rights of the estates, i.e., the common people as well as the nobles and clergy.

The Tsar did ratify a new Diet Act in 1869, but it did not reflect the glib promises of six years earlier, partly because the St. Petersburg functionaries had begun to feel uneasy over the influence of the pan-Scandinavian movement. Under the act, however, the Finns gained a constitutional law of their own in which the roles and limitations of the Tsar and the Diet were more carefully delineated. The Tsar was henceforth obliged to convene the Diet every five years, and he subsequently granted it a limited right to initiate legislation.

More important, perhaps, as a result of the financial turmoil the Crimean War caused in Russia, Finland was able gradually to establish its own currency. The Bank of Finland began to issue *markka* notes, equivalent to one-quarter of a ruble. In a significant move, Finland based its currency on silver while the ruble stayed on a paper standard. Later, in 1878, the Finnish mark joined most of the rest of Europe on the gold standard, while the Russian ruble, formally on a silver standard, remained in actuality only a paper currency.

J.V. Snellman, a major figure in the struggle to promote Finnish national interests, played key roles in establishing the independence of the banking system and in matters of culture and literature generally. Snellman served as a senator from 1863 to 1868, when he was forced to resign because of a dispute with the Governor-General. In that same year, the Bank of Finland was placed under the authority of the Diet and, in 1906, when a more democratic parliament (the Eduskunta) was formed, supervision of the banking system was transferred to it.

Establishment of a distinct Finnish national identity was complicated during the second half of the nineteenth century by the appearance of three rival political trends. Swedish speakers gravitated toward a Svecomen bloc inspired by A.O. Freudenthal, while Finnish speakers, including Snellman as well as G.Z. Forsman (later Baron Yrjö-Koskinen) and Agathon Meurman, tended to identify themselves with the Fennomen. The third faction, the Liberals, formed during 1870s under the leadership of Leo Mechelin, was comparatively indifferent to the linguistic issue, focusing instead on economic matters.

By 1882, however, most of the Liberals were drifting toward the Svecomen. Liberal ambivalence on the language issue eventually led to the party's political extermination because many of its Finnish-speaking members began to ally themselves with one of the two divergent Fennomen factions, the "Old" and the "Young." The Young Finns tended to be more radical on economic questions than their conservative elders and also less inclined to compromise on language issues. Representation in the Diet was by then almost evenly divided between Fennomen and Svecomen.

In 1889, the Young Finns founded a newspaper, which later became the *Helsingin Sanomat*, and followed this up in 1894 by establishing a new political party which was dedicated to the fight for the Finnish language and also to broadening the electoral franchise and improving social conditions, especially in the countryside. Linguistic antagonism continued to envenom the political debate. Until the 1890s, Swedish was still the dominant language

in the legislature, and when Yrjö-Koskinen used Finnish in addressing the House of Nobles in 1894, it was denounced as an impertin-
ence. But the Svecomen were by then railing in the face of history
(only about one-seventh of the population were in the Swedish-
speaking camp), and their defeat could be clearly foreseen.

Less easily predicted was the outcome of a renewed drive by
conservatives in Russia to impose their writ on the independent-
minded, Western-leaning Finns. Russian Slavophiles and pan-Slavs
regarded the decadent West as a source of ideological infection.
Eager to protect the purity of what they considered their superior
culture, they were determined to end this contaminating influence.
Russian liberals, on the other hand, had long seen Finland as a
model they hoped to emulate, and some even sought posts in the
Grand Duchy, where they could find a more agreeable life style.

By the 1870s, most European states had established a system
of universal conscription to staff their military forces, and Russia
followed suit in 1874. Faced with the likelihood of seeing their
young men forced into the Russian army, far-seeing Finns decided
to establish an army of their own. The Diet, in establishing the
new contingent, stressed its autonomous status by forbidding use
of the Finnish army beyond the national boundaries except in an
extreme emergency which threatened the Tsar's throne. Also, some
of the enabling legislation was termed "constitutional," meaning
that it could be amended only by the four chambers of the Diet
acting together. Moreover, the officer corps was to be composed
of Finns rather than Russians, and the three-year term of service
was only half that of the Russian term. Those Finns of military age
not called up for regular service were to receive a short period of
military training, thus providing a possible mobilization base for
a mass national army. Alexander II signed the Conscription Act in
1878, greatly reinforcing the Finnish sense of separation from the
rest of the empire.

On March 1, 1881, the Tsar signed a draft constitution
providing for the establishment of a Russian representative assembly. A notable step forward for Russians, this would have constituted a step backward for the Finns, who would have been subject
to the laws passed by the Russian assembly rather than those of the
Diet. But Alexander II was assassinated by terrorists only hours
later, before the new constitution could take effect, and his successor, Alexander III, pushed it aside.

The new Tsar was strongly influenced by Konstantin P. Pobedonostsev, a fervent pan-Slav, who later served as Procurator of the Holy Synod and in a number of other important posts. A fanatical reactionary, he had been Alexander III's tutor and considered representative government "the great lie of our time." Pobedonostsev preserved his influence under the next Tsar, Nicholas II, who assumed the throne in 1894, serving as his tutor also. Very much opposed to Finland's special status, he was even more opposed to any notion of constitutionalism in Russia itself and made it his priority to repress liberalism at home rather than in Finland.

Another of the new Tsar's advisers was K. Ordin, author of a book entitled *The Subjugation of Finland*, which appeared in 1889. Ordin argued that Finland was a conquered Swedish province with special rights that had been granted by a beneficent Tsar. What one Tsar had granted, therefore, another Tsar could take away. Alexander III, frustrated by the Western powers in his attempts to convert his military victories in the Balkans into concrete territorial gains, came under increasing pressure to stem Finland's gradual shift from St. Petersburg's control. Concern about Finnish separatism was exacerbated, it appears, by renewed signs of growth in the centuries-old influence of the Germans in Russia's Baltic provinces.[4]

Nationalist stirrings among the Finns and other nationalities on the dividing line between the Russian Empire and the rest of Europe were not the only targets of St. Petersburg's oppression. Religious extremist sects such as the Dukhobors were singled out for particularly harsh treatment. Roman Catholics and Lutherans, who formed the majorities in some western areas of the empire, were considered suspect and, for the first time in history, quotas were established for Jewish students at the secondary level and above. Simultaneously, efforts were made to substitute Russian for the native languages in Poland and the Baltic regions.

Alexander III proved to be luckier in his choice of advisers on foreign affairs than he was in the internal realm. Under the sober guidance of advisers such as Foreign Minister Nicholas Giers, a Swedish Protestant, he steered a careful course in foreign policy. Deferential as well as resourceful, Giers was able to control the Tsar's impulsiveness and thus avoid further aggravating the international atmosphere.

When Alexander's son, Nicholas II, succeeded to the throne he proved to be even more reactionary than his father. He appointed General Nikolai Bobrikov Governor-General of Finland in 1889, making it his task to extend to Finland the policy of Russification which was already under way in Poland and the Baltic provinces. Bobrikov's hand was strengthened in this by the Tsar's Manifesto of February 15, 1899, placing most of Finnish legislation under the direct surveillance of the Russian government.

Finns were sharply divided as to how best to combat the renewed menace from St. Petersburg. Many of the Young Finns joined the Swedish-speaking Liberals, led by Mechelin, to form an opposition group known as the Constitutionalists. They regarded the Tsar's manifesto as a kind of imperial coup and argued for passive resistance to it. "Compliant" Old Finns stressed that confrontation could destroy any influence Finland might have with the Russian authorities and called instead for compromise and negotiation. When it became clear that passive resistance could not succeed without support from the Compliants, a third, more extreme, group also appeared, known as the "Activists," who pressed for direct action through strikes and even military insurgency. The growing labor movement began to pursue broader aims than trade union issues, breaking finally with what its leaders considered *bourgeois* tutelage. The Finnish Labor Party, which Dr. N.R. af Ursin founded in 1899, was renamed the Social Democratic Party in 1903. The organization was badly split, but its majority still tended toward cooperation with the Constitutionalists.

Meanwhile, as in the Soviet Union of 1990-91, pressures were building in the Russian capital for a stronger hand over the restless borderlands in the West. One Russian minister reportedly stated, "We have not subjugated alien races in order to give them pleasure, but because we need them."[5] The Finns tried to stem the Russification measures by petitioning the Tsar himself. A petition against the February Manifesto, signed by more than a half million people (one-third of the total adult population), was carried to St. Petersburg by a delegation of 500 representatives. But the Tsar refused to see them, and a similar petition against the Conscription Act was also rejected. Finland's show of independence produced many sympathizers in Western Europe and, in June 1899, 1,000 well-known Europeans signed a petition to the Tsar. A delegation from that group was also refused an audience with the Tsar but received an enthusiastic reception from the Finns on their return journey from St. Petersburg.

In 1901, the separate Finnish defense force, numbering about 6,000 men, was abolished. The soldiers were to be placed under Russian officers, and the non-commissioned officers would be compelled to speak Russian. Because the entire Finnish army was too small to constitute an important supplement to Russia's enormous manpower reserves, it was clear that the real issue was Finland's continued autonomy, not military service as such. When the Russian Government made clear its intention to enforce the Conscription Act, many Finns refused to report for military service. A major party conflict then erupted between Compliants and Constitutionalists, and the leadership of the passive resistance movement was forced to go underground. The idealistic Constitutionalists took their stand on principle, arguing that justice would triumph in the end and that the struggle must be carried on with all the means available, short of violence. The Compliants, on the other hand, warned that Russia's prestige had become involved and that a policy of measured accommodation was required.

The division between opposing views was aggravated by the fact that most of the Svecomen minority rallied to the side of the Constitutionalists. Finnish speakers, highly sensitive to linguistic issues, were sometimes accused of readiness to sell out the country provided the deed of sale were written in Finnish. Later, however, many of the militant Fennomen among the Old Finns abandoned that group to form a Finnish-speaking Constitutionalist party.

In 1902, in an attempt to conciliate the Finns, the Russian government had suggested that only 1 percent of those eligible for the draft would be called under a lottery system. Three-fifths of those summoned refused to report, however, and there was simultaneously a heavy increase in the rate of emigration. This experience reinforced doubts in St. Petersburg about the reliability of Finnish troops, and after some time the Russian authorities abandoned the draft. The eligible Finns were required to make a nominal monetary payment, and the Finnish army was disbanded. Some Finns continued to serve in the Russian army as volunteers, including C.G.E. Mannerheim, who rose to the rank of Lieutenant-General, but there was no Finnish army during World War I. The Finns thus escaped the blood baths of the Great War, as did their Scandinavian brethren.

The Russian Minister of the Interior, V.K. von Plehve, a relative moderate on Finnish autonomy although a confirmed reactionary on other issues, sought a more enlightened policy in the Grand Duchy in spite of the adamant opposition of Bobrikov. Ironically, both von Plehve and Bobrikov were assassinated within weeks of one another in 1904, the first by the son of a wealthy peasant merchant, the latter by a young Finn who then committed suicide.

Throughout the first two decades of the twentieth century, Scandinavia, and Finland in particular, served as a kind of membrane through which more liberal or revolutionary elements in Russia could breathe. Lenin and Stalin met one another for the first time in Finland, and it was at Finnish initiative that a gathering of many of Russia's radical and revolutionary groups took place in Paris in September 1904, although neither the Bolshevik nor the Menshevik wings of the Russian Social Democrats were represented.

Russia's resounding defeat in the Russo-Japanese war in 1904–05 badly undermined the prestige of the Imperial government, in Finland as well as Russia itself. When the hated Bobrikov was assassinated in Helsinki in June 1904, the Russian Government wisely avoided raising its level of oppression in response. The new Governor-General, Prince Obolensky, followed a policy of relative conciliation within the general framework of Russification. A Finn of the Compliant faction was appointed minister of state for Finland. But when elections were held for a new Diet, the Compliants were heavily defeated, leaving the legislature a primary center of resistance to Imperial rule.

Spurred by the empire's defeat at the hands of the Japanese, leftist political factions in Russia called a general strike which spread to Finland. Although the labor movement took the initiative, Finnish business leaders supported the strikers in many instances by paying employees their wages during the period of the strike. The Socialists demanded a thorough reform of the Diet, and the Constitutionalists somewhat grudgingly acquiesced. The two factions later split over their fundamental approaches, however, and both of them organized armed forces — the Constitutionalists a White Guard, and the Socialists a Red Guard — forerunners of the units which were to clash more seriously in 1918.

Beset by his sea of troubles, Alexander III was forced to back down in Finland as well as in the rest of his domains. On November 4, 1905, he issued a proclamation rescinding the decrees based on the February Manifesto and canceled the governor-general's dictatorial powers. The Constitutionalists took the credit for the victory, although the Russo-Japanese war and the surge of revolutionary ferment in Russia which followed it played larger roles in assuring Finnish success.

At the invitation of the Tsar, a new senate drafted a bill establishing a unicameral legislature to be elected by universal suffrage, with equal voting rights for women and men as well as guarantees of civil liberty. A new parliament, the Eduskunta, composed of 200 deputies, was established on May 29, 1906. Finland's rudimentary political groupings then developed into modern political parties. In the first elections, the Social Democrats were the largest party, with 37 percent of the vote, but the Old Finns also did well, considering their earlier collaboration with the Russian authorities.

Among the Old Finn deputies was Juho Kusti Paasikivi, who took on the challenging post of envoy to Moscow after the Winter War of 1939–40 and eventually, in 1946, became President of the republic. The Old Finns distinguished themselves in the first Eduskunta by their consistent anti-Swedish attitudes, but the group evolved over time to become today's National Coalition Party (Kansallinen Kokoomus).

The Constitutionalists, or Young Finns, suffered a resounding defeat in the 1907 elections, but individual members later played important political roles as their interpretation of Finnish history became the dominant view in the country. All the presidents of Finland between the two world wars were former Constitutionalists, regardless of which party they had joined in the Eduskunta.

During the first decade of the twentieth century, there was also nationalist ferment in the Baltic provinces as well as in the Ukraine, Belorussia, and Georgia, complemented by a resurgence of unrest among the Moslem population of the empire. Riga was a Social Democratic stronghold, and revolutionary activity in the Baltic areas began there but soon spread beyond into Estonia. A nationalist conference in Riga on November 19, 1905, asked for autonomy for Latvia, while an All-Estonian Congress in Reval a few days later demanded that Estonian be made the official language in that area. A Lithuanian National Congress held in Vilnius the same month passed similar measures, but Lithuania's strongest political forces continued to be the Polish nationalists and (the predominantly Jewish) Social Democrats.

In Russia itself, the general strike which developed in October 1905 was centered in Moscow and St. Petersburg but spread quickly and effectively shut down most industrial activity in the country. Under the influence of senior statesman Serge Witte, just returned from successfully negotiating the Portsmouth Treaty which ended the Russo-Japanese war, the Tsar signed a manifesto proclaiming a constitutional monarchy. The October 17 Manifesto contained a guarantee of fundamental civil liberties, the extension of the franchise, and the promise that no law was to take effect without the approval of the State Duma (national assembly).

Witte, a former Minister of Finance of German descent, was called upon to head a new government. He made peace with the Finns by accepting their demands but turned a stern face toward rebellious elements elsewhere, especially the Poles. He also put down short-lived mutinies within the armed forces and, when a spontaneous back-to-work movement forced the St. Petersburg Soviet to call off the general strike, he arrested its leaders, including Leon Trotsky. An armed uprising which took place in Moscow a week later was savagely suppressed. More than 1,000 people were killed, including many who were taken prisoner, then executed.

The Finns, who had their own legislature, were not represented in either branch of the Imperial Assembly, although they were entitled to elect deputies to both. Accordingly, they did not participate in the four Dumas which were convened and dissolved between 1906 and the end of the Russian monarchy in 1917, but Poles, Ukrainians, and representatives of the Baltic peoples did take part. Most of them were associated with leftist Russian formations. Early in the First Duma, some 200 opposition deputies met in the Finnish town of Vyborg and issued a manifesto calling for passive resistance by the people. But the empire's widely dispersed population failed to respond, and the Vyborg participants were sentenced to three months in jail.

Building on the work of Witte, the next Prime Minister, Peter Stolypin, was an ardent Russian nationalist, and he pressed forward with a program that discriminated against, when it did not persecute, other nationalities within the empire. Finnish liberties were curtailed, Poles and Ukrainians were repressed, and he endorsed a law of 1911 which disenfranchised the Jews once again. In 1908, it was decreed that all matters relating to Finland had to be submitted to the Russian State Council, the second house of the Imperial Parliament, before being referred to the Tsar. The following year, the Finns were required to participate in fully funding Russia's military expenditures, although the Finns were no longer drafted for military service.

Stolypin was assassinated in September 1911, but his successors were unable to brake the country's momentum. Meanwhile, a series of reactionary governors-general held office in Helsinki, where they pursued the policy of Russification with more enthusiasm than common sense. Their zeal in attempting to re-establish control of Finland in this fashion may have been inspired by concern over impending war. The Swedish King's sympathy for Germany was well known, raising the possibility of a German-Swedish alliance in the event of hostilities and greatly increasing Finland's strategic importance to all the belligerents.

Notes — Chapter III

1. Eino Jutikkala and Kauko Pirinen, *A History of Finland* (New York: Dorset Press, 1988), 160.
2. Ibid., 161.
3. Ibid., 162.
4. Fred Singleton, *A Short History of Finland* (Cambridge: Cambridge University Press, 1989), 95.
5. Jutikkala and Pirinen, *History of Finland*, 195.
6. Alexander Gershenkron, *The Transformation of Russian Society*, ed. C. Black (Cambridge: Harvard University Press, 1960), 61.

IV

Neutrality in
The Great War

As the international outlook darkened in the Baltic region and rival alliances positioned themselves for the coming struggle in Central Europe, Scandinavia remained an oasis of calm, at least on the surface. In reality, ever since Denmark's loss of Schleswig, Holstein, and Lauenburg to Prussia and the founding of the German Empire following the defeat of France in 1871, the strategic situation of the Scandinavian countries had been worsening steadily.

Denmark had experienced a remarkable economic recovery from the Prusso-Danish war, but the country still suffered psychologically from the aftershocks of the conflict, while Sweden had been weakened by the loss of Norway in 1905. But in Stockholm, the government did find itself with a little more flexibility in the field of foreign affairs. Liberated from Norway's persistent fear of being drawn into international conflicts through Swedish activism, the government was more free to react to events from abroad.

Newly independent Norway was determined to remain a bystander in the developing situation. As its first Foreign Minister told the Parliament in 1905, the government's aim was "to avoid involvement in combinations and alliances that could drag us into belligerent adventures with any of the European warrior states."[1] Hoping to get the major powers to recognize, if not guarantee, the new state's neutrality, he worked for two years toward that end. Finally, in 1907, England, France, Germany, and Russia jointly and severally guaranteed Norway's territorial integrity but abstained from even mentioning the word neutrality.

Wilhelm II's Germany now exerted control over the entire southern shore of the Baltic, from the middle of the Jutland peninsula to Königsberg in the East. Russia's area of control was even more extensive, running from the German border through the Baltic lands and Finland to its border with Sweden high up in the Gulf of Bothnia. As a result, Sweden and Denmark were at considerable risk in case of a conflict between the two great powers. They were equally at risk if the Germans and Russians should decide to cooperate to the detriment of Nordic interests. Advanced technology, in the form of modern warships and expanding railway systems, only added to Scandinavia's sense of precariousness, as did Russia's renewed attempts to bring Finland's autonomy to an end.

Denmark and Norway remained essentially passive, but Sweden responded with a substantial modernization of its defenses, in spite of widespread pessimism about the military's ability to defend the country's neutrality in case of war. Of the two threatening empires, Sweden feared the Tsar's more and, in fact, demonstrated some popular sympathy for Germany's comparatively forward-looking autocracy. In an effort to "reinsure" themselves against a possible Russian attack, the Swedish Government in 1910 authorized secret conversations in Berlin between the Swedish and German general staffs.

> *The Germans, however, proved uninterested in giving promises of assistance in the event of an attack on a neutral Sweden. They wished instead to exploit Sweden's orientation toward Germany in order to alarm the Russians and cause them to place larger forces in northern Europe, thus lessening the Russian threat to Germany from the east.*[2]

There were also important reservations on Sweden's side. The Swedish political scene was envenomed at that time by a bitter struggle between left and right factions in the Parliament, with the growing labor movement strongly in favor of unadulterated neutrality in international affairs. In February 1914, the neutralist-minded Liberal government resigned over the King's demand that the period of military service be extended, and a government of conservative civil servants was appointed.

There was a significant difference between the Swedish Government's attitude toward the two belligerents: the Foreign Minister privately assured Berlin of Sweden's "benevolent neutrality" while promising Germany's enemies only "strict neutrality." Swedish ambivalence contributed to St. Petersburg's indecision over how to deal with Sweden's proclaimed neutrality. In August 1914, just after the outbreak of war, the Russian Baltic fleet headed toward the Swedish island of Gotland. Its mission was evidently to destroy the Swedish naval forces in that vicinity, but the commander was ordered back to base before reaching his objective. Later, in 1915, the German Government made offers to Sweden in an effort to bring it into the war on the German side but failed to pursue the matter vigorously.

The military stalemate in Central Europe throughout the war impelled renewed examination of peripheral operations, leading to the failed Western attempt at Gallipoli in 1915. Although the Nordic area was not brought into the theater of military operations, Denmark was forced by the Germans to lay mines to foil Britain's Royal Navy in the Belts between the Baltic and North Seas. All of Scandinavia suffered heavy losses in both human lives and shipping tonnage from submarines in World War I. By 1900, Norway had amassed the third largest merchant fleet in the world, after Britain and the United States, so that it was highly vulnerable to the submarine menace. During the war, the Norwegians lost some 2,000 seamen to hostile action, and the Danes lost about 100 ships.

The land-based stalemate spread to the high seas when Kaiser Wilhelm was unable to use the powerful High Seas Fleet he had so expensively conjured up as a challenge to the Royal Navy. Because of the German U-boat menace, England's admiralty was wary about operating in the North Sea, but units of Britain's First (Great) Fleet scored impressive if limited victories over the German navy at Heligoland Bight in 1914 and Dogger Bank in 1915. When the German High Seas Fleet finally tried to force its way out of the Baltic Sea on May 31, 1916, its tactical victory off the Danish coast of Jutland, in terms of ships destroyed, disguised its strategic defeat only momentarily. In Paul Kennedy's estimation, the German boast of victory, "based as it was on purely material considerations, was both misleading and irrelevant."[3] The Kaiser's much prized fleet had to remain bottled up in the Baltic for the remainder of the war, exiting only in 1919 on its way to surrender at Scapa Flow, and the critical importance of controlling the Danish Straits had been clearly highlighted for all future belligerents.

From the very beginning of the war, Britain was determined to exploit its naval superiority in order to interdict the flow of supplies to Germany's civil population, as well as the enemy's war production. London's imposition of a blockade in 1914 was at variance with fairly well-established doctrines of international law, and the Scandinavian governments, particularly Sweden's, protested vehemently. The United States also protested vigorously until its entry in the war on the side of Britain in 1917.

Stockholm was able at first to exert some moderating influence in London by threatening to cut off Britain's important transit route across Sweden to Russia, but following serious supply problems in 1916, the newly elected Swedish Parliament required the King to appoint a government prepared to accept the Western powers' control over the sea routes.

Denmark and Norway were also buffeted by the conflicting demands of the Central Powers and the Allies over the previously recognized distinction between contraband and non-contraband goods. Throughout the war, however, all the neutrals demonstrated considerable ingenuity in getting around the British restrictions. The Swedes turned copper ingots into little statues of Marshal von Hindenberg, which were adjudged to be non-contraband as *objéts d'art*. Denmark, not to be outdone, imported twelve times as much lard as it had before the war. This normally innocuous commodity was then sent to Germany to be turned into glycerine to produce explosives.[4] It was not until the November 1917 (Bolshevik) Revolution, when Russian absolutism was removed, that Scandinavia's sympathies shifted overwhelmingly in favor of the victorious democracies.

Throughout the war, Finland proved to be a haven for Russia's political dissidents, both Social Democrats and Social Revolutionaries. Lenin and his close associate, Grigori Zinoviev, were forced to remain in hiding in Finland throughout much of 1917, probably in fear that allegations about their activities as German agents would be substantiated. Lenin's host for part of his stay in Finland was, reportedly, the police chief of Helsinki, who was a secret Bolshevik sympathizer. Even within Russia, the special status of Finland was beneficial to the revolutionaries. Lenin for some time masqueraded successfully as a Finnish farmhand in order to evade the Tsarist police.

Although exempt from compulsory military service, the Finns suffered throughout the war from the blockade, food rationing, and wartime restrictions on their already limited civil rights. The disruption of Finland's foreign trade was only partly compensated for by the insistent demands of the Russian military machine. Moreover, the shift from peaceful exports to the provision of military goods introduced serious distortions in the Finnish economy. Agriculture benefited to some extent because of the new Russian demand for dairy products and meat. But shortages of previously available grain from Russia caused serious problems.

The outbreak of war in 1914 had stimulated Finnish aspirations for independence, and the idea of an armed revolt against Russian rule began gaining adherents, especially among university students. Many Finns served voluntarily in the Russian armed forces; however, other Finnish young men from the independence movement, who had not been subject to military training since the disbanding of the Finnish army ten years earlier, began to slip away to gain such experience. Approximately 2,000 men went to nearby Sweden and made the journey from there to Germany. Many of these Finns, organized into the 27th Prussian Light Infantry, paid with their lives for their training when their *Jaeger* unit was sent into action against Russian forces on the Baltic front.

After the March 1917 Revolution in Russia, the provisional Kerensky government restored Finnish autonomy. Finnish political prisoners in Russia were released, and the unpopular Governor-General, F.S. Seyn, was jailed. But such gestures were too little and too late to stem the tide of Finnish nationalism. The Finnish Government, headed by the Social Democratic leader Oskari Tokoi, assumed power within Finland, leaving only foreign and military affairs in the care of Petrograd, the new name for St. Petersburg. The Finns received some support within Russia from the All-Russian Congress of Workers and Soldiers Deputies, which favored full internal independence for Finland. But the new government held that when the Tsar abdicated, his powers as Grand Duke had passed to the new government. It responded by dissolving the Eduskunta. A new Finnish Parliament, elected in the fall of 1917, placed the Socialists in the minority once again, but they remained the largest single party.

When the Bolsheviks seized power in Russia in November 1917, the road was finally open for the Finns to make their leap to independence. Lenin had already promised that he would accept their decision, although he hoped that Finland would opt to remain in some kind of association with a Socialist Russia. But the new revolutionary government in Petrograd was too busy with more challenging matters to concern itself with the status of Finland. Accordingly, when the Eduskunta declared independence on December 6, 1917, Petrograd recognized the former Romanov duchy as an independent state.

Some 40,000 Russian troops remained in Finland, however, where relations between the Socialist and *bourgeois* tendencies had begun to deteriorate even before the Bolshevik Revolution. Red and White Guards, the former supported by Russia and the latter by Germany, began an armed struggle for control over Finland's future. An extremist minority in the Social Democratic Party executive, among which figured O.V. Kuusinen, declared a general strike, which led rapidly to chaotic conditions throughout the economy. Some of the Red forces reportedly ran amok, killing and looting indiscriminately.

In January 1918, the ultra-conservative P.H. Svinhufvud, head of the new Finnish Government and a former leader of the passive resistance movement, ordered the White Guards to expel the Russians from the country and to restore public order. As White Guard Commander Carl Gustaf Mannerheim mounted operations against the undisciplined Russians, the Red Guards seized power in the south of the country, leading to full-scale civil war in some areas. Approximately half of the Finnish population found itself on territory controlled by the Reds, which included Helsinki and the country's industrial centers, while the other half was on White territory. About 5,500 men on each side were killed in the fighting during the Finnish Civil War, but, in addition, 8,000 Reds were reportedly executed in reprisals by the White forces, and at least 70,000 Red prisoners were captured, of whom more than 10,000 died in prison camps.[5]

Mannerheim had accepted the role of Commander-in-Chief on the condition that no foreign troops would be brought in to assist his forces. There was also strong sentiment in the Eduskunta against contaminating Finland's struggle for liberation by invoking foreign assistance. As the struggle between the White and Red Guards dragged on, however, the Finnish Government looked to Germany for assistance. Meanwhile, the German Empire had reached an agreement with the Bolsheviks at Brest-Litovsk (March 3, 1918), which made the German Government reluctant to appear to be opposing Lenin's régime. But the German military, particularly Field Marshal von Hindenberg, felt otherwise. He believed that "Finland is Germany's natural ally, not only with the final period of the war but with the peace to follow in view."[6]

When the Kaiser sided with the military, Germany announced that it was intervening, not to "meddle in her domestic affairs but to help Finland in her fight against a foreign foe."[7] German troops were therefore ostensibly placed under Mannerheim's command, and Finland, in return, accepted a treaty limiting its conduct of foreign affairs. The same agreement gave Germany a highly preferential position in Finland's external trade.

In March, German naval forces made a landing on the Åland Islands, and, in early April, a German expeditionary force under General von der Goltz landed at Hangö and advanced toward Helsinki. The great Finnish composer, Jean Sibelius, who had taken refuge at a psychiatric hospital in Helsinki where his brother was a physician, described the German bombardment of the city as "a crescendo that lasted 30 hours and ended in a *fortissimo* — horrible but grand." With the German assistance, particularly from the *Jaeger* battalion, the Whites were able to win victory. On May 16, 1918, Marshal Mannerheim rode into Helsinki at the head of a victorious army.

A rump Parliament, from which virtually all members of the Social Democratic Party were excluded, then installed Svinhufvud as regent. The vice-president of the senate, Juho Kusti Paasikivi, a conservative banker who had earlier been an influential Compliant, served as Prime Minister. The two leaders, in spite of Svinhufvud's original preference for a republican form of government, then supported the idea of a monarchy under Prince Friedrich Karl of Hesse. Still under the impression that Germany would be victorious, a coalition of former Old and Young Finns, together with most of the Swedes, mustered a majority in the Eduskunta in his favor. Before any further action could be taken, however, Germany had been defeated. Svinhufvud and Paasakivi accepted the political consequences of their failed policy and both men resigned their posts.

Marshal Mannerheim, an aristocrat who had become the unlikely idol of rural conservatives, had resigned as head of the Finnish army shortly after his triumphal parade in May to protest what he regarded as undue German influence in Finland's military affairs. At Svinhufvud's request, he had gone to France and was visiting Britain, trying to overcome Finland's reputation for being too close to Germany, when the Eduskunta invited him to succeed Svinhufvud as regent. He served in that position until a republic was proclaimed in 1919. Kaarlo Juho Staahlberg, who had drafted the proposal for a republic, was elected its first president, 143 Eduskunta votes to 50 over Mannerheim, who was the candidate of the right. Staahlberg subsequently pardoned many of the hundreds of convicted Red prisoners, but a residue of bitterness carried over into Finnish political life for many years.

Sweden recognized Finland's independence on January 4, 1918, immediately after its recognition by Lenin's government made it safe to do so. During the Finnish Civil War, the White faction in Vasa had asked the Swedes to supply them with arms and to permit the transit of arms to them from Germany, which provoked a split in the Swedish Government and public opinion. Most Swedes, including the Social Democrats, criticized the conduct of the Finnish Reds but were unwilling to take sides in what had developed into a class war in a neighboring country. Although a very restrictive policy on White requests was adopted, limited quantities of arms were permitted to transit Sweden, partly on German transport vessels escorted by Swedish naval units.

> *A number of Swedish officers were also permitted to volunteer for service at the military headquarters of the Whites. Finland was not at war with any foreign power, and the laws of neutrality therefore presented no obstacle to Swedish military assistance to the Whites, but the government feared that involvement in Finland would in one way or another draw Sweden into the war between Germany and the western powers.*[8]

By 1917, Germany had already begun to make plans for its future domination of the Baltic area. It was then made clear in Stockholm that there could be an advantageous place for Sweden in the German scheme if it accepted the exclusion of the Western powers from all influence in the region.[9] Toward the end of that year, Germany offered to help Sweden acquire the Ålands, but the Swedes refused, fearing that German assistance would be incompatible with its policy of neutrality. When the Ålanders, who were Swedish-speaking, appealed for Sweden's intervention against Russian mistreatment, the government in Stockholm worked successfully to secure the evacuation of the Russian troops from the islands. The Swedes were also able to ensure that some small groups of Finland's Red and White Guards, which had moved over to the Ålands, left as well.

Stockholm then sent a small detachment of about 600 men to the islands to supervise the repatriation operations, which raised international suspicions about the *bona fides* of Sweden's neutrality. Both the White Finns and the Germans interpreted the Swedish action as an attempt to seize the islands for themselves and sent forces there to block any such eventuality. Sweden withdrew its forces in May 1918. Although the inhabitants were nearly unanimous in their desire to join Sweden, Stockholm failed in its postwar efforts to persuade the League of Nations that the principle of self-determination required that the Ålands be recognized as Swedish.

The League awarded the islands to Finland instead but required the Finns to guarantee the inhabitants' rights to govern themselves and preserve their Swedish language and culture. The League also stipulated that the Ålands were to be demilitarized and that any attempt to attack them or make use of them for military purposes was forbidden. The Soviet Union, as a non-member of the League, was not included among the guarantors, in spite of its close proximity to the islands.

Although the Bolsheviks suppressed independence movements in most of the former Tsarist Empire, the move toward independence in the westerly districts was more successful. Liberated from Russia by the draconian provisions of the Brest-Litovsk Treaty of March 1918, they were able to organize themselves even under German occupation to play an independent role in postwar Europe. During the Brest-Litovsk negotiations, Leon Trotsky had done his best to stir up revolutionary sentiments within the German army with his policy of "No Peace, No War," at one point declaiming that:

> ... *the terms proposed to us by the governments of Germany and Austro-Hungary are in fundamental conflict with the interest of all peoples. They are repudiated by the toiling masses of all countries, including the Austro-Hungarian and the German peoples. The peoples of Poland, Ukraine, Lithuania, Kurland, and Estonia feel in them the*

*violence inflicted upon their aspirations.... Imperialism is
writing with the sword on the flesh of living nations.*[10]

Faced with the dissolution of the Russian army and the
consequent lack of effective resistance to the continued German
advance, Trotsky was finally compelled to recommend acceptance
of the German *Diktat.* In spite of Nikolai Bukharin's adamant
opposition, Lenin sided with Trotsky, threatening to resign if the
Bolshevik Central Committee failed to agree.

Russia lost about 1.5 million square miles of territory under
the Brest-Litovsk treaty, including its Polish, Ukrainian, Lithuanian, Estonian, and Latvian districts, as well as Bessarabia. A
further serious blow to the Bolsheviks came during 1918, when
the German army overthrew pro-Communist risings in the Baltic
states. Although the treaty was formally annulled by the Armistice
of November 11, 1918, on the Western front, nearly all of the
territorial changes imposed under it stayed in force until the
Russo-German agreement of August 24, 1939, known as the
Molotov-Ribbentrop Pact.

Finland, in spite of its long existence as a quasi-autonomous
Grand Duchy, was in 1918 still new to the idea of real national
sovereignty and to the conduct of its own foreign relations. First
attention, of course, had to be accorded to its ties and conflicts with
Russia and Germany. Both of these neighbors were heavily involved
in Finland's internal affairs, militarily as well as politically, as both
had armed forces operating on Finnish territory. For that matter,
Finland was involved in what Russians considered their own internal affairs, occupying a significant amount of territory in Eastern
Karelia, a border region largely inhabited by peoples related to the
Finns. Next was the question of Finland's relationship to Sweden,
particularly the vexatious matter of the Åland Islands.

Relations with Russia remained the most critical item on the
Finnish agenda, as the Bolsheviks strove to hang on to as much
territory as possible from a disintegrating Russian Empire. Inspired by a feeling of brotherly concern for their neighbors to the
South, a Finnish volunteer force evidently played a significant role
in helping Estonia establish its independence in 1919. But Field
Marshal Mannerheim's open letter to President Staahlberg urging
Finland to join the White military offensive on Petrograd failed in
its purpose. Although not entirely unsympathetic to the White

cause, Staahlberg was evidently unwilling to join in this military adventure without support from the Entente powers, which did not materialize. Accordingly, the Red Army was able to repulse the attack by General Yudenich. Lenin himself reportedly noted that if the Baltic States (including Finland) had taken part in the offensive, the Bolshevik régime might have collapsed.[11]

When Trotsky's Red Army had demonstrated its ability to defend the new "workers' state" from both internal and external enemies, the Finnish Government decided to move toward a more stable peace. Opening the negotiations with an expansionist demand, the Finns asked for all of East Karelia, including the Kola Peninsula. After four months of negotiations, a compromise settlement was reached, and a Finnish delegation, headed by Paasikivi, signed the Treaty of Tartu (Dorpat) with the Soviet Union on October 14, 1920.

In addition to ending the state of war and reiterating Soviet recognition of Finnish independence, the treaty transferred to Finland the ice-free port of Petsamo and some nearby territory on the Arctic coast of Lapland. The Bolsheviks thereby finally honored the promise originally made by Tsar Alexander II in 1864 to exchange this area for two Karelian districts ceded to Russia at that time. As part of the new bargain, the Finns had to abandon their claims to East Karelia, which engendered considerable criticism from right-wing circles at home. Nevertheless, the acquisition of Petsamo gave Finland access to the Arctic Ocean and significantly enhanced the country's claim to be a Nordic nation rather than a purely Baltic one.

Meanwhile, the new Soviet Government in Moscow had to face the broader consequences of Russia's estrangement from the rest of the world, beginning with its exclusion from the postwar peace conferences. In an attempt to break out of its diplomatic isolation, the Soviet Government sent Maxim Litvinov to Stockholm to interest Allied representatives in a conciliatory proposal. But this gesture failed to elicit a positive response at Versailles, where Allied negotiators opted instead to invite representatives from all the warring factions in Russia to a conference on the island of Prinkipo (now Büyükada), in the Sea of Marmara. All of the anti-Bolshevik régimes rejected the invitation, believing that the Moscow government was on the verge of collapse. Soviet Foreign Minister George Chicherin returned the only favorable reply.

Yet the natural unwillingness of the Finns and Poles to side with the anti-Bolshevik (but Russian nationalist) Whites contributed notably to the eventual Bolshevik success in the civil war. Although Mannerheim had called for driving Lenin's troops out of northern East Karelia, he found it impossible to reach an understanding with the other ex-generals now leading the White forces.[12] Even after the Treaty of Tartu in 1920, Mannerheim and others still hoped to detach the border regions of Karelia by cooperating with the other succession states to that end. During 1921, while the East Karelians were still in revolt against Bolshevik rule, Poland, Latvia, Estonia, and Finland delivered notes to the Soviet Government protesting its failure to abide by the agreed-upon peace terms. Finland also brought this complaint to the League of Nations, and the Finnish Government opened negotiations with the states to its south with a view toward military collaboration. Foreign Minister Rudolf Holsti signed a political pact with Warsaw, but the Finnish Parliament repudiated his efforts, probably influenced in this direction by Paasikivi and the former Old Finns group. Later, also, the Western countries reportedly cautioned the Finns against any alliance with the Baltic states, whose external position they regarded as weak.[13]

The Finns remained as wary of the Polish Government's designs on the Baltic area as they were of the motives of the Russian Whites. They were thus unwilling to join in Poland's 1920 attempt to secure the contested territory between Warsaw and Moscow. The see-saw war between the Soviet Union and Poland in the spring and summer of 1920, during which Marshal Pilsludski's Polish forces and their Ukrainian allies took Kiev and the Red Army counter-attacked to the gates of Warsaw before it was repulsed, failed to resurrect the declining military fortunes of the Whites; instead, Poland and the USSR reached a peace of mutual exhaustion by the Treaty of Riga in March 1921.

When Wrangel's army, the last of the White forces, was at last evacuated from the Crimea at the end of 1920, the civil war had effectively ended, and the Bolshevik régime was thus free to concentrate on eliminating opponents at home. Internationally, the Bolsheviks moved forward simultaneously on two separate but related fronts, the diplomatic and the revolutionary. Officially, the new régime began to establish a network of diplomatic ties with some of its newly independent neighbors, notably the Baltic states of Estonia, Latvia, and Lithuania. The Treaty of Riga ending the war with Poland, which remained in force until 1939, established the Russo-Polish frontier along lines favorable to the Poles. In addition to granting Vilno (Vilnius in Lithuanian) to Poland, the treaty divided the Ukraine between Russia and Poland, in spite of strong Ukrainian claims to independence.

On the revolutionary front, Moscow's hopes for uprisings in Western Europe were encouraged by the establishment of short-lived "Soviet" régimes in Bavaria and Hungary. In order to play a more effective role on the world scene, Lenin concluded that the Bolsheviks had to amplify their own voices by means of an international organization. Contemptuous of the Second International because of its failure to block the 1914-18 war, he founded a new group, the Third International, or Comintern. Lenin's initiative had its origin in an appeal drafted by Karl Radek during the war and submitted to the third *Zimmerwald* Conference in neutral Stockholm in September 1917, but the new organization was not formally inaugurated until 1919. After the collapse of the Bolshevik-inspired revolts in Bavaria and Hungary, Lenin hoped to take advantage of the various "contradictions" he saw among the belligerents in the just concluded war — the contest between the victors and the vanquished and the rising conflict between the imperialist states and their colonies.

At its second congress in July 1920, the Comintern adopted a set of twenty-one conditions, largely drafted by Lenin, emphasizing the need for discipline and highly centralized leadership. All decisions were to be unconditionally binding on the member parties. But the heavy Russian control so evident in this supposedly international organization significantly reduced its appeal to the more sophisticated socialists of Western Europe, especially those of Scandinavia. Most of the original first-echelon leaders of the Comintern were either Russian citizens or East Europeans with close ties to Moscow. G.E. Zinoviev was head of its executive committee, while the committed Bolshevik but more cosmopolitan Karl Radek, still in jail in Germany at the time, was designated secretary.

The apparent success of the Bolsheviks in "expropriating the expropriators" in 1917 naturally generated interest and some enthusiasm in labor circles throughout Scandinavia, as well as in Finland. The Norwegian Labor Party (*Arbeiderparti*) had become radicalized during the war when it fell under the influence of its left wing, headed by Martin Tranmael. This group led the party into the Comintern in 1919, but moderate elements refused to accept the Third International's centralization, breaking off to form the Norwegian Social Democratic Labor Party in 1921. The moderates regained control of the old party in 1923 and withdrew from the Comintern at that time, while the more Bolshevik-minded elements established the Norwegian Communist Party. The moderate socialists then reunited and revived the Labor Party organization in 1927. Similar tensions between extremist and moderate labor circles also troubled Denmark, where the struggle was greatly complicated by the resurrection of the old issue of Schleswig. There, in 1920, pro-Danish elements pressed for a plebiscite to resolve the nationality question. The new German Republic agreed to a plebiscite, and the resulting poll closely reflected linguistic preferences. North Schleswig, down to the present frontier with Germany, voted roughly three to one to return to Denmark, while the southern districts of the province favored Germany in about the same proportions.

In retrospect, it is clear that the Comintern's attempt to bind European Communist Parties to the procrustean bed of Russian experience seriously undermined the possibility that its "brother parties" would develop into mass parties in their own countries. The Norwegian labor movement ended its brief flirtation with the Comintern in 1923, leaving behind a rump Communist Party that eventually (1975) merged with a coalition group known as the Socialist Left Party. Except for the war years, 1940–45, when the far left joined in the national resistance to the German occupiers, its adherents have failed to play a significant role in Norwegian politics.

Comintern doctrinal rigidity was even less appealing in Denmark. There also, the far left gained a modicum of popular support during the German occupation, but only after Danish Communists followed the lead of Moscow in resisting Nazi aggression. Absent a German occupation and buffered by the almost uninterrupted rule of the Social Democrats in Sweden and Norway, Denmark offered few opportunities for a Moscow-leaning Communist movement to develop.

Iceland, which was still part of Denmark at the end of World War I, proved to be a different case. Communist-oriented parties played a significant role there even before Icelandic independence was gained in 1944. The Labor Party, founded in 1916 (later to become the Social Democratic Party), gave birth to various splinter groups, one of which in 1970 became the People's Alliance. Whether as an occasional partner in coalition governments or in opposition, it has exerted considerable pressure on a succession of Icelandic governments to restrict or eliminate the American military presence at Keflavik and to withdraw from NATO. Much of its electoral support appears, however, to stem from traditional Icelandic insularity and a desire to avoid outside contamination rather than a keen ideological sympathy with Communist principles.

Scandinavia as a whole emerged from World War I with some damage but fully aware of its comparatively fortunate position. The German, Austro-Hungarian, Ottoman, and Russian Empires had been dismantled, and those of France and Britain were seriously wounded. Other belligerents, such as Italy and Belgium, suffered physical and psychological harm. In such circumstances, it is not surprising that the relative success of a neutral stance in the struggles among the great powers burned itself into the consciousness of all the Nordic peoples.

Notes — Chapter IV

1. Olav Riste, ed., *Western Security*, 129.
2. Wahlbäck, *Roots of Swedish Neutrality*, 21.
3. Paul M. Kennedy, *The Rise and Fall of British Naval Mastery* (Malabar, Fl.: Robert E. Krieger, 1982), 246.
4. Marc Ferro, *The Great War 1914–1918* (London: Unwin, 1977), 108.
5. Jutikkala and Pirinen, *History of Finland*, 220.
6. Ibid., 219.
7. Ibid.
8. Wahlbäck, *Roots of Swedish Neutrality*, 27.
9. Ibid.
10. George F. Kennan, *Russia and the West Under Lenin and Stalin* (Boston: Atlantic Monthly Press, 1960), 48.
11. Jutikkala and Pirinen, *History of Finland*, 228.
12. Ibid., 226-27.
13. Ibid., 238.

V

Neutrality Between the Wars

A t the conclusion of World War I, the Scandinavian states found
themselves in a more favorable international position than they
had enjoyed for many years. The German and Russian Empires were
gone and with them their acute rivalry for dominance in the Baltic.
An independent Finland now stood between the mass of the Soviet
Union and the rest of Scandinavia, while Denmark had re-acquired
the Danish-speaking areas of Schleswig. Sweden was particularly well
insulated from the great powers, but none of the Nordic states
needed to fear inordinate pressure from larger nations.

The twenty-seven nations which assembled in Paris in January 1919 to settle the map of the postwar world negotiated for
three months. Plenary meetings of the Peace Conference were
relatively unimportant, as all key decisions were taken by the Big
Four — Wilson for the United States, Lloyd-George for Britain,
Clemençeau for France, and V.E. Orlando for Italy. The three
European leaders had little confidence in Wilson's proposed
League of Nations, but they yielded to him on that issue in return
for concessions on other matters which, in their view, were of more
immediate consequence. Germany at first refused to sign the
Treaty of Versailles but eventually did so, detailing two virtually
unknown representatives to perform the repugnant task. The
League of Nations then took up its functions in Geneva, but the
United States, in a fit of renewed isolationism, refused to join,
gravely weakening the organization from the very beginning.

In accord with their modern practice of reasoning together to
solve problems, all the Scandinavian countries were enthusiastic
supporters of the new League of Nations and its system of collective
security. Nevertheless, some dissent was voiced on both the right
and the extreme left of the political spectrum. Critics observed that

both Germany and the Soviet Union were excluded and that joining the League would oblige members to cooperate in maintaining the *status quo* for the indefinite future. This could require the abandonment of neutrality and the acceptance of unknown risks if the world situation developed in an unfortunate direction.

Supporters of the League replied that all states were expected to join the League in due course and that, while member states would be required to take part in economic sanctions against an aggressor, the obligation to take military sanctions was less binding. Moreover, joining the League would provide some assurance of receiving assistance from others if their own nations were attacked.

During the course of the following two decades, the fears of the League's critics proved to be as exaggerated as the claims of its supporters. France soon failed in its attempts to strengthen the obligations of League members to participate in sanctions, largely because of Great Britain's refusal to cooperate. Many Scandinavians were sympathetic to the so-called Geneva Protocol of 1924, which would have marked an important step toward effective military sanctions, but the protocol failed to win general acceptance. In spite of this shortfall, the Nordic states continued to play a vigorous role within the League as conciliators, a role they have continued to exercise in the rather different framework of the United Nations.

Not surprisingly, the two pariah states, Germany and Russia, which had not been invited to participate in either the Conference or the League, soon took steps to draw together for mutual support. The semiautonomous German army, under the leadership of General Hans von Seeckt, began its secret military and military-industrial cooperation with the Red Army, a policy which was to continue until the 1930s. In the spring of 1922, during a general economic and financial conference in Genoa, Germany and Russia found themselves frustrated by their lack of acceptance on Europe's emerging economic scene. On Easter Sunday, they repaired a short distance down the Italian coast to Rapallo, where they quickly negotiated an agreement canceling their war damage claims on one another. This, in Adam Ulam's considered view, "enabled both sides to emerge from isolation with a diplomatic partner to play off against Great Britain and France."[1]

But signature of the agreement also permitted both parties to move forward more openly and effectively in the military field.

George Kennan's evaluation of the significance of this 1922 marriage of convenience between bourgeois Germany and revolutionary Russia seems to be definitive. "For the Western Allies, Rapallo meant the forfeiture of the collaboration of Germany as a possible partner in a united Western approach to the problem of Russian Communism.... [It] could justly be described as the first great victory for Soviet diplomacy."[2]

That victory was only temporary, however, and the path was left open for further disappointments in Moscow. At Locarno, in 1925, a series of agreements were signed which were designed to remove some of the sting inflicted on Germany at Versailles. Under the new agreements, which amounted to a dramatic diplomatic defeat for the Soviet Government, Germany guaranteed the frontiers of France and Belgium. Great Britain did likewise, pledging military assistance to them in case of a violation.

In addition, Germany signed arbitration pacts with Poland and Czechoslovakia, promising not to seek changes in their borders except by mutual agreement or arbitration. For its part, France tried to enhance its security *vis-à-vis* Germany by linking its future to those same two East European states, plus Romania, which taken together constituted the "Little Entente." But Britain did not extend its guarantee to Poland, Czechoslovakia, or Romania.

At the same time, the German Foreign Minister, former Chancellor Gustav Stresemann, adroitly kept the Rapallo relationship alive as a means of maximizing Western receptivity to the Weimar government's views. Russo-German relations were formally reaffirmed in the Treaty of Berlin, signed on April 24, 1926, in spite of German resentment over clear Soviet responsibility for the Comintern's support to the abortive uprising of the German Communist Party in 1923. That support was not limited to unofficial Party channels either, because Soviet diplomats sought promises from the Baltic states and Poland that they would not interfere in the German struggle and would permit the USSR to send materiel and personnel through their territories to the Communist factions in Germany. In a ploy to be repeated more than twenty years later, Warsaw's acquiescence in this scheme was reportedly sought by promising East Prussia to the Poles.[3]

One more link in the paper chain of interlocking agreements was provided by the signature in 1928 of the Kellogg-Briand Pact. Named after the U.S. Secretary of State and the French Foreign

Minister, this agreement was ultimately signed by sixty-five states. Its signatories condemned "recourse to war for the solution of international controversies" and renounced war "as an instrument of national policy." Fearful that Soviet representatives might indulge their penchant for merely rhetorical disarmament proposals, the fifteen original signatories declined to permit them to take part in the negotiations. Soviet Foreign Minister Chicherin thereupon denounced the pact as an attempt to encircle the USSR, but he relented when the Soviet Union was invited to adhere to the document.

Moscow then moved quickly to negotiate what became known as the "Litvinov Protocol," putting the general international pact into force immediately with its Western neighbors. The Soviet Union also tried to conclude a bilateral nonaggression treaty with Poland. Although initially reluctant to tie its interests too closely to those of the USSR, Poland was soon concerned enough about the threat from Germany to sign on the dotted line, although only after Moscow had yielded to Warsaw's insistence that the other border states be included as well. As the USSR had already negotiated a treaty of friendship and neutrality with Lithuania in 1926 and a trade pact with Latvia in 1927, the Soviets did not find the Polish stipulation onerous and were pleased to sign treaties of nonaggression with all three Baltic states as well as with Poland and Romania in 1929.

Like the rest of Scandinavia, Finland had entered the post-World War I era with high hopes, as had the Baltic states and all the other newly independent states of Europe. Soon, however, the economic consequences of the peace proved too much for their fragile political structures to bear. Those caught geographically and economically between the two pariah states, Germany and the USSR, were struck particularly hard. The commercial and transport links tying Finland and the Baltic states to their former metropole in the Russian Empire increased the difficulty of establishing viable economies in a world on the brink of the great depression of the 1930s.

Before the Revolution, Russia had absorbed three-quarters of Finland's exports and supplied it with two-thirds of its imports. The gap resulting when the Russian market virtually collapsed in 1917 was, therefore, nearly overwhelming. Moreover, not until Finland had broken with Germany at the end of 1918 was it possible for the American Relief Administration headed by Herbert Hoover to send food assistance. When the aid arrived, however, it saved thousands of Finns from starvation and gave their language a new cliché, "to live by Hoover," i.e., on the dole.

Fortunately for Finland, better times soon arrived as postwar reconstruction in Western Europe led to a growing demand for Finnish forest products. By 1922, Finland's limited industrial production had returned to prewar levels. Industrial output then grew significantly, in parallel with the growth of investment in industry.

Farmers were less fortunate; many of them were forced into bankruptcy. Land reforms introduced by the Agrarian Party leader, Kyösti Kallio, who served as Minister of Agriculture and, later, Prime Minister, in the 1920s helped to mitigate the plight of small landholders. The growth of the cooperative movement also helped by permitting farmers to regain their equilibrium. But, by 1929, the world economic crisis began to take a heavy toll on exports of Finnish timber and food products.

Part of the adverse effect on Finland's economy came as a result of the re-entry of the Soviet Union in international markets for grain, timber, and other commodities. The USSR, as part of its initial Five-Year Plan, was prepared to sell at dumping-level prices in order to finance its ambitious industrial and military buildup. Consequently, Finnish farmers found themselves severely undercut in world markets, and prices of their products fell in 1930 to 64 percent of their 1928 level.

In spite of these blows, by investing in industry and emphasizing export-led growth, Finland emerged from the world depression more quickly and in better shape than many of its neighbors. By 1939, the share of gross national product derived from metalworking industries had advanced from its 1924 level of 15 percent to 21 percent. In line with that progress, the size of the population working in industry had doubled, and the proportion of the population dependent on agriculture had fallen, from two-thirds in 1920 to one-half. Although still much poorer than their Scandinavian neighbors, the Finns were steadily closing the gap.

Political life in independent Finland continued to be troubled by the language conflict which had so marked its nineteenth-century experience. A group dubbing itself the True Finn movement pushed vigorously for a monolingual Finland, in opposition to the insistent demands of the Swedish-speaking minority. But the clash between *bourgeois* and Socialist elements in society provided even more fireworks than the linguistic divide. That bitter struggle was kept alive largely by Finnish-speaking university students. Students returning from volunteer military service in East Karelia, where they had fought against the Bolsheviks on the side of the native East Karelians, formed the Academic Karelia Society (AKS), which dominated Finnish-speaking student life for a decade.

A Finnish Communist Party (SKP) had been founded in Petrograd in 1918 by O.V. Kuusinen and others, but it was illegal in Finland. Its leaders in Stockholm and Moscow were therefore obliged to operate through various front organizations. Their chief representative in Finland was Arvo Tuominen, editor of the left-wing journal *Suomen Työmies* (*Finnish Worker*), who was also secretary of the Socialist Worker's Party (SWP) and vice-chairman of the Trade Union Federation. The SWP had been formed in 1920 by a faction which was to the left of the Social Democrats but unenthusiastic about the SKP's plans to smuggle arms into Finland for a renewed insurrection.

In spite of his relatively moderate approach, Tuominen was arrested in 1922 for expressing his pro-Soviet views too openly and served four years in prison, as did a number of the party's other leaders. O.V. Kuusinen, however, spent a great deal of time underground in Finland and led the new party along the Moscow party line, persuading Lenin, among others, that his faction was more viable than the émigré Communists in Petrograd.

In the 1922 elections, the Communists captured twenty-seven seats in the Eduskunta, exactly the number lost by the Social Democrats in the same elections. But, the following year, Prime Minister Kallio indicted the whole Communist group in Parliament for treason and outlawed the party itself. A front party, under the rubric of the Socialist Workers' and Small Holders' Election Organization, collected twenty-seven seats again in the 1929 elections, but it too was suppressed in 1930 and did not re-emerge until 1945. At that time, it took the form of the Finnish People's Democratic League (SKDL), forming an open electoral alliance with the Communist Party, which had by then been legalized.

Finland's relations with the USSR between the wars were complicated by the activity of pro-Soviet organizations in Finland and the domestic reaction to their perceived threat to the country's independence. The character of Finnish foreign policy during the same period was determined largely by a succession of conservative German-oriented presidents, whose antipathy to the Soviet Union was well known. Under their leadership, the Finnish Government entered a loose alliance with Estonia, Lithuania, Latvia, and Poland, all of which succession states owed their independence to the break-up of the Russian Empire. The Eduskunta, however, disavowed the alliance, stressing the Scandinavian option instead and the need to avoid too provocative a stance toward Finland's enormous neighbor.

The resurgence of extreme right-wing activity which surfaced in Finland in 1929 can be seen as a reaction to an increase in Communist pressure, particularly from the Communist-controlled Young Workers Educational Association. When 400 red-shirted members of the association rallied in the market town of Lapua in November, the rally was broken up by force and their red shirts were torn to shreds. Soon afterwards, a organization called the Lock of Finland was formed for the ostensible purpose of stamping out overt Communist activities by legal means. This group was quickly succeeded by the more extreme Lapua movement, which often resorted to violent methods.

It was not long before it became clear that the Lapua movement was commanded by right-wing extremists with leanings toward Fascism. A right-wing government, headed by then Prime Minister Svinhufud, proved unable to curb the Lapua gangs, who beat up suspected Communists and sometimes forcibly expelled them over the border into the USSR. They even asked that the Social Democratic Party, as well as the Communists, be banned.

In February 1932, however, when a large group of armed militants gathered at Mäntsälä, near Helsinki, and demanded that their "Lapua law" be accepted as superior to parliamentary law, Svinhufud, who had been elected to the presidency in 1931, called a halt. The new President persuaded them to disband peaceably; then, using the emergency laws the Lapua movement had originally championed to suppress the left, he effectively put an end to what had become an incipient counter-revolution. A number of prominent members of the AKS, who resented that organization's support for the Mäntsälä mutiny, withdrew from the group and joined the Agrarian Union, reinforcing its True Finn character.

An organization which was even more obviously Fascist than the Lapua movement, termed the Patriotic People's movement (IKL), and directly inspired by the Nazi movement in Germany, then strove to replace it. Fortunately, subsequent parliamentary elections revealed that its electoral strength was limited. In 1933, it collaborated with the Conservatives, obtaining fourteen seats in Parliament (at the expense of its collaborators) and retained them at the polls in 1936. In the 1939 elections, however, the IKL dropped to only eight seats, and it was dissolved in 1944 under laws prohibiting Fascism.

President Svinhufud, who had narrowly edged out Staahlberg in the elections of 1931, immediately appointed Marshal Mannerheim chairman of the nation's Defense Council. When the presidency passed to Kallio in 1936, he and Mannerheim collaborated effectively in building up the country's defense potential. In 1938, under their leadership, the Parliament approved a large military appropriation bill, although only a small part of the arms could be procured before war broke out. At the same time, the wounds of the earlier clash between Reds and Whites finally showed clear signs of healing. The auxiliary Civil Guard units, which had formed the basis for the White Army in the War of Liberation, moved toward a reconciliation with the Social Democrats, and later, during World War II, the Guard was integrated in the regular army.

The Baltic states of Estonia, Latvia, and Lithuania were even less experienced in 1918 at dealing with their political and economic problems than formerly more or less autonomous Finland. The Soviet Union had agreed to accept their independence even before negotiating its treaties of peace with Poland and Finland, recognizing the sovereignty of all three in 1920. However, the Baltic states were destined to remain entrapped geographically and economically between Germany and the USSR, being much affected as well by the instability of their other Slavic neighbor, post-World War I Poland.

Estonia declared its independence immediately after the Bolshevik revolution, and an Estonian Government was installed shortly thereafter. Attempting to orient its foreign policy and economy toward Western Europe, the new state was ruled by short-lived coalition governments from 1920 to 1933. Four of those governments were headed by Konstantin Päts, a seasoned campaigner for an independent Estonia. Buffeted by the world economic crisis of the 1930s and the consequent turmoil in neighboring states, Estonia moved as they did toward an authoritarian régime. Under a new constitution, adopted in 1933, Päts took on dictatorial powers, which were confirmed in another constitution promulgated in 1938.

Latvia's brief period of independent existence was similar to that of Estonia. Latvian territory south of the River Daugava (Dvina) had been occupied by Germany during the war, but the break-up of the Tsar's Empire and that of his German cousin at the end of that conflict made it possible for the Latvians to move toward freedom. Latvia's original declaration of independence in 1918 led to a period of confused fighting, but by 1920, both Germany and the Soviet Union had extended recognition. Like Estonia, Latvia tried to pursue a pro-Western orientation in foreign policy and economic development under democratic coalition governments until 1934. At that stage, Latvia followed the example of its neighbor to the North by adopting an authoritarian régime. Emulating Konstantin Päts, the Latvian Premier Karl Ulmanis assumed dictatorial powers.

The Lithuanians enjoyed an even more truncated period of democratic governance than their Baltic neighbors. The Lithuanian area had not been treated as a separate political entity under the Tsars but was split into different provinces. Moreover, a strong Russification campaign during the second half of the nineteenth century had considerably damaged development of its indigenous culture. The Russian Revolution of 1905, which provided a modicum of free speech, stimulated a cultural renaissance as well as demands for political autonomy.

Occupation by the Germans during World War I did nothing to assuage the nationalist urge, and a Lithuanian Council was formed in September 1917 to pursue self-determination. The Council declared Lithuania an independent state at Vilnius in February 1918 and moved to form a government on Armistice Day, November 11, 1918. However, when German troops evacuated Vilnius in January 1919, Bolshevik forces took over the city, establishing a pro-Soviet régime there. The new Lithuanian Government then required the assistance of the German army to install itself in Kaunas, which it had to accept as its seat for the next twenty years. Although the Bolsheviks were driven out of Lithuania in

August 1919, the Poles seized Vilnius the following year and held
it until the outbreak of war in 1939. Lithuanian nationalists could
take only limited consolation from the fact that the Klaipeda, or
Memel, district of East Prussia was detached from Germany and
incorporated in Lithuania in 1923.

Lithuania enjoyed only a few years of rule under a democrat-
ically elected coalition government. Well before its Baltic neighbors had succumbed to antidemocratic forces, a military *coup
d'état* in Lithuania brought Antanas Smetona to power. Assuming
dictatorial powers to govern his largely agrarian country, he curtailed civil liberties and abolished opposition parties. The Smetona
régime avoided diplomatic relations with Poland, because of tensions arising from the Vilnius dispute, and maintained only the
coolest of relations with the Soviet Union.

The economic situation between the wars in Denmark, Sweden, and Norway was not much more favorable than that in the
Baltic states, but their firmly grounded political systems were more
successful in weathering the interwar storms. The Nordic states
were hit, as were all the advanced industrial countries, by a series
of currency crises, which further complicated the already difficult
task of re-establishing their overseas markets after the 1914–18
war. As the importance of industry grew, old political parties lost
some of their support, and workers' organizations improved their
relative standing.

In Denmark, for example, the Social Democrats in 1924
displaced the Liberals as the largest party, although they failed to
gain an absolute majority. As a result, those two parties held office
in turn. The Liberals (in 1920–24 and 1926–29) and the Social
Democrats (in 1924–26 and 1929–40) governed in coalition with
the Conservatives and the Radical Liberals, respectively. Two new
parties, the Communists and the Single-Taxers, also made themselves felt during the interwar period, while the National-Socialist
Labor Party, which came into existence during the heyday of the
Nazi Party in Germany, lasted only a few years.

The depression of the 1930s had a nearly catastrophic effect
on the Danish economy, dependent as it was on foreign trade,
particularly in agricultural products. Unemployment reached un-
precedented levels, and in 1933, the Liberals collaborated with
the Stauning-Munch (SDP/Liberal) government on an emergency program. This combined a currency devaluation with other

exceptional measures, such as production and price controls, guaranteed farm prices, and a ban on strikes and lockouts.

Norway was equally hard hit; unemployment reached a level of 18 percent in 1921 and remained at about that rate throughout the decade. Norway's first Labor (Social Democrat) government was formed in January 1928 after that party captured the largest number of parliamentary seats in the 1927 elections. This government lasted only a few weeks, but in 1935 the Norwegian electorate turned once again to Labor, installing as Prime Minister Johan Nygaardsvold, who retained that position for ten years. In fact, the moderate approach of the Social Democrats, based on social reforms and the spread of the welfare state, gained such widespread approbation that it remained in office until 1965, a full thirty years.

The tenure of Sweden's Socialists proved to be even longer, as their leaders occupied the Prime Minister's office in Stockholm for forty-four consecutive years, beginning in 1932. As in Norway, this remarkable achievement was built on an extensive program of social welfare, going back to the establishment of old-age pensions in 1911.

The substance of Scandinavian foreign policy *vis-à-vis* the Soviet Union throughout the 1919–39 interregnum can be fairly characterized as more passive than pacifist. Denmark had purely minimal relations with the USSR during that period, although it retained a certain importance in Soviet eyes as the cork in the mouth of the Baltic Sea. Norway's geographic importance was more clearly defined, producing a marked feeling of insecurity among some Norwegians who were conscious of the strategically exposed position of their northernmost province. This province, Finnmark, a large but thinly populated area with only 60,000 inhabitants, would be of great value to the USSR as a means of extending its short ice-free northern coastline. The resulting access to Norway's northern ports might effectively transform the Soviet Union into an Atlantic power as well as a Pacific one.

Sweden's dealings with the USSR between the wars were almost as superficial as those of its Nordic cousins. Stockholm began the period with a feeling of relief that a formerly threatening great power headquartered in St. Petersburg had been supplanted by a fragmented and weak state unable to project power beyond its immediate frontiers. As the USSR grew in power during the

1930s, however, Finland once again became the keystone to Swedish-Soviet relations. Moscow, which had come to accept Finland's increasingly Nordic orientation politically and economically, was not at all prepared to countenance Finnish military cooperation with its Scandinavian neighbors, especially Sweden.

In reviewing the history of the early 1930s, Bolshevik theoreticians could take some pride in the way their convictions about the inevitable decay of capitalism seemed to be confirmed. The great depression had shown even the most powerful of the capitalist giants to have feet of clay. Moreover, Marxian postulates about the inherent contradictions and rivalries among capitalist states also proved to be valid, although there was little beyond doctrinal consolation to be gained by this. Moscow found itself impelled to create a defense barrier around the Socialist homeland, composed, ironically, of just such contradictory elements. But the chief stumbling block on the road to the desired mutual security was not the clash of interests among the capitalists; rather, it was the continued antagonism between Bolshevik Russia and its capitalist, or precapitalist, neighbor Poland, a nation with which it shared a long land border as well as maritime and naval interests in the Baltic. Their antagonism was based on more than ideological grounds, moreover, being rooted firmly in 1,000 years of national and religious conflict.

Max Beloff makes it clear that "the Polish attitude was to be, in the end, responsible for the failure to achieve even a limited version of an Eastern European security scheme."[4] Nevertheless, as late as December 1933, Poland joined with the Soviet Union in asking the Baltic Republics and Finland if they would accept a joint guarantee against German aggression. The smaller nations were reluctant, however, and Poland failed to pursue the question.

Poland's lack of enthusiasm for the abortive mutual security proposal was to some extent conditioned by its continuing dispute with Lithuania over the city of Vilnius, plus concern about finding itself in the middle of the quarrel between Lithuania and Germany over Memel. Poland's claims against Czechoslovakia regarding the Teschen district provided still another complication, aggravated by Polish resentment over Czechoslovak hospitality for Ukrainian nationalist émigrés from Polish-owned areas of Ukraine.

Although the Poles' reluctance to tie themselves to a mutual security scheme with the USSR was substantially based on historical antipathy to the Russians, there were *Realpolitik* considerations as well. By early 1934, the Polish Government had become convinced that France, Poland's most important ally, had become an unreliable source of support. Rather than put its safety in the hands of Russia and the smaller countries of Eastern Europe, Poland opted to strengthen its ties with Germany, concluding in January 1934 a ten-year nonaggression pact with the Nazi government. Although still afraid of Germany, some Poles evidently considered its new Nazi leaders less dangerous than the earlier Prussian-dominated government because their ambitions were believed to be directed toward such "indubitably German" territories as Austria and the Sudetenland rather than toward Poland.

At the same time, the Polish Government wished to hedge against other contingencies and, in May 1934, renewed its nonaggression pact with the Soviet Union. Just before that event, the Soviet Union had also tried to reach a direct agreement with Germany, proposing a joint Russo-German guarantee of Finland and the Baltic states, but Germany declined. Almost immediately thereafter, the USSR prolonged its existing nonaggression pacts with all three Baltic states — until 1945.

In September 1934, the Baltic states took further steps to link their fates together by setting up a Baltic Conference framework through which they could conduct a common foreign policy. The following spring, a second meeting of the Baltic Conference reaffirmed that the three governments were still convinced of the value of broader regional security pacts, but made it clear that they would not enter into any such agreement without the participation of Germany.

The rise of Adolph Hitler naturally increased the apprehensions of Soviet leaders over the situation on the northern shore of the Baltic, which would constitute their Scandinavian flank in case of hostilities with Germany. In the circumstances, the Swedish Government believed a policy of caution was mandatory and stood aside from Helsinki's suggestion of a Fenno-Swedish defense alliance. Foreign Minister Rickard Sandler favored instead a "Nordic" neutrality which would parallel that of Sweden itself. But he also indicated a willingness to examine whether there were "limited areas or questions where a certain degree of coordination between the armed forces of all or some of the Nordic countries might enhance our chances of avoiding war."[5]

Sandler probably hoped to build on this limited pro-Nordic position to develop a more substantial degree of cooperation in the future. However, although there was considerable support throughout Scandinavia for a coordinated approach to security policy, there were also significant differences in perspective among the nations and their fears were aroused from different directions. Their policy preferences proved, accordingly, to be fundamentally incompatible.

For the Danes, for example, the primary danger lay in Germany, which had been stirring up irredentist sentiments in northern Schleswig and had an obvious interest in gaining control of the Danish Straits. The Danish Government therefore shunned anything more than moral support from the other Nordics and went out of its way to assure the Germans of its pacific intent, going so far as to intimate that only symbolic resistance would be offered if the Wehrmacht attempted to use Danish territory.

Norway, which felt itself more removed from the likely center of military action, was less inclined toward a completely pacific stance but was still unwilling to consider any defense cooperation with its fellow Nordics. Finland, on the other hand, thought with good reason that the threat came from the East and prepared itself for an armed encounter with the Soviet Union. At the same time, although not sympathetic to Nazism, it anticipated some support from Germany because of Berlin's interest in keeping Soviet power in Scandinavia in check. Finland was even more eager to obtain support from its Nordic neighbors, in spite of their reluctance to adopt too high a profile at its side. Finland therefore refused to accept the nonaggression treaty offered by Germany and solemnly declared its intention of following a Scandinavian line in foreign policy.

Sweden naturally favored the continued independent existence of all its Nordic neighbors as well as the avoidance of links between any of them and one of the great powers. The Swedes took some comfort in the thought that the great powers would try to avoid acquiring new enemies in the dangerous situation then prevailing. Nevertheless, the Swedish Government was aware of the concern in Moscow over Finland's long-standing sympathy for Germany, if not for Nazism.

In the absence of an effective League of Nations role in defending the Åland Islands, Sweden would probably be the first state to be asked by the Council of the League to assist Finland should the islands be attacked. Sweden's own defense planning was based on closing the Gulf of Bothnia to naval operations by any of the great powers. Stockholm did not want any of the major powers to gain a foothold in the Ålands from which to mount an assault on the Swedish mainland. The Swedes therefore considered that possession of the islands by one of the great powers could be more of a threat to them than to the Finns.

Accordingly, the Swedish Government in 1938 responded to Finland's desire for a greater degree of defense cooperation by asking that the Finnish Government join it in proposing to the League Council a plan for joint defense of the Ålands. But Sweden's own involvement would depend on a political decision in Stockholm in each particular case, and Sweden itself would be willing to accept even such a limited obligation only if the plan received the approbation of the interested big powers. Therefore, in 1939, when the Soviet Union, under its new Foreign Minister, V.M. Molotov, showed itself hostile to such an arrangement, Sweden backed away. Moscow simultaneously stepped up its efforts to engage the Finns in bilateral security discussions.

Meanwhile, the general European situation continued to deteriorate. Increasingly worried by developments in Germany, France had been seeking support from the Soviet Union and in 1934 was instrumental in bringing its potential ally into the League of Nations, where it was accorded a permanent seat on the Council in recognition of its status as a great power. At the League, Foreign Minister Maxim Litvinov reiterated his famous dictum that "Peace is indivisible" and implied Soviet support for the idea of a multilateral agreement that would parallel the Locarno Pact in the West. Solemnly, he assured his international audience that this would not be an attempt to encircle any country.

Throughout the first half of 1935, there were numerous diplomatic excursions and alarums among the major powers over possible security *combinazione*. Hermann Goering was known to be intriguing in Poland with Foreign Minister Josef Beck and President Pilsudski. In January, France and Italy reached an agreement on Danubian security, which also raised apprehension in Moscow. More ominously, France and Britain together tried to reach an agreement with Germany. When the German response to the Franco-British initiative tried to separate the twin issues of

Eastern and Western security, this called forth strong objections from the Soviet Government.

The exchange of diplomatic notes was illuminated, but not arrested, in March 1935 by the announcement of rearmament measures on the part of France and Great Britain, plus the reintroduction of conscription by Germany. In April, France, Britain, and Italy met at Stresa to consider their response to German conscription, at which time French Foreign Minister Pierre Laval informed his colleagues of France's intention to proceed with negotiation of a mutual assistance pact with the USSR.

The Germans, in May, condemned the proposed Franco-Russian pact as incompatible with the Locarno Pact, which France denied. That denial was seconded by Great Britain, Belgium, and Italy (which at that point had still not yet cast in its lot with Nazi Germany). But the abrupt deterioration in its relations with England and France which followed Mussolini's invasion of Abyssinia soon removed the possibility of an Italian contribution to the Western side of the European balance of power.

Italy's conquest of Abyssinia in 1935 generated great public disapproval in the West but little effective opposition. Hitler, in contrast, supported his fellow dictator's position and, with the outbreak of the Spanish Civil War in 1936, he and Mussolini were drawn even closer together. Their alliance was not made formal, however, until November 1936, when the world was informed a Berlin-Rome axis had been born.

Even after the Franco-Soviet pact was signed on March 2, 1935, Laval stalled its ratification and aroused Soviet concerns by his frequent conversations with the Poles and Germans during the delay. The pact was not finally approved by the French Chamber of Deputies until February 11, 1936, after a debate which reflected considerable domestic opposition to it. Hitler immediately seized the occasion as a pretext to reoccupy the Rhineland on March 7, but the French Senate was not intimidated and confirmed the treaty's ratification later that month.

The terms of the Franco-Russian treaty of mutual assistance were tied to the Covenant of the League and the Locarno Agreement. In practice, therefore, the pact would come into effect only if the feared "aggression by a European state" were recognized by the Council of the League. In the absence of the League's recognition, military cooperation against an attack could not be relied upon.

An even more serious shortcoming of the Franco-Russian treaty was geographical. The Soviet Union had no common border with the anticipated aggressor, Germany; hence, Soviet assistance in case of a German attack on France could be extended only if one of the states between the USSR and Germany were willing or forced to permit the passage of Soviet troops. Soviet forces could move against East Prussia with the concurrence of Latvia and Lithuania but could not attack the rest of Germany without Polish approval.

Almost simultaneously, the USSR signed a parallel mutual assistance treaty with Czechoslovakia, in which it promised military help to that country, but only if France did the same. Moreover, because the USSR at that time had no common border with Czechoslovakia, the acquiescence of Poland or Romania would have been necessary if Soviet troops were to go to the aid of their new ally. These inherent limitations strongly suggest that both pacts were considered by all signatories more as political gestures than as effective military alliances. In the case of the Soviet Union, it appears likely that Moscow in the mid-1930s was less interested in a military alliance with France than it was in preventing any understanding between France and Germany that might have encouraged an ambitious Germany to expand in Russia's direction.

Somewhat similar considerations of *Realpolitik* seem to have been behind the Soviet Union's role in the prolonged agony of the Spanish Civil War (1936–39), where Stalin made both Hitler and the Western powers compete for his favor. Soviet support in the form of tanks, aircraft, and military advisers succeeded in saving Madrid in the first year of the war. But such aid diminished markedly soon thereafter, probably because Moscow lost hope of any significant French or British help for the embattled republic.

The Comintern, as the USSR's handmaiden, was instrumental in recruiting thousands of volunteers from the Western democracies to form the International Brigades. However, no such "volunteers" from the Soviet Union made an appearance at any stage in the conflict. Moreover, few of the many Comintern representatives who took an active role in the civil war were Soviet citizens, although many of them had been long-time residents of the USSR.

Stalin's principal objective, apparently, once he had prevented an early nationalist victory, was to curry favor with the Western democracies while avoiding an overcommitment of his own limited resources. Throughout Europe, including the Scandinavian and Baltic states, Communist Parties under Comintern guidance moved quickly to adhere to a changing party line. From an original position favoring a "United Front" (i.e., joint action with Socialist and other leftist parties), they moved to "Popular Front," which broadened the spectrum to include democratic and nonleftist elements, and finally to a "National Front," open to anyone against international fascism.

Scandinavia's Social Democratic Parties, in office in Norway and Sweden and sharing governmental responsibility in Denmark, were naturally sympathetic to the plight of the Spanish Republicans. But they were unwilling to abandon their neutral stance in international politics, particularly given the threat to themselves from resurgent Germany. More surprisingly, few Scandinavians served in the International Brigades.

In spite of his resource limitations and the complicating differences among Spain's anti-Franco factions, Stalin was prepared to make reasonable efforts to keep the republic alive. Such efforts also supported his real objective, which was to solidify the estrangement between Germany and the Western democracies. For one thing, continuation of the war would keep part of the German military machine occupied far from Soviet borders, even if the Wehrmacht gained important military experience in the process. Neither did Hitler, although for different reasons, seem to feel any urgency about concluding the war. In November 1937, he reportedly observed that its continuation would be more to Germany's advantage than a speedy victory by the right.[6]

Stalin's cynical policy was reflected in the way he and his representatives continued to support the conflict until the very end, although by early 1939 the war was clearly lost. This delayed the surrender of Madrid until March 29, 1939, when its capitulation effectively ended the war. By that time, Spain had long since been replaced on the front pages of the world's newspapers by other crises, first by the West's abject sellout of Czechoslovakia at Munich in the fall of 1938, and then by Hitler's march into Prague on March 15, 1939. On that same date, in a major speech to the Eighteenth Congress of the Communist Party of the Soviet Union (CPSU), Stalin practically washed his hands of the Spanish affair, mentioning Spain only in passing as included among the territorial ambitions of the Axis powers.

The Soviet Party Congress was still in session when Hitler took his next step toward massive confrontation, occupying nearly all of what was left of Czechoslovakia. The Germans tried to demonstrate some self-denial by permitting Hungary to occupy the Carpatho-Ukraine region and later told Moscow that this was intended as a gesture of conciliation to the Soviet Union because it eliminated a possible source of Ukrainian nationalist agitation. It seems more likely, however, that Berlin's restraint was really an attempt to induce a similar gesture on the part of Poland with regard to Danzig.

The British, including Prime Minister Neville Chamberlain, were outraged by Germany's final sweep into Czechoslovak territory and tried to bring the USSR back into the framework of collective European security. The Soviet Government played along to the extent of proposing a conference to look into the matter, at which Britain, France, Romania, Poland, Turkey, and the USSR would be represented. But Poland and Romania refused to participate so the proposed meeting never took place.

Meanwhile, Hitler took Memel (now Klaipeda) from Lithuania and maintained a high level of pressure on the Polish Government, pressure its leader Jozef Beck was still reluctant to recognize publicly. At that stage, according to Gordon Craig, the hapless Beck still entertained illusions about building a "Third Europe" under Polish leadership to control the balance between Germany and the Soviet Union.[7]

Some Westerners were apparently almost equally naïve in assuming that the ideological hostility between Communists and Nazis would rule out complicity between them, pointing to the Anti-Comintern Pact signed by Germany and Japan late in 1936 and subsequently by Italy. But this proved to be just another "piece of paper," which impeded neither a Russo-German agreement in 1939 nor a Russo-Japanese understanding two years later.

Finally, Prime Minister Chamberlain determined to issue an unequivocal guarantee to Poland, and in a statement to the House of Commons on March 31, 1939, he announced that the British and French Governments would lend "all support in their power" if the Polish Government felt compelled to resist aggression. The Soviet Ambassador in London evidently encouraged the British Government to make its statement as strong as possible, without explicitly endorsing the British position. Adam Ulam is probably correct in his view that the Chamberlain declaration

> ... *made possible the whole chain of events leading to the Molotov-Ribbentrop pact of August 23, 1939, and thus was indirectly responsible for the most momentous development of Soviet foreign policy since Brest-Litovsk. On its face, the British Government's pledge guaranteed Poland; in fact, its timing and circumstances provided a guarantee to the U.S.S.R. and doomed the Polish state.... A few words spoken by Mr. Chamberlain transformed the U.S.S.R. from being in a hopeless diplomatic situation to being the arbiter of Europe's fate.*[8]

After initially backing off from its informal encouragement of the British initiative, Moscow seemed to relent and, in mid-April, Litvinov made proposals for multilateral guarantees covering all the Eastern European states, including the successor states of Finland, Estonia, Latvia, and Lithuania. But such guarantees were bound to raise a host of problems for the British Government, and negotiations on them were certain to be time-consuming. Simultaneously, the Soviet Ambassador in Berlin made secret overtures to State Secretary Ernst von Weizsäcker about a possible improvement in Russo-German relations. The Germans were slow to respond but, late in April, Hitler renounced both the Anglo-German naval treaty and the Polish-German nonaggression pact, clearing the decks for his attack on Poland.

Suddenly, on May 3, 1939, Litvinov was replaced as Soviet Foreign Minister by Vyacheslav Molotov, and the Russo-German *rapprochement* took on real momentum. This personnel change was triply significant. Not only was Litvinov a Jew, and therefore an interlocutor difficult for the Nazi regime even to contemplate, he was also closely identified with the Soviet regime's public quest for collective security. Replacing him, therefore, held out the possibility that the Soviet Union was now prepared to envisage a *Realpolitik* alternative to its much publicized "idealism." Most important, perhaps, was the fact that Molotov retained his positions as Prime Minister and member of the Politburo. As a result, he became the first front-rank Soviet leader since Trotsky to serve as Foreign Minister.

The Western powers evidently got the message, for they attempted to accelerate their slow-moving negotiations in Moscow, but the Germans indicated little interest until July. It was then the Soviet turn to show no sense of urgency while the Germans quickly developed an intense interest in coming to an agreement. It is now clear that Ribbentrop was under pressure to assure Soviet passivity when German troops advanced into Poland and that the attack was scheduled to commence before the end of August.

Molotov continued to stall, but in the face of a virtual ultimatum from Berlin, Stalin agreed to receive Ribbentrop in Moscow on August 23. Their talks have since been likened to those at Tilsit between Alexander I and Napoléon, more than 100 years earlier, when the two major land powers carved Europe up between themselves. Meanwhile, Soviet officials in Moscow had presented a series of difficult demands to the Western negotiators, who were still in the Soviet capital. On August 21, those talks were adjourned on the pretext that Soviet military representatives were required at maneuvers.

Not until the Molotov-Ribbentrop agreement had been signed on August 23 were the Soviet talks with the West broken off, at which time Defense Minister Kliment Voroshilov blamed Poland for their lack of success. By that time, the Russians were convinced that the West would go to war if Germany attacked Poland. But Hitler evidently believed that they would not, particularly in the absence of Soviet support for the anti-Nazi cause. When he realized that Britain and France would, in fact, meet their commitments to Poland, Hitler postponed his attack for a few days but finally ordered it to proceed on September 1, 1939.

With the Wehrmacht attack on Poland, France and Britain suddenly found themselves at war with Nazi Germany. Czechoslovakia had already been sacrificed to Hitler's ambitions at the Munich Conference, and Moscow's eagerness to join in Poland's partition meant that the two democracies would soon be without an ally in the East. In addition to its half-share in Poland, the USSR then quickly occupied the three Baltic states and incorporated them in its union of "Socialist" states.

The conquest of Poland was concluded quickly in spite of a valiant Polish struggle. By the end of September, Nazi Germany and the USSR controlled all of the territory on the southern shore of the Baltic. The Allies hoped to weaken Germany through economic warfare and peripheral operations, so their forces on the Western front took no offensive action while Germany readied its onslaught on them. In the circumstances, attention shifted to the North, where the Western Allies, the USSR, and Germany all had interests to protect. In consequence, all of the Nordic states except Sweden were quickly drawn into the conflict.

Notes — Chapter V

1. Adam B. Ulam, *Expansion and Coexistence* (New York: Holt, Rinehart and Winston, 1974), 150.

2. Kennan, *Russia and the West*, 222.

3. Ulam, *Expansion and Coexistence*, 155.

4. Max Beloff, *The Foreign Policy of Soviet Russia* (London: Oxford University Press, 1956), vol. 2, 156.

5. Wahlbäck, *Roots of Swedish Neutrality*, 35.

6. Ulam, *Expansion and Coexistence*, 245.

7. Gordon A. Craig, *Germany 1866–1945* (New York: Oxford University Press, 1978), 710.

8. Ulam, *Expansion and Coexistence*, 267.

VI

War on the Northern Front

Intent on strengthening its defenses around Leningrad, the Soviet Government quickly seized the opportunity offered by its agreement with the Nazis to present sweeping territorial claims on Finland, which had been allotted to the Soviet sphere of interest in the Ribbentrop-Molotov agreement. As early as August 1938, Soviet Embassy officials in Helsinki had voiced their concerns to their Finnish contacts about the possibility of a German attack through Finland. Although the Soviets offered military assistance to the Finns, Helsinki's response was limited to the statement that Finland would allow no foreign power to gain a foothold on Finnish soil.

At the beginning of October 1939, the Soviet Union dramatized its concern by indicating it wished to take up certain "concrete political questions." Stalin then reportedly demanded of the Finnish negotiators, Paasikivi and Tanner, that Finland cede a small area on the Karelian isthmus and the fortified island of Koivisto, near Viipuri, as well as part of the Petsamo area, and that it lease the Hangö peninsula at the mouth of the Gulf of Finland to the Soviet Union. In recompense, Finland would be given a slice of territory in East Karelia.

The Finns were convinced that giving in to Soviet coercion would only make it more difficult to resist when further, inevitable demands were levied against them. But the meeting of Scandinavian heads of state which took place during the Moscow negotiations showed that there was no possibility of help from Finland's neighbors. When Tanner asked Swedish Prime Minister Albin Hannson whether Sweden would promise effective military help if a rejection of the Soviet demand led to war, Hannson replied that Helsinki should not count on it. Even Marshal Mannerheim considered it necessary to adopt a conciliatory approach, but when Paasikivi then offered Stalin a naval base on Jussarö, a small island near Hangö, it proved to be not good enough. The Soviet authorities manufactured a frontier incident on November 26, breaking off negotiations and tearing up the 1932 nonaggression pact. With the virtually unanimous support of all elements of Finland's population, the Finnish Government began to mobilize.

At the end of November, Moscow launched an attack with forty-five divisions on its thinly populated neighbor, establishing a puppet government, headed by O.V. Kuusinen, in the border area at Terijoki. But the Finnish army resisted strongly, and the Soviet forces were thoroughly embarrassed by their inability to operate effectively under severe weather conditions.

The USSR's lack of success was unsurprising in view of Stalin's recent thoroughgoing purge of the Red Army's leadership. Marshal Mikhail Tukhachevsky and seven other leading generals had been executed in 1937 after a secret trial, and the ranks of the Soviet officer corps were then savagely reduced. A majority of the officers, down to battalion level, were purged, and many were executed. Moreover, the Soviet air force was hampered in Finland by obsolescent aircraft and poorly trained pilots. As a result, Soviet casualties during the three months of combat totaled more than 200,000, including 50,000 killed.

The Finnish Government responsible for the Moscow negotiations resigned as soon as the war began, and President Kyöst Kallio replaced it with a new government under Risto Ryti. Tanner became Foreign Minister, and Paasikivi was named Minister Without Portfolio. They appealed to the League of Nations for support, and influential Western statesmen, including Winston Churchill, applauded the Finns' tenacious courage. The USSR was expelled from the League in December 1939, although Moscow continued to maintain that it was not at war with Finland but had merely intervened on behalf of the lawful Terijoki government of the "Finnish Democratic Republic." Public outcry in the West at this obvious falsification was severe, particularly in the United Kingdom and the United States.

In February 1940, French and British military representatives arrived in Helsinki and presented an Allied plan for sending an expeditionary force to Finland. The plan envisaged sending the expedition through the Arctic regions of Norway and Sweden, even if their governments did not agree to permit their passage. The new British Minister in Helsinki spoke of sending 20,000 men to take over the northern sector of the front by mid-April, and Clement Attlee later stated in the House of Commons that 100,000 men had been ready to proceed to Finland. In a curiously muted remark, the Soviet Ambassador in London, Ivan Maisky, urged the British to follow the Spanish Civil War model of intervention "so that it did not interfere with Anglo-Soviet relations on other fronts."[1]

Although the political fallout in Germany from the Soviet military debacle in Finland was as severe as it was among the Western democracies, Hitler and Ribbentrop played the role of good allies. Inevitably, those Nazi leaders eager to let the Wehrmacht have a go at the stumbling Red Army were encouraged, particularly because the Winter War was interfering with the supply of badly needed materials from Finland. There was also embarrassment in Berlin at the sight of one of Germany's "natural allies," a Nordic nation, being ravaged by the Bolsheviks.

Sweden, which had not issued a neutrality declaration in the Winter War and was therefore at liberty to assist the Finns, provided financial and material assistance to them, and a group of about 8,000 men volunteered to fight in Finland. Norway also sent material support, although not as much as its more prosperous neighbor.

It was soon clear from Mannerheim's reports that Finnish military resistance could not last much longer. Moreover, it was generally felt that Norway and Sweden might refuse to permit the passage of Allied reinforcements. If so, assistance was unlikely to arrive in sufficient strength in time to save the deteriorating military situation. The Swedes made no secret of their reluctance to allow Anglo-French troops to cross their territory, fearing that their real purpose would be to interrupt the export of Swedish iron ore to Germany. More concretely, the Swedish Government was convinced that the arrival of Allied troops in Norway and Sweden would trigger an immediate retaliatory move by the Germans.

Perhaps Moscow shared Stockholm's apprehensions on this point, because it would hardly be in Soviet interests to have the Germans ensconced in Sweden. On January 29, 1940, the Soviet Government informed the Swedes that it did not in principle rule out a peace settlement with the Helsinki government. Christian Günther, who had succeeded Sandler as Foreign Minister in December 1939, reportedly played a significant role in facilitating the subsequent Fenno-Soviet negotiations. The Soviet Union's nominal ally, Germany, was probably concerned that continuation of the war could help the Western Allies to intervene in Scandinavia and to block its shipments of iron ore from Sweden. Finally, on March 12, 1940, yielding to German advice as well as Soviet aggression, the Finnish Government was obliged to capitulate and cede the territories demanded by Moscow, bringing the Winter War to a close.

The settlement imposed by Moscow cost Finland more than 10 percent of its territory. The Karelian isthmus, including the port city of Viipuri, and the whole of Lake Ladoga were put into Soviet hands. Also, a salient in the Salla area, which had brought the Finnish frontier within 80 kilometers of the strategic Leningrad-to-Murmansk railway, was wiped out. But the Finns were able to retain the port of Petsamo. The Hangö peninsula was leased to the Soviet Union for thirty years, giving the USSR a naval base which could control the northern approaches to the Gulf of Finland. Finally, both sides agreed that neither would conclude any alliance directed against the other.

The more than 400,000 Finns who inhabited areas ceded to the Soviet Union were permitted to move into Finland, and their fellow countrymen strove to make new farms, shelter, and employment available to them. Finland's plight aroused great sympathy throughout the Western democracies, particularly in the United States, where many Finns had settled in the Midwest and where the Finnish Government was remembered for its unique willingness to repay its World War I debts. Stalin's reluctance to antagonize the West further at that point may have contributed to the relatively lenient settlement accorded the Finns, in comparison with their neighbors in the Baltic Republics.

Finland's intrepid but futile attempt to defend its national integrity did more than focus the attention of world opinion briefly on the High North. It also aroused the fears and greed of several of its European neighbors stimulated by the area's potential role in the rapidly developing struggle for domination of the Eurasian continent. The Scandinavians themselves were acutely sensitive to their vulnerability. Most clearly hoped that the Western Allies would prevail in their struggle against the Nazi menace. Few, however, were willing to sacrifice themselves for the benefit of the Allies, whose conduct before the war had been so feckless.

The President of the Norwegian Storting, C. Hambro, pointed to the magnitude of the problem in February 1940:

> ... *nobody believes the present British Government or would take their word for anything.... We have to fight the common belief that England is willing to fight to the last Pole, the last Norwegian and the last Finn, as long as England does not suffer ... and the British Government has done nothing to counteract this belief.*[2]

In addition to the Soviet Union, both the Western Allies and Hitler's Germany quickly elevated the relative significance of dealing with Scandinavian problems. As usual, Winston Churchill was among the first to recognize the problems and to draw the appropriate historical analogies. By September 1939, the future Prime Minister was already a prime mover on defense policy as First Lord of the Admiralty, and he commented at length in his memoirs of World War II on the crisis in the North. As he noted in the first volume, "The thousand-mile-long peninsula stretching from the mouth of the Baltic to the Arctic Circle had an immense strategic significance."[3]

Churchill recalled Allied plans, in the closing stages of World War I, to mine Norway's territorial waters, known as the Leads, as an extension of the great antisubmarine mine belt the Allies had already placed across the North Sea. The Allies had worked hard in 1917–18 to persuade the Norwegian Government to take the necessary action itself, but by the time Oslo had agreed, in September 1918, the need for closing its waters to the U-boats had evaporated, and nothing was done.

Norwegians also remembered World War I and drew their own conclusions from that conflict, which had dramatized Norway's strategic importance in any conflict in the North Atlantic. As Nils Ørvik of Queens University in Ontario has pointed out:

> *Even during the trying times in 1917–1918, when the British started to put heavy pressure on the Norwegian Government, the Norwegians had remained confident that it was not, could not and would not be in the British*

national interest to occupy Norway or to impose any perma-
nent restrictions on Norway's national independence. Tem-
porary measures, such as the 1918 mine barrage, were of
course flagrant violations of Norwegian sovereignty. They
were also harmful to her international status. But seen from
Britain they were emergency measures of a short duration.
The real dangers came from the other side — through a
German retaliation caused and triggered by British viola-
tions of Norway's neutrality and of Britain's use of Norwe-
gian waters and territory for warlike acts against Germany.[4]

Such assumptions lay at the base of Norway's neutrality policy
during 1939-40 as well as during World War I. Accordingly,
Norwegian apprehensions focused more on Britain than on Germany because of the fear that trouble would start with British
pressures on Norway. Logically, Oslo's focus had to be on defense
against Norway's friends, rather than its enemies. "If Norway
could prevent the British from blatantly violating her neutrality, it
would not be in Germany's interest to do so on her own. This was
the lesson from World War I."[5]

These views were widely held throughout Norwegian society,
not least among Social Democrats, who had opposed all appropriations for defense until 1935, when they formed a minority
government. At that time, they joined with the Liberals and
Christian Democrats in funding a limited defense effort. Under
this compromise, Norway's armed forces were designed not so
much to repel an enemy attack as to "mark the country's neutrality" and thus to provide a "neutrality guard" as a basis for protests
against any violation.

At the same time, Norwegian leaders knew very well who
were the "good guys" and who the "bad guys" in any likely
conflict. As Foreign Minister Halvdan Koht noted, "I often said
in secret meetings ... that if we against our will were forced into
the war, I did not want us to drift in on a side where we did not
want to be."[6] Some Conservative critics correctly interpreted this
view, which was widely shared in the Norwegian Parliament, to
mean, "If our neutrality is violated by the British, we capitulate. If
someone else comes, we don't."

In 1940, in contrast to 1918, mining the Leads would have
had significance far beyond its antisubmarine task. By using the

Norwegian territorial corridor to the open sea, Germany would be able to render the British blockade largely ineffective. This was particularly important because one of the two most vital imports required by the German war machine, iron ore, came mainly from the mines at Gällivare in the far north of Sweden, via Norway. Churchill also had hopes of impeding the supply of the second vital commodity, oil, which came to Germany from Romania and the area around Baku in the USSR, but he realized that this task was, at least in its initial stages, largely in diplomatic hands.

"Winston was back" in the Admiralty, however, and from that vantage point he could play a critical role in forging British policy on the sea lanes. He pointed out that in winter, when the Swedish port of Lulea on the Gulf of Bothnia was iced over, Sweden's iron ore could be sent to Germany only through the small port of Oxelosund, in the Baltic, or from Narvik, far to the north on Norway's Atlantic coast. Attempts were already being made to negotiate with Sweden about reducing its supply of ore to the Germans, he observed, essentially by pre-emptive purchase for England's own account. Churchill also floated the possibility of chartering all the free neutral shipping available, in addition to the many bottoms already contracted for from the Norwegians, and extending to that vast flotilla the benefits of the Royal Navy's convoy system. But if those expedients did not succeed, he concluded, more drastic action might be required.

The other government departments, particularly the Foreign Office, were reluctant to follow Churchill's advice to violate international law by mining Norway's territorial waters without Oslo's consent. There was also some fear in London that the Norwegian response to such action might deny Britain the 2 million tons per year of Swedish iron ore it was itself importing through Narvik. Although only about one-fifth the amount going to Germany, its loss would have been a significant blow to Britain's wartime economy.

Churchill recognized that the use of Narvik and its rail line to Finland "as a line of supply for the Finnish armies affected the neutrality both of Norway and Sweden. These two States, in equal fear of Germany and Russia, had no aim but to keep out of the wars by which they were encircled and might be engulfed. For them this seemed the only chance of survival. He also recognized his own colleagues' reluctance to violate Norway's territorial waters for Britain's singular advantage against Germany. But the First Lord calculated that in the Narvik supply operation his government was "moved by a general emotion, only indirectly connected with our war problem, towards a far more serious demand upon both Norway and Sweden for the free passage of men and supplies to Finland."

Churchill welcomed what he called

> ... *this new and favorable breeze as a means of achieving the major strategic advantage of cutting off the vital iron ore supplies of Germany. If Narvik was to become a kind of Allied base to supply the Finns, it would certainly be easy to prevent the German ships loading ore at the port and sailing safely down the Leads to Germany. Once Norwegian and Swedish protestations were overborne, for whatever reason, the greater measures would include the less.*[7]

Taking advantage of this new breeze, Churchill penned a note to the cabinet on December 16 in his characteristically eloquent style. Arguing that Norway's sympathies were on Britain's side and that it would retaliate against his recommendation for mining the Leads only if compelled to do so by brute force, he suggested that such force would be applied in any case

> ... *if Germany thinks it in her interest to dominate forcibly the Scandinavian peninsula. In that case the war would spread to Norway and Sweden, and with our command of the seas there is no reason why French and British troops should not meet German invaders on Scandinavian soil.... It cannot be too strongly emphasized that British control of the Norwegian coast-line is a strategic objective of first-class importance. It is not therefore seen how, even if retaliation by Germany were to run its full course, we should be worse off for the action now proposed. On the contrary* **we have more to gain than lose by a German attack upon Norway or Sweden.** *This point is capable of more elaboration than is necessary here*[8] *(emphasis added).*

The First Lord concluded that Britain had taken up arms in accordance with the principles of the Covenant of the League of Nations and that no technical infringement of international law could deprive his nation of the good wishes of neutral countries.

> *The final tribunal is our own conscience. We are fighting to re-establish the reign of law and to protect the liberties of small countries. Our defeat would mean an age of barbaric violence, and would be fatal not only to ourselves, but to the independent life of every small country in Europe.... Small nations must not tie our hands when we are fighting for their rights and freedom.... Humanity, rather than legality, must be our guide.*[9]

By January 1940, the French had also become alert to the possible significance of the Scandinavian flank. General Maurice Gamelin considered that "the opening of a new area of hostility in Scandinavia might be of considerable value to the Allies." He thus wrote to Prime Minister Edouard Daladier about opening a new theater of war there, appending a plan to land an Allied force at Petsamo. Gamelin foresaw the need to seize ports and airfields on the west coast of Norway as a precautionary measure. His plans also envisaged the possibility of "extending the operation into Sweden and occupying the iron-ore mines at Gällivare."[10] Because the British First Lord of the Admiralty considered Narvik to be the only possible route to Finland for aircraft, materiel, and volunteer forces, his priorities were the opposite of General Gamelin's. Churchill consistently regarded aid for Finland as a mere covering operation for the major effort, which was cutting Germany off from deliveries of Swedish iron ore through Norway.

Under Churchill's prodding, plans were drawn up to interrupt the flow of ore from Narvik to Germany, initially by naval action in Norwegian territorial waters, as soon as Lulea was closed in December. Later, sabotage was to be used to impede shipments from Oxelosund. A major operation to seize the port of Narvik, code-named Avonmouth, was projected for early spring and assumed the acquiescence of the Norwegian and Swedish Governments. Avonmouth was also designed to secure the rail line from Narvik to Gällivare, which was to serve as a channel for assistance to Finland. The Avonmouth forces were to be largely British and under British command but with support from a brigade of French *Chasseurs alpins*, troops specially trained to operate in winter conditions.

Early indications that Sweden might adopt a hands-off policy in the case of British military action were dispelled in January

1940 when the Swedish Government was advised of Allied intentions to undertake naval operations in Norwegian waters. In an
emotional interview with a British diplomat in Stockholm, Eric
Boheman, the Secretary General of the Swedish Foreign Office,
completely reversed his previous tolerant attitude. "The consequences of this step would probably be the German occupation of
Denmark, and possibly the end of the independent existence of all
Scandinavian countries." He added: "I should have thought that
the British Government had the fate of a sufficient number of
small states on their consciences as it was."[11]

In the face of Nordic protests and opposition from Dominion
leaders, Neville Chamberlain and his government decided to defer
any action in Norwegian waters, to the chagrin of Churchill and
the French allies. Shortly thereafter, the King of Sweden declared
his support for his government's efforts to prevent great power
involvement in the Fenno-Soviet war, ending any Allied hopes of
influencing Swedish public opinion in their favor.

In the interim, some German eyes had also turned in a
northerly direction. Admiral Erich Raeder invoked the threat of
British action in asking whether it would not be possible for his
forces to gain bases in Norway under combined pressure from
Germany and the USSR.

> *I stressed the disadvantages which an occupation of
> Norway by the British would have for us; the control of the
> approaches to the Baltic, the outflanking of our naval
> operations and of our air attacks on Britain, the end of our
> pressure on Sweden. I also stressed the advantages for us of
> the occupation of the Norwegian coast; outlet to the North
> Atlantic, no possibility of a British mine barrier, as in the
> years 1917–18.*[12]

Even earlier, German Vice Admiral Wolfgang Wegener had
argued that Germany's naval strategy in World War I had been
fundamentally flawed by failing to move aggressively into the
Atlantic and allowing itself to be boxed into the Baltic and the
North Sea. In contrast to the British policy of a "near blockade"
of Germany, he advocated a "far blockade" of the United Kingdom, which he was convinced would have brought the 1914–18
war to a successful end before the United States could have entered
the conflict effectively. Wegener's views may have been flawed, but

it seems clear that they had an direct effect on the thinking of Raeder and his colleagues. Inherent in that thinking was the requirement for at least one major naval base in Norway, preferably Trondheim, to support the German navy's projected operations in the Atlantic.

On the political plane, Nazi Party propagandists had long been active in attempting to convert the peoples of Scandinavia to the idea of a Nordic community under the "natural leadership" of Germany. A willing Norwegian instrument soon came to hand in the person of Vidkun Quisling, a former Defense Minister, and head of a small party with pro-German and pro-Nazi sympathies. Quisling was invited to meet with Raeder and, later, on December 14, 1939, with Hitler himself, to whom he stressed his belief that Britain would soon move to occupy Norway.

Hitler was reluctant to accede to Quisling's bid for German assistance in mounting a coup against the Norwegian Government. In what Churchill later considered dissimulation, the Führer reportedly commented that "he would prefer Norway, as well as the rest of Scandinavia, to remain completely neutral," as he did not want to enlarge the theater of war. In retrospect, it appears that Hitler genuinely would have preferred Norwegian neutrality at that time. Germany's principal goals with regard to Norway in 1940 were to assure passage through the Leads for its ships and the uninterrupted transport of Swedish iron ore from Narvik. Although establishment of naval bases on Norway's Atlantic coast would have been advantageous, it was of long-term rather than immediate interest, as the Wehrmacht was gearing itself up for the demanding campaign into France.

But Hitler did agree that "if the enemy were preparing to spread the war, he would take steps to guard himself against the threat."[13] Quisling was, therefore, given a subsidy, and the Germans promised that further study would be given to his request for military support. According to Admiral Raeder, Hitler decided on the very same day to authorize a small-scale study (*Studie Nord*) of a possible landing in Norway. Although Quisling's visit may have played a role in directing Hitler's attention to the Scandinavian front, other developments were also pushing him in that direction. In particular, the Soviet attack on Finland at the end of November 1939 raised the possibility that the British might seize on the Fenno-Soviet conflict as an excuse to establish themselves in Norway.

The Allied Supreme War Council, in a meeting in Paris on February 5, 1940, agreed to prepare two British divisions and a slightly smaller French contingent, both forces camouflaged as volunteers, for an expedition to the Far North. The French at the same time accepted British arguments that a landing at Petsamo would be what General Ironside called "a military gamble without a political prize" which could amount to a reprise of the disaster at Gallipoli in 1915. "While it would neither save Finland nor gain control of the iron ore mines, it would ensure war with Russia and divert Allied strength from the Western front without forcing a corresponding German diversion."[14] The French then concurred in moving into Narvik with a view to getting control of the Gällivare ore field. It was also agreed that the ore field was to be the main objective and that only a part of the joint force was to push on to aid Finland.[15]

The Germans' *Studie Nord* was completed by the end of December, but Hitler did not release it to the services at that time, still persuaded that Norway's continued neutrality was in Germany's best interest. Unfortunately, a Churchill broadcast on January 20, 1940, calling upon the neutrals to join the fight against the Nazis, stimulated more of a response from Germany than from the neutrals. On January 27, "Hitler gave explicit orders to his military advisers to prepare comprehensive plans for an invasion of Norway if necessary. The special staff formed for the purpose met for the first time on February 5th."[16] But it was not until March 1940 that the need to postpone the Nazi *Blitzkrieg* in the West gave Hitler time to focus on the situation in Scandinavia, and continued reports of London's intentions there persuaded him to pre-empt a possible British move. The *Studie Nord* group was then replaced by a new planning group within the Defense High Command (OKW) and given a new code name, *Weseruebung*. An Army general, Nikolaus von Falkenhorst, who had acquired some Scandinavian experience in the expeditionary corps sent to Finland in 1918 in support of the Whites during the Finnish civil war, was put in charge of the operation.[17]

In the meantime, British diplomatic pressure on Sweden failed to generate the desired reaction in Stockholm. As Lord Cadogan reportedly told Anthony Eden, "Diplomacy is rather hamstrung by being deprived of the necessary apparatus — military strength. Words don't do anything."[18] At the same time,

Churchill's attempt to seize the military initiative in neighboring Norway was bedeviled once again by the kind of lackadaisical execution so characteristic of Britain's forces in the early days of the war.

Although Finnish acceptance of a Soviet-dictated peace settlement on March 12 appeared to lessen the likelihood of a British move into Norway, Hitler apparently was convinced that Britain would not abandon its strategic aim of shutting off Germany's ore imports. The Scandinavian area "had become a decisive sphere of interest for both belligerents and would remain a permanent seat of unrest."[19] Hitler's conclusion was evidently based on his interpretation of the *Altmark* incident, which occurred in mid-February.

The *Altmark* was a German naval auxiliary vessel which was transporting captured British merchant seamen from the South Atlantic. Intercepted by British warships on its journey to Germany, it took refuge in Jösing Fjord on the coast of Norway. Although the British pursuers did not at first attempt to examine the vessel, which was attended by two Norwegian gunboats, Churchill personally ordered that it be boarded. During a hand-to-hand fight, several German seamen were killed, and about 300 British prisoners were liberated. The Norwegian gunboats did not attempt to intervene, but the Norwegian Government protested vehemently this infringement of its territorial waters.

Neither the British nor the Germans were persuaded by the vigor of the Norwegian protest, and Hitler was convinced that it was merely a gesture designed to hoodwink him. Thus, a short-term tactical triumph for Churchill led quickly to a strategic reversal of major significance. In Ørvik's analysis, the *Altmark* incident was decisive. The fact that no attempt other than protests was made by the Norwegians to stop the British seizure led Hitler to the following conclusion:

> *The British would not respect Norway's neutrality and the Norwegian Government would not use what little force it had to prevent the British from helping themselves as they saw fit. The reading was that Admiral Raeder and others who had joined him in warning against a British-Norwegian 'plot' to deny Germany the advantages and benefits it had gained from Norway's neutral status, had been proven right.*[20]

On the assumption that Norway was already Britain's willing accomplice, Hitler ordered General von Falkenhorst to ensure that German forces reached Norwegian territory before the British could land there. His directive of March 10 specified, "The strategic objectives were to be to forestall a British intervention in Scandinavia and the Baltic Sea area, to provide security for the sources of Swedish iron ore, and to give the Navy and Air forces advanced bases for attacks on the British isles."[21] Later, at the Nuremberg trials, von Falkenhorst reported the Führer as saying:

> *The occupation of Norway by the British would be a strategic turning movement which would lead them into the Baltic, where we have neither troops nor coastal fortifications. The success which we have gained in the East and which we are going to win in the West would be annihilated, because the enemy would find himself in a position to advance on Berlin and to break the backbone of our two fronts.*[22]

On April 2, Hitler ordered that *Weseruebung* be carried out before the impending great offensive in the West and set April 9 as the date for the operation to begin. It had become clear to German military planners by then that the security of *Weseruebung* could be assured only if the airfields on the Jutland peninsula were in their hands. Accordingly, an attack on Denmark was scheduled to take place on April 9, the same date as the landings in Norway. The Danes, who had received intimations from Britain the previous year that they could not rely on U.K. support in case of war, had accepted Germany's offer of a nonaggression pact, in spite of well-founded doubts as to its usefulness.

According to Swedish diplomat Krister Wahlbäck, "The Swedish government had received quite reliable information that an invasion of Denmark and Norway was imminent several days before it occurred. The Swedish legation in Berlin was well informed and its reports on the subject proved to be accurate."[23] Sweden's Nordic neighbors were not so well informed, so both Denmark and Norway were taken completely by surprise.

The British, who had received indications of German naval activity in the area, failed to take effective action. Three small German transports were thus able to land an expeditionary force in Copenhagen early in the morning of April 9, meeting no resistance. The subsequent German crossing of the land frontier on Jutland provoked an exchange of gunfire, but the struggle was brief. The Danish Government protested but had to acquiesce. The Germans undertook to respect Denmark's independence and integrity. The two major opposition parties entered the government, hoping to forge a national coalition which could maintain some vestiges of self-rule. Denmark was also coerced into signing the Anti-Comintern Pact and was obliged to take action against the country's small number of Communists. It stipulated, however, that it had taken on no obligations outside of Denmark itself.

The situation in Norway was more complex, due in large part to the isolated nature of much of the country. The initial German landings were carried out by rather small detachments, but the Norwegian military, distracted by Britain's mine-laying activities, which had begun on April 8, was unable to respond effectively. Mobilization was not ordered until a few hours before the invasion began, and by then it was clearly too late.

Although the British had planned to move into Norway in substantial force at the first sign of a German move on Scandinavia, advance warning of the Nazi assault failed to trigger an early response from the British. In the view of James A. Bayer, "This inexplicable lapse ... likely lost the battle for Norway. It was a blunder of incalculable proportions."[24] As a result, the Germans, who began their preparations much later than the British, managed to land in Norway just before the Allied forces arrived.

To the astonishment of nearly everyone, the Nazi onslaught extended as far north as Narvik, 1,200 miles from the German naval bases. German destroyers landed a small party there after a sharp engagement with two Norwegian coastal defense ships, and by the time a British flotilla arrived the following day, the German troops had established themselves in and around the port. The lightning seizure of Narvik put an end to British hopes of securing a foothold there from which they could strangle the vital supply of iron ore to the Nazi war industry.

Farther to the South, the German landings were equally successful at Trondheim, which gave them access to central Norway, and at Bergen, Norway's second largest city. The Norwegian capital, Oslo, proved more difficult, as torpedoes from the Oscarborg fortress sank the German cruiser *Blücher*, with the loss of many staff officers. The same afternoon, however, paratroopers who had landed at Fornebu airfield secured the city for the Germans. Nevertheless, the short delay in gaining control of the capital permitted the King and the government to make their escape and eventually to mount a serious resistance to the invaders.

British efforts to retake Trondheim by landing 13,000 men to do battle with some 2,000 German occupiers failed ignominiously because of a series of mishaps and the Royal Navy's sudden awakening to the dangers posed by German aircraft and U-boats in that area. At Narvik, 20,000 Allied troops had little more success against another 2,000-man contingent of Germans. Britain's military ineffectiveness at this stage of the war was in part caused by their commanders' reluctance to use their naval artillery because of the collateral damage it would inflict on the civilian population.

The British did manage to expel the enemy temporarily from Narvik on May 27. By that time, however, military disaster had overcome the Allies in France, and their forces in Norway were recalled. King Haakon and his government escaped into exile in England at the same time. The British, meanwhile, had occupied Denmark's Faeroe Islands, due west of Bergen, following up later by occupying the other two Danish possessions in the North Atlantic, Iceland and Greenland, where they were joined the following year by American forces. As "unsinkable aircraft carriers," all three were to play important roles in the forthcoming "Battle of the Atlantic" against German submarines.

The Soviet Government presumably took some comfort from the German move into Denmark and Norway, not because it welcomed their incorporation in Hitler's "New Order" in Europe but because it made his eventual reconciliation with the Western Allies less likely. But Sweden was a great deal closer to the Soviet heartland, and a Nazi presence there could have negative consequences for the USSR's security. To make the Soviet position clear to its temporary ally, Molotov asked Graf Werner von Schulenburg, the German Ambassador in Moscow, about "rumors ... that Germany would soon be forced to include Sweden in her Scandinavian operations." The new Soviet Foreign Minister took the occasion to point out that "in his opinion, Germany and definitely the Soviet Union were vitally interested in preserving Swedish neutrality."[25]

The Soviet definition of Swedish neutrality was a limited one, as Molotov had illustrated shortly after the Winter War, when he told the Swedish Ambassador in Moscow that the Soviet Government was opposed to ideas of a defense union among Sweden, Norway, and Finland. That, he said, would violate Sweden's neutrality as well as Finland's peace treaty with the USSR. "If Sweden changed its neutral policy, the Soviet Union would also change its policy toward Sweden."[26]

The Swedish Government regarded the conflict in Norway as part of the overall struggle among the great powers and was even less inclined to intervene there than it had been earlier in Finland. Any suggestion to the contrary evaporated quickly with the collapse of the Allied struggle against the invader. Sweden's armed forces were mobilized when the Germans landed in Denmark and Norway, but those dilapidated forces could not have presented a credible opposition to similar attacks on their own territory. The German Minister in Stockholm on April 9 demanded that the Swedes follow a policy of strict neutrality, avoiding mobilization measures and military deployments directed against the German occupation of its Nordic neighbors. The Swedish Government responded that it would follow its declared policy of neutrality but reserved the right to take any measures necessary to preserve and defend that neutrality.[27]

It soon became clear that Sweden's efforts to maintain strict neutrality, which included the denial of Swedish territory to any of the belligerents, would prove more of a disadvantage to the Germans than to the Western Allies. On May 16, Ribbentrop demanded that Sweden allow the transport of armaments through Sweden to its temporarily beleaguered forces in the Narvik area. The Swedish Government rejected this demand but agreed reluctantly to allow limited consignments of food and personnel (described as "male nurses") to pass through its territory.

German aircraft reportedly violated Swedish airspace on numerous occasions during this period, and about twenty of them were shot down by antiaircraft artillery.[28] The Swedish armed forces were also placed on full alert to protect the Åland Islands, but no hostile action ensued.

Sweden's early hopes for successful Allied intervention in Norway evaporated with the withdrawal of the Western forces from Narvik. German victory in the Far North signified Berlin's full control over Norway's ports and put a temporary end to demands on Stockholm for the transit of Wehrmacht forces. It also underlined Sweden's almost complete isolation from the West and its enclosure within Germany's sphere of dominance. The Soviet Government informed the Swedes on April 13 that it had told the Germans it wished to see Sweden's neutrality respected. However, not much comfort could be derived from this in Stockholm, especially after Hitler's crushing defeat of the Allied forces in France in June 1940.

The Swedes took somewhat more seriously the assurances given by the USSR's trade negotiator, Anastas Mikoyan, who told them in April that the Soviet Union could supply them with attack aircraft and large quantities of oil and gasoline in return for ammunition and railway equipment. Soon, however, Mikoyan's initial claims were watered down considerably, and the trade agreement subsequently negotiated by the two countries did not provide for any major exchange of goods.

Paris fell on June 13, and two days later the Germans demanded that all restrictions be removed on the passage of their personnel and materiel through Sweden to occupied Norway. The Swedish Government quickly agreed in principle and, under an agreement concluded on July 8, German soldiers stationed in Norway bound for Germany on leave were allowed to cross Sweden. The Swedes also conceded orally that their railroads could be used to transport German military units between central and northern Norway.

As a result of these agreements, the Germans were not obliged to transport their troops through Atlantic waters to Norway or between central and northern Norway, where they would have been subject to attack by the Royal Navy. The Swedish Prime Minister, Per Albin Hansson, reasoned that his country's "dear and strict policy of neutrality was broken because of our realization that it was unreasonable to risk war in the present circumstances."[29]

Publicly, the Swedish Government admitted that the transit agreement was not in accord with the strict line it had followed during the fighting in Norway, but it argued that it could not be said to conflict with international law. The Norwegian Government in exile in London, as well as the British Government, protested, citing the Hague Convention on land warfare, which forbids the passage of belligerent troops across the land of neutral states. Stockholm denied that such stipulations applied to the transport of belligerent troops to an occupied area after hostilities there had ceased. The Swedes observed further that soldiers on leave could not be equated with units being sent into battle.

In truth, by July of 1940, there seemed to be little chance for Sweden to deny the victorious Germans much that they demanded. Its bargaining chips were very few. The Swedish navy was relatively strong in comparison with the German navy, but Swedish foreign trade was almost entirely dependent on Germany, leaving it at a severe disadvantage in any test of will in the Baltic. The Swedish Government had not troubled to conceal its preparations to destroy the mining facilities at Gällivare in case of a German attack, which provided some disincentive to the Berlin authorities. However, Germany's dependence on Swedish iron ore was largely counterbalanced by Sweden's dependence on German armaments for its own defense.

Meanwhile, to the West, Denmark lay prone under the Nazi boot, and the Quisling government was cooperating with the German occupiers in their savage attempts to exterminate the Norwegian resistance. In the East, Finland was licking its wounds from the lost battle with the Soviet Union, reinforcing Sweden's sense of isolation in the face of German power. Nevertheless, in spite of their psychological and military vulnerability, the Swedes made concerted efforts to exploit their limited advantages in dealing with the Germans and with the British as well.

When Berlin asked for an increase in the numbers of German troops on leave allowed to transit Sweden, Stockholm argued that such an increase would risk provoking a Royal Air Force bombing campaign against the railroad. Although this was never a real possibility, the British did take action against Swedish interests in June 1940 by seizing four destroyers Sweden had purchased from Italy as they lay in the harbor of Torshavn in the Faeroes. Stockholm protested to London that Germany might seize the occasion to insist that Sweden break off relations with England. After several days the British Government agreed to release the vessels, in spite of Churchill's objections, in which he reiterated his view that a German attack on Sweden could prove to be in Britain's interest.

In the fall of 1940, Sweden made an agreement with Great Britain to permit a small number of Swedish vessels to pass through the British (and German) blockade. Although the so-called Gothenburg Arrangement permitted only limited traffic, it did allow Sweden to import some vital supplies, including oil, and it had important political connotations because it signaled London's belief that Sweden should not be forced to be entirely dependent on Germany. The German authorities agreed to the Gothenburg traffic only after a delay of several months, although it was apparent that Germany's own interest dictated that its Swedish supplier maintain a viable economy.

Because of the limited resources available from the Gothenburg traffic, Sweden found itself constrained throughout the war not only to cooperate economically with the Germans but to preserve a discreet silence on German policy. In return for supplying the German war effort with iron ore and ball bearings, the Swedes received coal, coke, iron products, and artificial fertilizers. Both the outgoing and incoming aspects of the exchange were profitable, and given the importance of foreign trade to the Swedish economy, the Swedes would have been strongly disadvantaged by its cessation.

Although most of the Swedish public sympathized with the Allied cause, the government took care to remind the newspapers of the dangers of possible Nazi reprisals if they criticized German behavior. Sweden, in the government's view, should avoid attracting the attention of Nazi policy makers so that contacts with Germany could be carried on in routine fashion between the civil servants on both sides. Prime Minister Hansson attempted to set the framework for this policy of restraint as early as July 1940 when he observed that "our position towards foreign countries has not been determined and will not be determined by considerations of political ideology. We stand by our right to order our own affairs and do not interfere in the political concerns of others."[30]

A new crisis now presented itself in the eastern portion of the Baltic Sea. By May 1940, there were only six independent states left in Europe north of the Alps: Switzerland, Sweden, Finland, and the three Baltic nations. But the Soviet Union had, already in October 1939, prevailed upon the small Baltic threesome to sign "mutual assistance" pacts with their enormous neighbor and to accept Soviet garrisons at key points in their countries. Early in June 1940, while the attention of Germany and the rest of the world was focused on the closing phases of the French campaign, Soviet forces occupied Lithuania, Latvia, and Estonia.

Moscow then demanded, and got, the return of Bessarabia and northern Bukovina from Romania. Hitler bridled at both actions, but especially at the seizure of Romanian territory, which put Soviet forces dangerously close to the Romanian oilfields he needed for his military campaigns. As early as August 1940, the Germans started to transfer two armored divisions and ten infantry divisions to Poland as a hedge against further Soviet moves.

Almost simultaneously, the Germans demonstrated a renewed interest in Finland. Even before then, however, the USSR had presented new demands on the Finns requiring that the fortifications on the Åland Islands be demolished and the USSR be permitted to open a large consulate there. In addition, the nickel mines at Petsamo were to be brought under Soviet control, and transit on Finnish trains for Soviet troops stationed at Hangö had to be assured. Soviet representatives also intervened blatantly in Finnish domestic politics, forcing Väinö Tanner from the government.

When Molotov visited Berlin in November 1940, he asked Hitler for a free hand in dealing with Finland, on the model of the Baltic states, declaring ominously that "the Finnish question is still unresolved." As Finland had been consigned to the Soviet sphere of influence, "there must be neither German troops in Finland nor political demonstrations in that country against the Soviet--Russian Government." Hitler assured him that Germany desired no war in the Baltic and, while it had economic requirements in Finland, it was not politically interested in that country. When Hitler asked whether the Soviet Union intended to go to war again with Finland, Molotov was evasive. He later explained that there was no question of a war in the Baltic but of a settlement "on the same scale as in Bessarabia and in the adjacent countries."[31] Shortly thereafter, in December, Hitler directed that planning begin for an attack on the USSR, code-named Operation Barbarossa, with the assumption that Finland would be Germany's ally in the campaign.

During the same month, the Soviet Union informed the Finnish and Swedish Governments of its strong objections to a proposal, advanced by the Finns, for a defense and foreign policy union between the two Scandinavian states. Germany also criticized the idea, illustrating that both of the temporary allies wanted to use Finland against the other. The Swedes, who had hoped to use the proposed union as a way of keeping the Finns from committing themselves irrevocably to the Germans, were obliged to shelve the proposal.

In their discussions with the Finns, the Swedish Government had made it clear that a joint foreign policy would have to be determined in Stockholm. Moreover, Finland would have to abandon any intention of regaining the territories it had lost in the Winter War. The Finnish Government had agreed to those conditions. In reality, however, revanchist sentiment was far from dead in Finland, and the desire to regain the large losses of territory in Karelia was particularly strong. Meanwhile, the compromise settlement of the Winter War was no more popular in Soviet military circles than it was in Finland. But the Red Army, in deference to German views, was prepared to forgo armed action as a means of improving its strategic position, at least for a time.

Most Finnish leaders probably calculated that the proposed union with Sweden could garner both Swedish and German support, not simply as an alternative to reliance on Germany. Accordingly, when the idea of union had to be abandoned, the Finnish military, with the concurrence of the political leadership, began consultations with their German counterparts.[32]

By the autumn of 1940, it was clear that the Royal Air Force had won the Battle of Britain and that a German invasion of England was no longer an active possibility. Germany appeared to be preparing to strike instead at the Soviet Union. In conversations with the Swedish authorities, the Finns maintained that they would try to remain neutral in an eventual Soviet-German war.

Early in June 1941, however, Swedish intelligence sources learned that in the course of relieving one of Germany's divisions in northern Norway, both that division and its replacement would be present in northern Finland at the same time. Realizing that Finland would take part in the coming conflict between Germany and the USSR, Stockholm had to assume that Sweden would be subject to a new series of German demands for transit rights. Finland was evidently going to form the northern flank of a German attack on the Soviet Union, and the Wehrmacht would insist that it be permitted to transfer troops from Norway and Germany through Swedish territory into Finland.

Indeed, the Germans did expect to encounter a more favorable attitude in Sweden toward its campaign in the east than it had on the Western front. On June 22, 1941, the very first day of the German invasion, as Hitler proudly proclaimed, "In alliance with their Finnish comrades, the victors of Narvik stand on the shores of the Arctic Ocean," they presented a list of ten demands on the Swedish Government. The first and most controversial was that a German division in Norway, known as the Engelbrecht Division after its commanding officer, be permitted to reach Finland via the Swedish railway system.

The Finns, who were once more at war with the USSR, supported the German demand, promising to take over responsibility for the transportation of the division's 15,000 men as soon as they had reached the Finnish border. Because of Finland's endorsement, some Swedish officials were prepared to interpret the granting of transit rights as being in line with Sweden's earlier policy of assisting its Scandinavian neighbors. More persuasively, it was felt, failure to meet the German demand would inevitably bring Hitler's wrath down upon them. Although it seemed unlikely that the busy Wehrmacht would be able to punish Sweden in the immediate future, Stockholm's refusal would impel the Germans to retaliate as soon as they found a convenient occasion to do so.

Somewhat gratified that the Germans had not demanded military bases on Swedish territory, the Swedish Government agreed on June 25 to permit passage of the Engelbrecht contingent, describing its decision as a one-time concession only. When the Germans requested passage for another division one month later, the request was refused with the suggestion that they be sent by sea along the Swedish coast.

Although passage of the Engelbrecht Division constituted a clear breach of Sweden's neutrality, it provoked little reaction from the British Government. London's low public posture reflected the views of the British Legation in Stockholm, which had reported that the Swedes believed the Soviet Union and Communism to be a greater threat to Scandinavian security and European civilization than Germany and Nazism. As one of its senior staff members wrote as early as January 1940,

> ... *it seems to me that, provided that German aggression is neatly wrapped up in a parcel labelled 'protection from Bolshevism,' the temptation to submit quietly must be very great for the Swedes, who do not at heart believe that the Germans will treat them too badly if they submit willingly. If the Allies win, they will regain their independence anyhow,*

*and if the Allies lose, they stand a chance of being treated
better than if they had resisted the victor.*[33]

Even the Soviet protest, which came only after a month's
delay, was couched in unantagonistic terms, suggesting that Moscow, as well as London, was relieved that the Germans had not
demanded more from Sweden than they had.

Domestically, however, the new German demands provoked
lively political controversy within Sweden, with the Social Democrats arguing that they should be refused. The opposite side was
upheld by Swedes who accepted the German view of the war or
who simply wished to preserve good relations with Berlin in case
Germany succeeded in establishing its "New Order" in Europe.

Prime Minister Hansson tried without great success to medi-
ate the issue, but he did manage to keep his government together
while yielding to most of the German demands. Germany was
allowed to send armaments and supplies to its troops in northern
Finland via Sweden, and a strip of Sweden's territorial waters was
mined, effectively completing a German minefield across the
Baltic. This began on the coast of Lithuania and was designed to
keep the Soviet navy out of the southern Baltic.

Swedish antiaircraft units did not seriously engage the German warplanes that violated Swedish airspace, merely firing warning shots at them, while courier aircraft were allowed to pass
without hindrance. In tacit recognition that Sweden's hallowed
policy of neutrality was no longer in effect, the government avoided
using the very word "neutrality" during the last half of 1941.[34]

Notes — Chapter VI

1. James A. Bayer and Nils Ørvik, *The Scandinavian Flank as History* (Kingston: Centre for International Relations, 1984), 78.
2. Ibid., 70.
3. Winston S. Churchill, *The Second World War* (Boston: Houghton Mifflin, 1948), vol. 1, 531.
4. Bayer and Ørvik, *The Scandinavian Flank as History*, 25.
5. Ibid., 26.
6. Halvdan Koht, *Norway, Neutral and Invaded* (London: Hutchinson, 1941), 41.
7. Churchill, *The Second World War*, vol. 1, 544.
8. Ibid., 546.
9. Ibid., 547.
10. Liddell B.H. Hart, *History of the Second World War* (London: Pan Books, 1974), 59.
11. Bayer and Ørvik, *The Scandinavian Flank as History*, 125.
12. Churchill *The Second World War*, vol. 1, 537.
13. Hart, *History of the Second World War*, 59.
14. Bayer and Ørvik, *The Scandinavian Flank as History*, 111.
15. Hart, *History of the Second World War*, 60.
16. Ibid., 59.
17. Ibid., 60.
18. Bayer and Ørvik, *The Scandinavian Flank as History*, 118.
19. Ibid., 50.
20. Ibid., 49.
21. Ibid., 50.
22. Churchill, *The Second World War*, vol. 1, 564-5.
23. Wahlbäck, *Roots of Swedish Neutrality*, 46.
24. Bayer and Ørvik, *The Scandinavian Flank as History*, 146.
25. Orjan Berner, *Soviet Policies Toward the Nordic Countries* (Lanham, Md.: University Press of America, 1986), 32.
26. Ibid., 31.
27. Wahlbäck, *Roots of Swedish Neutrality*, 46.
28. Ibid., 47.
29. Ibid., 49.
30. Ibid., 53.
31. Berner, *Soviet Policies Toward the Nordic Countries*, 34.
32. Wahlbäck, *Roots of Swedish Neutrality*, 58.
33. Bayer and Ørvik, *The Scandinavian Flank as History*, 37.
34. Ibid., 62.

VII

An End and a Beginning

Hitler's original directive for Operation Barbarossa, dating from December 1940, had stated that one of its objectives was "to secure the Petsamo region and its ore mines as well as the Arctic Ocean route and then to advance jointly with Finnish forces against the Murmansk railroad."[1] Finland at first announced its neutrality in the conflict between the Nazi and Communist behemoths but, when Soviet aircraft bombed its territory, the government declared war on the USSR. Field Marshal Mannerheim, in an order of the day on July 10, 1941, proclaimed a "holy war" and spoke of liberating the people of Karelia. By early 1942, operating in conjunction with German forces, the Finns had regained the territories they were obliged to yield to the USSR in 1940, and their troops occupied large areas in East Karelia as well.

Many Finns thought they saw the beginning of an end to their subjection to Soviet dictates. For Finland, and most of the rest of Scandinavia, however, the Nazi attack on the Soviet Union in June 1941 marked the end of the beginning of World War II rather than the beginning of an end to the conflict. There was much anguish and bloodshed still ahead.

On November 29, 1941, the Eduskunta unanimously passed a resolution emphasizing that Finland wanted no more than the restoration of its 1939 frontiers. Finnish prudence in this regard may have been encouraged by a statement in the House of Commons by the British Foreign Secretary on October 10, 1939. He noted then, "If the Finnish Government persist in invading purely Russian territory, H.M. Government will be forced to treat Finland as an open enemy, not only while the war lasts but also when peace comes to be made."[2] The Finnish Government subsequently made it very clear that it had no interest in pushing on beyond the

1939 borders and, in accordance with Mannerheim's advice, it refused to participate in the German siege of Leningrad.

As Fred Singleton has recorded in his *Short History of Finland*, the Germans who besieged Leningrad for more than a year in 1941–42 came from German bases in the Baltic states rather than Finland. In fact, once the Finnish armed forces had established their defensive battle line in the winter of 1941, it remained virtually unchanged until 1944. Nonetheless, the Finns did make a contribution to the German military campaign. For example, they fulfilled Hitler's Barbarossa directive by cutting the main line of the Murmansk railway at Petrozavodsk. In spite of this, supplies were still able to get through from Arctic ports via the branch line, skirting the southern shore of the White Sea to a junction with the Archangelsk-to-Vologda line.[3]

The British Government, yielding to Soviet pressure, declared war on Finland as well as Romania and Hungary on December 6, 1941. But the Japanese attack on Pearl Harbor the following day brought the United States into the war against the Axis powers, creating a major shift in the balance between the contending powers. The Wehrmacht failed to break through the Soviet defenses around Leningrad or in front of Moscow late in 1941, and as the momentum of the German advance slowed, Sweden began to work discreetly toward extending its limited freedom of maneuver. During December, Stockholm refused a German request for transit rights through Sweden for its troops in Finland.

When proposals were made to involve Sweden in possible peace talks with Finland, the Soviet Ambassador understood that Stockholm could not be active in such an endeavor for fear of German reprisals. Later, as the Soviet military situation improved, Moscow's message became more demanding. Swedish economic aid to Finland was interpreted as helping to prolong Finnish participation in the war, thereby indirectly helping Germany. The USSR made it clear its interests should receive higher priority in Sweden than Finnish and German ones did.

In February 1942, Sweden ordered partial mobilization of its armed forces in response to reports that Germany was contemplating the preventive occupation of Sweden, but this proved to be a false alarm. Although German forces continued to enjoy considerable success, both in the North Atlantic submarine campaign and on the Eastern front, Hitler, in March 1942, implied some reduction in German demands on Stockholm by assuring King Gustav V that Germany intended to respect Sweden's neutrality. Shortly thereafter, the Germans accepted in part a Swedish proposal to reduce the number of German soldiers passing through Sweden from Norway because of reputed technical difficulties on the railway.

In May 1942, the indefatigable Churchill presented a new plan for an Allied landing in Scandinavia, code-named Operation Jupiter. This was conceived as an alternative to an early but weak cross-channel operation and was designed to assist the Soviet Union by preventing Luftwaffe attacks on Allied shipping to Murmansk and Archangelsk. Britain had started sending convoys to the USSR via the Arctic route in September 1941, concentrating on Murmansk as the only available ice-free port. When the Germans realized how many Allied ships were carrying aid to the Soviet Union along this route, they reinforced their air and naval strength in Norway and mounted a relentless attack on them.

One convoy, designated P.Q. 17, which sailed at the end of June 1942, was particularly hard hit when its ships were forced to scatter in the Barents Sea. Only thirteen of the original thirty-six vessels survived, and fourteen American ships were sunk. Only two British, six American, one Panamanian, and two Russian ships managed to reach Archangelsk, delivering 70,000 tons of cargo out of the 200,000 tons which had started the journey in Iceland. Over the vehement protests of Stalin, Churchill had to defend the Admiralty's insistence on suspending the Arctic convoys until summer's continuous daylight had passed. The next convoy was not sent until September, with a much stronger escort, permitting twenty-seven out of a total of forty ships to get through to Archangelsk.

Operation Jupiter's objective was to eliminate the Luftwaffe's seventy bombers and 100 fighters stationed at two airfields in the north of Norway, which were protected by 10,000–20,000 soldiers. Once Royal Air Force fighters and bombers had been established in Murmansk, a division was to be landed in the Petsamo area. Receiving little support from the Allies for his northern initiative, however, Churchill turned his attention to North Africa, where the first large assault on the Axis forces eventually took place.[4]

The arctic convoys had to be suspended again in March 1943 so that escort ships could be diverted to the Atlantic, where they were instrumental in defeating the German U-boats in the following months. When the convoys were resumed in November, much stronger escorts had become available, including escort carriers. The already weakened German forces were unable to stop them from delivering large cargoes to the Soviet ports.

During the war, 811 ships sailed with aid for the USSR. Fifty-eight of them were sunk, and thirty-seven had to turn back, but 720 made it through safely. The convoys, which included American as well as British ships, delivered about 4 million tons of cargo, including 5,000 tanks and more than 7,000 aircraft. In the process, the Allies lost eighteen warships and a total of ninety-eight merchant ships, including those sunk on the return trip. In trying to stop the deliveries, the Germans lost the battle-cruiser *Scharnhorst*, three destroyers, thirty-eight U-boats, and a large number of aircraft.[5]

By the fall of 1942, as the Red Army continued to hold off the German onslaught at Stalingrad, the Swedish Government ordered that German warplanes violating its airspace be fired upon for effect if they failed to respond to warning shots. Shortly thereafter, Churchill assured a senior Swedish official (then Under Secretary of State Boheman) in London that the Allies did not wish to bring Sweden into the war. But, he emphasized, Stockholm should follow a more neutral line because the likelihood of German reprisals seemed much reduced.[6] The Swedes soon adopted a firm attitude in their commercial negotiations with the Germans, and the Swedish Government relaxed its attempts to restrain press criticism of the Nazis. In February and March 1943, Sweden also repeated its partial mobilization in order to discourage any possible hostile intentions on the part of Germany.

A trade agreement between Sweden on one side and Britain and the United States on the other was drafted by mid-summer 1942, but Stockholm delayed its ratification until September. As part of this bargain with the Allies, Sweden canceled its transit agreement of July 1940 with Germany, explaining that the occupying forces had used terror methods which had increased, not decreased, tension in Norway. Berlin accepted the cancellation without strenuous objection. At a meeting in Moscow of the three Allied Foreign Ministers in October 1943, Molotov proposed "that the three Powers suggest to Sweden to place at the disposal of the Allies air bases for the struggle against Germany." Although he had assured the Swedes in October 1942 that their participation in the war was not desired, Churchill was still well aware of their potential importance in the campaign and did not wish to appear to be rejecting the Soviet proposal. In a message to Foreign Secretary Anthony Eden in Moscow on October 31, 1943, the Prime Minister pointed out that

> *It would be a great advantage to bring Sweden into the war. We do not think the Germans have the strength to undertake a heavy invasion of Sweden. We should gain a new country and a small but valuable army. Our gains in Norway would be far-reaching. Valuable facilities would be afforded to Russian air forces.*[7]

Two days later, Churchill clarified his intentions when he indicated that he did not want to "discourage the Russian desire that Turkey and Sweden should *of their own volition* become co-belligerents or actual allies. The Russians should not be put in the position of arguing for this and we of simply making difficulties. We should agree in principle and let the difficulties manifest themselves, as they will certainly do, in the discussion of ways and means"[8] (italics added).

Stalin, who might not have stressed the voluntary aspect of Swedish participation quite so much, was reportedly disappointed when the Allies failed to endorse his proposals on Turkey and Sweden enthusiastically. The Soviet leaders undoubtedly believed that the Swedes should be in their debt because they owed their continued independence and their precious neutrality not to their own cleverness but to the Soviet Union's success in thwarting Hitler's plans for European hegemony. Such sentiments grew also in Britain and the United States as the war progressed and Allied casualty totals mounted.

Nevertheless, the Allies continued to be interested in Swedish cooperation, both as a channel to the Finns and as a possible member of the anti-Nazi coalition. In November 1943, at the Teheran Conference of the Big Three leaders, Stalin replied to U.S. President Franklin Roosevelt's query about getting Finland out of the war by reporting a conversation between the Soviet Ambassador in Stockholm, Alexandra Kollontay, and Swedish

Under Secretary Boheman. Boheman had explained Finland's fear of being turned into a Soviet province. Stalin insisted that the Soviet Government had no wish to make Finland its province unless the Finns forced them to do so. Churchill recounted Stalin's remarks:

> *Madame Kollontay had then been instructed to tell the Finns that the Soviet Government would have no objection to receiving a Finnish delegation in Moscow; but they wished the Finns to state their views about dropping out of the war. In Teheran he had just received the gist of the Finnish reply, which was conveyed to him through M. Boheman. The reply did not make any mention of Finland's desire to dissociate herself from Germany. It raised the question of frontiers. The Finns suggested that as a basis of discussion the 1939 frontier should be adopted, with some corrections in favor of the Soviet Union. Stalin believed that the Finns were not really anxious to conduct serious negotiations. Their conditions were unacceptable, and the Finns well knew it. The Finns still hoped for a German victory; and some of them at any rate had a strong belief that the Germans were going to win.*[9]

In the three-cornered discussion which ensued, Churchill expressed his understanding that Russia must have security for Leningrad, and its position as a permanent naval and air power in the Baltic must be assured, but the Finns should not be incorporated in the Soviet Union against their will. Moreover, it would not be useful to ask for indemnities. Stalin insisted that the Soviet Union did not want money but that the Finns could make appropriate compensations within a few years by supplying the USSR with such things as paper and wood. Churchill then noted that he would like to have Sweden on his side in the war and Finland out of the war by the spring, and Stalin agreed.

The conversation then turned to Viborg ("Nothing doing about Viborg," said Stalin), the Karelian Isthmus, and Hangö. "If the cessation of Hangö presents a difficulty," said Stalin, "I am willing to take Petsamo instead." "A fair exchange," said Roosevelt.

When Churchill stated his hope that Marshal Stalin would handle the question of Finland with due regard to the possibility of Sweden coming into the war in time for the general offensive in May, Stalin agreed, but with the following conditions:

1. Restoration of the 1940 treaty;
2. Hangö or Petsamo (here he added that Hangö was leased to the Soviet Union, but he would propose to take Petsamo);
3. Compensation in kind up to 50 percent for damage. Quantities could be discussed later;
4. A breach with Germany;
5. The expulsion of all Germans;
6. Demobilization.

Churchill and Roosevelt argued against large indemnities, but Stalin was not persuaded. He proposed that the USSR occupy part of Finland if the Finns did not pay, withdrawing within a year if they paid. Agreeing that they had much bigger things to think about, such as the projected landings in France, the three leaders then passed to a discussion about the future of Germany, specifically whether it should be split up and, if so, how.[10]

At Teheran in 1943, and later at Yalta at the end of 1944, Roosevelt and Churchill were necessarily hesitant to damage their working relationship with Stalin. Roosevelt, in particular, hoped that good faith on the part of the West, plus the organizational stiffening provided by the new United Nations, would call forth reciprocal good faith from the Soviet Union.

The Soviet Union, still in need of military and economic aid from the Western Allies in 1943, was also circumspect, having in effect declared a cease fire on the ideological front by formally dissolving the Comintern in May 1943. This move proved to be good propaganda, although the dissolution does not seem to have had an inhibiting effect on the CPSU's ability to "coordinate" the activities of its brother parties. Many of its experienced cadres later resumed their activities in its successor organization, Cominform, which was founded in Poland in October 1947, and focused on Europe rather than the Comintern's worldwide mission.

The Allies continued to be concerned about the importance of Swedish exports to Germany and, in April 1944, demanded a serious cut-back in Sweden's exports of iron ore and ball bearings to their enemy. Ball bearings had evidently overtaken iron ore in importance in Allied calculations, as they believed them to be an essential component of German aircraft production. In spite of U.S. insistence that it was prepared to take strong measures to assure Swedish compliance, Stockholm refused. Instead, the Americans were advised to take the matter up with SKF, the company which produced the bulk of the ball bearings. After talks with the Americans, SKF agreed on June 8, two days after the Allied landings in Normandy, to reduce its shipments of ball bearings to the Germans.

Although some Western critics maintained that Sweden was only making cheap gestures to placate the Allies, Stockholm insisted that it needed to maintain ties with Germany to have any chance of influencing Berlin on its policy toward the other Nordic nations. Later in 1944, however, Sweden virtually put a stop to all trade with Germany, first by withdrawing war risk insurance from Swedish vessels calling at Germany's Baltic ports and then by banning all foreign shipping from Swedish territorial waters.

Meanwhile, the Finnish Government was showing a distinct interest in a separate peace and indicated that it hoped to work out a cooperative arrangement with Sweden after hostilities had ceased. In July 1943, the Finns asked Sweden for a promise of military support after the war. The Swedes refused, arguing that Moscow would probably regard a defense alliance between the two Scandinavian states as a provocation. The Swedish Foreign Ministry did promise material and moral support to Finland after the war, however, and opined that a calmer Soviet attitude toward the situation in the North could best be achieved if Moscow concluded that both Finland and Sweden were well disposed toward the USSR.

Late in 1943, the far northern portion of the Eastern front, which had been quiet since the Finns had adopted defensive positions early in 1942, came under strong pressure from the resurgent Soviet forces. In December, as the Germans were pulling back from their defeat at Stalingrad, the Agrarian Party leader, Urho Kekkonen, made a speech in which he called for a "good neighbor" policy with the Soviet Union as the only basis on which Finland could preserve its freedom and independence. This speech, squarely in the Compliant tradition, was also in line with public opinion, which had come to the conclusion that Finland was on the losing side in the war. Accordingly, the Finnish Government was reconstituted under a new Prime Minister, Edwin Linkomies, and the representatives of the pro-German Peoples Patriotic League (IKL) were excluded.

The new government, with encouragement from Sweden's King Gustav V and the Swedish Government, began to put out cautious peace feelers, and in February 1944, the Eduskunta asked it to seek terms "which would permit us to withdraw from the war." In March, J.K. Paasikivi, who had left public life in 1941 after his service as Finnish Minister in Moscow, returned to the Soviet capital to start negotiations. But the terms the USSR offered, including a demand for the Finns to expel or intern the Germans by the end of April, plus a large war indemnity, were unacceptable to the Finnish Government.

Stockholm was aware that the Germans would inevitably cast a hostile eye on Swedish efforts to broker a peace between the USSR and their Finnish ally. They feared in particular a German attack on the Åland Islands in an attempt to secure communications with the 150,000 German troops in northern Finland. In fact, it appears that in February 1944 Hitler ordered that the Ålands be occupied if Finland did make a separate peace with the Soviet Union. Soviet suspicions of Swedish policy gradually lessened as they became convinced Stockholm was genuinely trying to influence the Finns toward a peace settlement.

On June 7, 1944, as part of a general advance, Soviet troops under Marshal Semën Timoshenko crossed the Isthmus of Karelia into Viborg. Von Ribbentrop visited Helsinki on June 25 and pressured President Risto Ryti into signing an agreement forswearing a separate peace. In recompense, Germany provided substantial additional military aid to Finland. However, Ryti, who had been re-elected for two years in March 1943, signed the agreement with Ribbentrop in his personal capacity, without submitting it to the Eduskunta, and when he resigned on August 1, 1943, the agreement lapsed, so the Finns maintained.

Finland eventually blunted the Soviet summer offensive when Red Army forces were shifted to the Central front for action against the Germans. On August 4, 1944, however, Mannerheim was elected President, replacing Ryti, and he immediately called for peace negotiations. On September 4, diplomatic relations with Germany were broken, and the following day an armistice was declared. Negotiations on a more permanent cessation of hostilities opened in Moscow on September 14 between a Finnish delegation headed by Prime Minister Antti Hackzell and a Soviet delegation headed by Molotov. The latter was supported by

Marshal Voroshilov and the temporarily rehabilitated Maxim Litvinov, among others.

The conferees were able to reach an agreement by September 18 requiring the withdrawal of Finnish troops to their 1940 lines and the disarmament of all German troops on Finnish soil. The Finns complied with the requirement to expel the Germans, but they lost 1,000 men in the process. This campaign, which lasted nearly six months, involved driving the German forces northward along the Torne valley into Norway. Progress there was slow, and fighting continued until May 1945 as the German troops in Lapland resorted to scorched-earth tactics.

The points included in the September settlement were closely patterned on those presented to Churchill and Roosevelt at Teheran some nine months earlier:

1. Hangö was returned to Finland in exchange for a fifty-year Soviet lease on the Porkkala area, a peninsula on the coast about 30 miles west of Helsinki.
2. Petsamo was handed over to the Soviet Union.
3. A war indemnity equivalent to $300 million (at 1938 prices) was to be paid to the USSR in specifically named goods over a period of six years.

Several provisions were added when the armistice agreement was incorporated in the Paris Peace Treaties on February 10, 1947:

1. Finland's armed forces were limited to an army of 34,400 men, a navy of 4,500 with 10,000 maximum tonnage, and an air force of 3,000 men, with sixty aircraft.
2. The Åland Islands were demilitarized.
3. Finland was prohibited from manufacturing or possessing atomic weapons.[11]

Finland reportedly lost 85,000 men in its two wars with the Soviet Union between 1939 and 1945, with another 50,000 permanently disabled. In addition, the Finns had to resettle a flood of refugees from Karelia for the second time in four years. More important, however, was the fact that Finland was the only one of Germany's Eastern Allies to escape Soviet occupation. Thus, although the Finns found themselves within the Soviet sphere of influence, they were able to maintain a real degree of independence. Finland's freedom of action in foreign policy was obviously constrained, but its internal affairs were largely unaffected, provided that certain groups and individuals were kept away from sensitive political positions.

The Allied leaders, in both East and West, had become markedly more assertive as their armies moved into the developing vacuum created by their destruction of Hitler's "thousand-year Reich." Nevertheless, Western efforts to mitigate the punishment meted out to Finland as a consequence of its wartime affiliation with Nazi Germany were fairly successful. This is dramatically revealed in the difference between its fate and that of Poland and the three Baltic nations at the end of the war. To be sure, Poland and the Baltic states were conquered by the Red Army whereas Finland was not, but the Finns by mid-1944 would have been unable to repulse a serious Soviet offensive if Stalin had wished to demonstrate his power to do so.

By the end of 1944, Western concerns were mounting over Soviet intentions everywhere, but especially in Eastern Europe. Stalin's refusal to countenance a compromise approach to the question of Poland's future was a particularly bitter pill for all the Western nations to swallow. Britain and France had gone to war in 1939 precisely because of the Nazi attack on Poland. At Yalta, President Roosevelt pushed unsuccessfully for a compromise resolution of the Polish question, dramatizing his *démarche* by noting that there were five or six million Poles in the United States who were vitally interested in the fate of their homeland.

Stalin was unwilling to heed Roosevelt's pleas, or those of Churchill, as he proceeded to establish a Soviet regime in Warsaw as the keystone in the broad glacis he was intent on building between his turf and a possibly hostile West. It is not an exaggeration to say that Poland, which provided the issue that started World War II, was the issue that started the Cold War that followed.

But Stalin was evidently prepared to accept less control over Finland. He may have felt that the Finnish Communists were strong enough to gain control via political and subversive means. In any case, he apparently was confident that the Finns were less likely than the Balts or the western Slavs to serve as a source of political contamination or as a path of possible military aggression. The Finnish experience in the immediate postwar period was, accordingly, quite different from that of the Baltic states and Poland.

Perhaps the relaxed attitude of Soviet military leaders toward Finland stemmed from their failure to comprehend the growing significance of strategic air power, particularly after the creation of atomic weapons. The United States Army seems to have had a much earlier appreciation of how important Scandinavia would become in the dawning era of polar air routes. Stalin, who was ridiculed by Khrushchev for allegedly planning his military campaigns in Eastern Europe on a globe rather than a map, may have underestimated the importance of Scandinavia. He did, nevertheless, insist on taking the Petsamo area, depriving Finland of its access to the Arctic Ocean.

Until 1945, Denmark and Norway were held in Germany's secure grip in spite of persistent efforts by resistance groups to make that occupation as painful and expensive as possible. The Norwegians were more active in this regard, favored by their more rugged terrain, particularly in the north. But a significant resistance movement also arose in Denmark, where the elderly King Christian X endeared himself to his fellow Danes by refusing to bow the knee to the German occupiers. Danish opposition to the Nazis was demonstrated during the 1943 elections, when 97 percent of the votes were cast for democratic parties and the Nazis won only one seat out of 150.

In August 1943, the *modus vivendi* worked out with the Germans on April 9, 1940, finally broke down. Following strikes and disturbances in several Danish towns, including the capital, German troops went on a rampage, shooting people in the streets and taking 500 individuals as hostages. After the Danish Government resigned, German authorities took over direct control of the country. Attacks were launched against Danish army barracks and naval depots, and twenty-three Danish lives were lost.

By September, a Freedom Council was formed to coordinate the numerous sabotage and resistance groups which had sprung up around the country, serving from then on as a kind of underground government. Sabotage activity increased, followed by German "countersabotage" designed to destroy Danish property and thereby discourage support for the resistance. The Nazis also began a systematic campaign of plunder, taking huge quantities of industrial and agricultural products and making vain promises of eventual reimbursement.

Throughout the war, the Danes in blacked-out Copenhagen were able to look out their windows at night and see the twinkling lights of old Danish towns such as Malmö and Hälsingborg across the sound in neutral Sweden. During the war, many Danes and Norwegians sought refuge across the Øresund via a brisk but illegal traffic in small boats. In one particularly spectacular effort in October 1943, many Danes collaborated in evacuating virtually all of Denmark's Jewish population to Sweden just before they were to be rounded up by the German authorities for shipment to the extermination camps.

Although the Danes were spared the embarrassment of a native Nazi régime such as that afflicting the Norwegians, a voluntary corps of Danish Nazis was formed during the occupation. This stirred considerable indignation and demonstrations, particularly in Copenhagen, and the Germans imposed a curfew in the capital in retaliation. German patrols again began firing in the streets, wounding hundreds of people. When the Germans then announced that eight Danish saboteurs had been executed, a general strike was called. The strike was maintained in spite of appeals from prominent Danish political figures and was not abandoned until the Germans gave in to a series of demands posed by the Freedom Council.

Members of the former government also sought contact with the Freedom Council, and the remnants of the national military command structure accepted its leadership. Links were established with the British clandestine forces in London, who brought a welcome degree of professionalism to the local sabotage teams. Many Danes journeyed to England for training and afterward were dropped back in Denmark, where they helped organize the campaign against the German-controlled railroad system. In all, more than 2,500 instances of industrial sabotage were reportedly carried out, as well as 2,000 attacks against railways.

As for Norway, when King Haakon fled to England in June 1940, his government fled with him, representing the legally elected Storting. In London, the main parties formed a national government-in-exile, which operated throughout the war. Its main contribution to the Allied cause was to control Norway's vast merchant fleet. More than 40 percent of the tonnage entering

British ports during the Battle of the Atlantic in 1941 was
Norwegian.

At home, under the occupation, governmental affairs were
turned over to Vidkun Quisling, whose name became a synonym
for collaborator. Norway's Nazis never lived up to the expectations
of their German masters, however, as Nazi ideology failed to take
root anywhere in the country. An active underground network
soon emerged, carrying out an extensive campaign of sabotage.
There were heavy reprisals on Norwegian citizens for the activities
of resistance groups. In addition, some 35,000 Norwegians were
arrested during the war, and many were shipped off to concentration camps in Germany. Among them were about half of Norway's
Jewish population, the other half having managed to flee to Sweden. Britain's Special Operations Executive worked closely with the
Norwegian resistance throughout the war. Among their notable
joint missions was the destruction in February 1943 of a large
supply of "heavy water" at the German installation in Vermork,
Norway, which may have delayed Nazi atomic bomb research by as
much as a year.

The mere fact of a "resistance organization in being" may
have been almost as much of a problem to the German occupiers
as their actual operations.

> The threat of an armed rising in Norway by the
> Resistance movement called Milorg in cooperation with
> allied forces constrained Hitler to detail thirteen army divi-
> sions, 90,000 naval personnel, 6,000 SS men and 12,000
> para-military troops to watch and control a country with a
> total population of only three million, and at the end of the
> war Milorg received the surrender of 400,000 Germans
> (ten times Milorg's own strength) and liberated 90,000
> prisoners of war, nearly all of them Russians.[12]

By 1943, a number of young Danes and Norwegians had fled
to Sweden for training in a so-called police corps. The Swedish
Government maintained that the corps was designed to keep order
after the Germans were driven out of their countries, not to fight
them, and stressed that its weapons would remain under Swedish
control. In April 1944, Germany demanded that the training
cease, but the Swedish Government rejected the German
démarche. The men were then organized in more regular military

units in the hope that they might participate in the liberation of their homelands. Few of the Danes actually took part in the subsequent military campaign, but a number went on to play prominent roles in the postwar development of their country, including the future trade union leader and Social Democratic Prime Minister Anker Jørgensen.

Norway's émigré battalions were able to play a more active role than their Danish colleagues when German forces began to evacuate Finnmark in the far north of their country. The Swedish Government in December 1944 agreed that the Norwegian units could be transferred to the newly liberated areas, and they were transported to Kirkenes by American military aircraft. Although this meant that belligerent warplanes were permitted to operate from neutral territory, Germany raised no objections.

In mid-April 1945, the Norwegian government-in-exile asked for Swedish military intervention in Norway to make it clear to the German troops there that their position would be untenable after the Reich's impending collapse. The Swedes refused this request as well as a less precise inquiry from Denmark, insisting on their commitment to keep Sweden out of the war. Nevertheless, military planning for a possible move into either or both of its neighbors began, in case an unforeseen contingency required such action.

Sweden became active in the closing months of the war, working with no less a figure in the Nazi régime than Heinrich Himmler. In March 1945, he made it possible for the Swedes to bring Danish and Norwegian prisoners back from German concentration camps. Himmler then asked the leader of this expedition, Count Folke Bernadotte, for Swedish assistance in meeting General Eisenhower so that he could capitulate on the whole Western front.

The Western Allies refused Himmler's offer because it appeared to be "a last effort to make trouble" between them and the Soviet Union. But the Swedish Government instructed Bernadotte to suggest an alternative proposal as his own idea. Accordingly, Himmler was asked to carry out that part of his offer which pertained to Denmark and Norway, in return for which Sweden might agree to intern the German units remaining in Norway, comprising several hundred thousand men. Agreement along those lines was reportedly reached in principle on April 30, but, before any action could be taken, Hitler dismissed Himmler and committed suicide, designating Admiral Karl Dönitz as his successor. The German forces in northern Europe surrendered to Field Marshal Sir Bernard Montgomery on May 4, 1945, and British forces entered Denmark the following day. Crown Prince Olav returned to Norway as commander in chief of the armed forces a few days after the Germans surrendered, followed soon by King Haakon. Vidkun Quisling and about twenty of his fellow collaborators were tried for treason, sentenced to death, and shot.

Notes — Chapter VII

1. Berner, *Soviet Policies Toward the Nordic Countries*, 35.
2. Singleton, *A Short History of Finland*, 136.
3. Ibid.
4. Churchill, *The Second World War*, vol. 4, 312.
5. Hart, *History of the Second World War*, 410.
6. Wahlbäck, *Roots of Swedish Neutrality*, 63.
7. Churchill, *The Second World War*, vol. 5, 289.
8. Ibid.
9. Ibid., 398-99.
10. Ibid., 397.
11. Singleton, *A Short History of Finland*, 139.
12. Peter Calcovoressi and Guy Wint, *Total War* (New York: Penguin Books, 1979), 273.

VIII

Europe Reconfigured

In 1945–46, the Nazi surrender and the resulting cease-fire lines had established the boundaries of a settlement which neither East nor West could alter without risking war. Inevitably, given the divergent Soviet and Western views on how best to structure the new Europe to ensure their own security, there would be competition, but both East and West could point to some positive aspects of their situation, imperfect as it might be.

The USSR had pushed the threat of German aggression hundreds of miles to the West and was able to build a formidable defense in the intervening space. The West's share of Europe included all of France and Italy, and its troops occupied major parts of German and Austrian territory. On such foundations, the West could create a viable defensive position in the event of continued Soviet intransigence. Aside from the special case of Finland, moreover, the situation in Scandinavia seemed to be quite satisfactory. There was certainly little or no sympathy for Communism in Norway, Denmark, or Sweden, although Stockholm's markedly independent policy on all international issues was bound to create frictions with some of the Western Allies from time to time.

Possible Soviet designs on Bear Island as well as Spitsbergen (one of the islands in the Svalbard archipelago which had suffered from both British and German occupation and raids during the war), seemed more likely to constitute a genuine concern. In 1944, Molotov had proposed that the Svalbard group be put under joint Norwegian-Soviet administration and that Bear Island be transferred outright to the USSR. But sovereignty over Svalbard had been awarded to Norway by a multilateral treaty signed in 1920, and the Soviet Union had accepted this settlement without reservations. When Molotov tried to reopen the question of Svalbard in 1946–47, Norway rejected his proposal on grounds of impracticality, and the Soviet Union did not pursue the matter. The strategic balance sheet in the North therefore showed a number of Western assets with only a few troublesome questions, largely the result of Soviet sensitivity about their sea routes to and from the Murmansk area.

The delayed peace conference designed to put an end to World War II finally assembled in Paris in July 1946, with twenty-one nations in attendance. They were unable to agree on peace treaties covering Germany and Austria, territories already serving as unstable buffers between East and West and under joint occupation by the forces of the Big Four. By February 1947, however, the negotiators were able to reach agreement with Italy, Hungary, Romania, and Finland.

The Paris agreements effectively sanctioned the Soviet Union's spread into Central Europe and formalized its territorial acquisitions in Finland. Moreover, its seizure of Ruthenia (from Czechoslovakia), and northern Bukovina and Bessarabia (from Romania), together with its retention of the three Baltic states and the addition of much of eastern Poland, gave the USSR a common border with all the countries of Eastern Europe, including Hungary. In spite of the territory which still separated the Soviet Union from Yugoslavia and Albania, its acquisitions farther north significantly increased its ability to maintain pressure on its developing satellite network.

An encouraging factor for Western statesmen immediately after the war was the existence of the United Nations. President Roosevelt had placed great hope in the UN as a forum for dealing with postwar problems. He had, accordingly, been prepared to make substantial concessions at Yalta on concrete political and territorial issues. He was delighted when the USSR accepted the U.S. proposals on voting in the Security Council, which established a great power veto in that group. The U.S. Senate, the President felt sure, would not accept the UN charter without such a provision.

Although Stalin had originally asked that all sixteen Soviet republics be represented in the General Assembly, he contented himself at Yalta with obtaining only three votes — the USSR itself, the Ukraine, and Byelorussia. He pointed out, with some justification, that the USSR would be badly outvoted in any case because the votes of the British dominions (Canada, Australia, India, and South Africa) would be strongly influenced by London, and nearly all of the Latin American votes would be in Washington's pocket. Curiously, the Soviet Union at first asked for a total of four voting members, including Lithuania, on the grounds that it, like Ukraine and Byelorussia, had suffered so heavily in the war.

Most accounts consider Churchill's speech at Fulton, Missouri, in March 1946 as the *de facto* declaration of the Cold War. He observed, "From Stettin in the Baltic to Trieste in the Adriatic, an iron curtain has descended across the Continent," a declaration which notably did not include any of the Scandinavian countries. A month before, Stalin had made a speech on the incompatibility of capitalism and communism and called for a series of three Five-Year plans "to ensure against any eventuality."

Washington, concerned about aggressive Soviet behavior, had already asked the American Embassy in Moscow to explain Stalin's position. The Embassy's Counselor, George F. Kennan, was only too glad to oblige and, in his record-breaking 8,000-word telegram of February 22, 1946, called Washington's attention to what he considered to be the roots of Soviet conduct, an analysis that later found its way into the pages of *Foreign Affairs* under the pseudonymous "X," Kennan pointed out that the Soviet leaders saw the world as divided into two camps and that they needed to justify their autocratic rule at home by evoking a foreign enemy. However, he cautioned that this did not mean that Moscow was seeking world revolution. By and large, the nations of Scandinavia were inclined to accept Kennan's analysis, but they emphasized the "no world revolution" caveat.

As John Lewis Gaddis has noted, American strategists had recognized as early as August 1944 that a German defeat would leave a power vacuum in Europe into which only the Russians would be well-positioned to move. A U.S. Joint Chiefs of Staff memorandum of that time had viewed the change in the European balance of power as "more comparable indeed with that occasioned by the fall of Rome than with any other change occurring during the succeeding fifteen hundred years."[1] This was something of an overstatement for, as John Spanier pointed out in his popular *American Foreign Policy Since World War II*, "The power vacuum created by Germany's defeat, which permitted Soviet power to extend into the center of Europe and which precipitated the cold war, was virtually a replay of the struggle that erupted after the end of the war against Napoléon ... with Stalin taking Tsar

Alexander's place and the United States playing the role of England in rearranging the new balance of power."[2]

The new U.S. role took shape when Secretary of State George Marshall made his memorable address at Harvard on June 5, 1947, when he called upon the European nations to present a plan for their common needs and common recovery. Within a month, the Europeans had responded by setting up a committee to coordinate their joint planning. This group, later expanded to seventeen members, became the nucleus for the Organization for European Economic Cooperation (OEEC).

Marshall's invitation was extended to all Europe's suffering nations, including the USSR and Eastern Europe. Failure to do so would have cast doubt on American *bona fides* and led to charges that Washington was to blame for dividing Europe along ideological lines. The gesture toward the USSR would, in Washington's view, place the onus for continued division of Europe on Moscow. Foreign Minister Molotov threw a scare into the American Government by arriving in Paris with a large retinue of experts for the first meeting on the European recovery plan. Within a few days, however, he had denounced the U.S. proposal, alleging that its program for European economic integration would require the USSR to abandon its own plans for resuscitating the Soviet and Eastern European economies. On July 2, 1947, the Soviet Union withdrew from the conference, and its neighbors were obliged to follow suit. Moscow prevailed upon the Edward Beneš government in Czechoslovakia to rescind its initial agreement to participate.

In a typically prescient move, Finland had declined the invitation to attend the Paris meeting in the first place, in spite of a recommendation to the contrary from the Foreign Relations Committee of the Eduskunta. The Finns reasoned that the Marshall Plan was becoming the source of serious differences among the great powers. Accordingly, Finland, desiring to remain outside great power politics, "regrets that it does not find it possible to participate." As there were no similar inhibitions on Finnish membership in such Western-oriented organizations as the International Monetary Fund and The World Bank, however, Finland joined them both in 1948, seven years before it was admitted to the United Nations.

An important stimulus behind the Marshall Plan had been U.S. concern over French fears that German economic recovery would eclipse France's performance and place its national security once more in jeopardy. Similar concerns among France's neighbors led in 1948 to the creation of a military framework which was to parallel that of the Marshall Plan on the economic side. "The reluctance of the French to visualize a rearmed Germany was only echoing what was felt in a far stronger fashion in smaller countries such as Bénélux and Denmark, if not indeed Norway."[3] Responding to a speech of January 22, 1948, by British Foreign Secretary Bevin, representatives of five Western European countries (France, the UK, and the Bénélux countries) gathered together in March to pledge their close cooperation on a number of security and armament questions. A number of European leaders, most notably Belgian Prime Minister Paul-Henri Spaak, showed themselves cool to the idea of trying to build an effective defense pact without U.S. participation. The "coup" of February 1948 in Prague, which pushed Edward Beneš out and the Communist leader Klement Gottwald into the Czechoslovak presidency, did much to remove earlier American reservations over such an arrangement. It had a similar effect in France, whose leaders had earlier hoped to rebuild its former alliance with Moscow. As the American historian Timothy Ireland noted, "One of the results of the Prague coup was to make more explicit the linking of French security against Germany to the wider question of European security against the Soviet Union."[4]

Almost simultaneously with the Prague coup, Moscow showed a renewed interest in the Soviet Union's northern flank, proposing a treaty of "friendship, cooperation, and mutual assistance" with Finland, which was signed on April 6, 1948. Although the Finns were relieved that nothing more was demanded of their country, their fellow Nordics were not nearly so pleased with the result. The atmosphere was further clouded by signs that the Soviet Government was prepared to exert pressure to persuade the Norwegians to sign a similar agreement.

The five-power talks in Brussels began on March 6 and resulted less than two weeks later in the signature on March 17, 1948, of a Treaty of Economic, Social and Cultural Collaboration and Collective Self-Defense. The five signatories invited other states with similar ideas to join them. The treaty did not exclude eventual German membership in the pact, but it referred specifically to a possible renewal of German aggression. The Brussels Pact on "Western Union" is recognized as the nucleus around which the North Atlantic Treaty Organization was built, but its original anti-German orientation is often passed over. It is true that Foreign Secretary Ernest Bevin held open the possibility of Germany's eventual accession to the new group, but fear of a resurgent Germany was the glue which held both the Brussels Pact and NATO together in their early years. NATO's first Secretary General, Lord Hastings Ismay, spoke truly, if jocularly, when he observed that the Alliance was designed to "to keep the Russians out, the Americans in, and the Germans down."

President Truman expressed the U.S. position in an address to a joint session of Congress, also on March 17:

> *"Since the close of the hostilities, the Soviet Union and its agents have destroyed the independence and democratic character of a whole series of nations in Eastern and Central Europe. It is this ruthless course of action, and the design to extend it to the remaining free nations of Europe, that have brought about the critical situation in Europe today. The tragic death of the Republic of Czechoslovakia has sent a shock throughout the civilized world. Now pressure is being brought to bear on Finland, to the hazard of the entire Scandinavian peninsula.... I am confident that the United States will, by appropriate means, extend to the free nations the support which the situation requires. I am sure that the determination of the free countries of Europe to protect themselves will be matched by an equal determination on our part to help them protect themselves."* [5]

Early thinking in the U.S. tended to favor a unilateral guarantee to its European associates, which would not necessarily involve agreement on a treaty. In line with that thinking, the Brussels group would eventually be expanded beyond the five signatories of the Brussels pact to include Norway, Denmark, Iceland, and Italy, as well perhaps as Sweden and Portugal. Later adherents might be Spain, Germany, and Austria, or at least the western zones of the last two countries.

A number of Western European leaders, however, favored a formal treaty arrangement, but for diametrically opposed reasons, as they believed that only thus would the U.S. commitment be binding on future administrations. Paul-Henri Spaak told American officials that, while he himself did not believe a treaty to be essential, "All of western Europe, particularly France, would welcome such a move." Bevin was even more explicit, noting, "If the new defence system is so framed that it related to any aggressor it would give all the European states such confidence that it might well be that the age-long trouble between Germany and France might tend to disappear."[6]

In the face of growing evidence of Western resolve to resist Soviet pressures, Moscow and the Communist Parties of Western Europe in the spring of 1948 launched the first in a series of "peace offensives," designed to capitalize on the pacifist sentiment widely prevalent in the West. By the end of June, however, the Soviet Government abruptly changed tactics and imposed a blockade on Berlin, preventing any overland traffic from reaching western zones of that city, 110 miles deep in the Soviet Zone of Germany. This stimulated the governments and air forces of the Western powers to supply Berlin with essential quantities of food and fuel through the following winter.

The blockade also galvanized public opinion in the United States and Western Europe, including Scandinavia, and thus facilitated Western efforts to meet the Soviet challenge. A military organization for the Brussels treaty had been created by September 1948, and the U.S. quickly transferred military supplies from its stocks in Germany to the French forces there. The Berlin blockade was not lifted until May 1949, after confidential discussions between American and Soviet negotiators at the United Nations. By that time, Western, especially American, tenacity in maintaining Allied rights in Germany evidently persuaded Moscow that nothing further was to be gained by continuing the blockade. On the other hand, Soviet leaders derived some satisfaction from demonstrating that the United States was not prepared to risk direct confrontation, even in regard to such a vital area as Germany.

The question of Scandinavian participation had been on the minds of a number of the Brussels conference participants, even though Bevin had not mentioned the Nordic countries at all in his speech. In fact, according to Magne Skodvin, Professor Emeritus at Oslo University, Denmark and Norway were not approached or even indirectly informed when discussions on a Western European bloc were first initiated.[7] Although neither the northern nor southern flank European states had been invited to join the Brussels

Treaty group, Bevin apparently envisioned the eventual participation of Norway, Denmark, Italy, and Greece in a security system of the Western democracies.

All of the Nordic countries were firm believers in the UN ideals, including the charter's requirement that all member states participate in both military and economic sanctions against an aggressor. Some objections had been raised in Scandinavia, particularly in Sweden, about this requirement on the grounds that adherence to the charter would, at least theoretically, be incompatible with a policy of neutrality. After some discussion, however, majority opinion in Sweden agreed with the government that, as a practical matter, there was no such conflict. Sweden's policy of neutrality was seen as designed to prevent the country from being automatically drawn into a war between the great powers. But as sanctions could be imposed only if all permanent members of the Security Council supported them, there was no risk of being ordered by the Security Council to take action against one of the major powers. Sweden's new Foreign Minister, Östen Undén, set forth his nation's view in October 1945 by pointing out that the new organization would be able to function in the event of future wars only if all permanent members of the Security Council worked together.

> *The Swedish people must for their part earnestly desire — both because of their own vital interests and for idealistic reasons — that a political division of states into mutually hostile groups does not occur. We are willing to join a common security organization and in the event of a future conflict to abstain from neutrality to the degree that its Charter requires. However, if against expectation a tendency for the great powers to divide into two camps manifests itself within the organization, our policy must be to avoid being drawn into any bloc or group.[8]*

In the immediate aftermath of World War II, Denmark, Norway, and Sweden had tried to adopt their traditional neutral policy with regard to disputes between other nations. However, Norway's experience with the Nazi invaders had persuaded many of its people that close association with a powerful neighbor was a surer way to preserve the nation's security in an uncertain world; Moscow's threatening stance served only to reinforce that belief.

Nevertheless, both Norwegian Foreign Minister Trygvie Lie and his successor, Halvard Lange, in 1946 had been unequivocal in refusing to join any form of regional political or military bloc. The basic Norwegian "bridge-building" approach was that cooperation among the victors of World War II should continue and that, if it did, the UN Security Council would be able to harmonize national differences and play its proper role in conflict resolution.

Even after Britain's proposal for a Western Union in January 1948, initial Norwegian official reactions were reserved, and Lange made clear his preference for a Nordic solution, possibly in association with Great Britain. But the Soviet Union's suggestion of a bilateral pact with Norway provoked apprehensions about possible "Finlandization," both within that country and elsewhere. In March 1948, the Norwegian Parliament authorized an extraordinary expenditure of 100 million kroner for military preparedness and authorized the call-up of extra personnel.[9]

By January 1949, even Lange had to recognize that the possibilities for bridge-building were virtually exhausted. He also had to admit the profound differences of opinion which had emerged during negotiations with Sweden and Denmark about a possible Scandinavian defense pact. In his view, such a pact had to rest on the idea of "regional collaboration within an area large enough to constitute a factor of real power."[10]

Lange received strong parliamentary support in reaching those conclusions. Many of his supporters praised Norway's "Atlantic Policy" during the war and welcomed a close association with the Western nations as a supplement and reinforcement of the nation's support for the UN. His supporters "also rejected as unfounded the opponents' allegation that Norway was destined to become the advance bastion of a Western Alliance directed against the Soviet Union, or a forward base for American nuclear bombers."[11] Proponents of the alliance denied that Norway's defense policy would in fact be altered. Much stress was put, instead, on the benefits to be expected from the American Mutual Defense Assistance Program, which promised to supply arms and equipment for the common defense on reasonable terms.

Lange and Defense Minister Jens Christian Hauge had, as early as March 1948, begun asking Western ambassadors and military attachés what kind of help Norway might expect if it were attacked. Neither the United Kingdom nor the United States was particularly forthcoming, the British because of worries about their lack of resources and the Americans simply because no decision had yet been reached by their complex legislative-executive procedures. Nevertheless, the military forces of both countries had earlier shown considerable interest in the strategic advantages inherent in Scandinavia's geographic position. In June 1947, the British Chiefs of Staff and the Joint Planning Staff had pointed out the potential benefits of controlling Scandinavia:

> *(a) We would have advanced air bases which would halve the distance to Moscow. We would also be very favorably placed for rocket and air attacks on Russian communications with Western Europe.*
>
> *(b) Our early warning system would be greatly improved. We would, moreover, be well placed far forward on the direct air route between Western Russia and the industrial East of the North American continent.*
>
> *(c) We would be well placed to cover naval and air operations in northern waters and the Baltic.*
>
> *(d) Additional man-power and valuable raw materials would be available to assist our war effort.*[12]

The American Army had been even more enthusiastic about Scandinavian real estate and had moved to take advantage of it much earlier. In May 1945, the Joint Chiefs of Staff had recommended "that eight bases in France, Italy, Denmark and Norway be acquired for the use of units of the U.S. air forces during the occupational period." The Norwegian base in question was Sola, by Stavanger, and it was made clear that it was to serve the needs of combat units — heavy bombers to be supported by fighters — and not transport aircraft. The personnel strength for the Sola base alone would amount to about 4,500 men.[13]

In a foreshadowing of what later came to be known as the Nordic Balance, the Department of State and the American Ambassador to Norway both counseled against this recommendation. Acting Secretary of State Joseph C. Grew asked the military leaders to reconsider their desires for bases in Norway and Denmark, since "it would open the door to Russia for similar requests." Ambassador Lithgow Osborne, in Oslo, similarly warned that "the establishment of a strategic air base for heavy bombers by the United States would very probably, it seems to me, contribute to a continuation of Soviet occupation in Finnmark and also a Russian demand for an air base in Norway."[14] By the end of September, General Eisenhower agreed that the recommendation for bases in Norway and Denmark should be dropped, and the Joint Chiefs of Staff concurred.

Although the alarm occasioned in the spring of 1948 by Soviet behavior in Czechoslovakia and Scandinavia stimulated renewed interest in the idea of Nordic air bases, General Karl Spaatz, Chief of Staff of the United States Air Force, saw little advantage in bases on the continent since they could be so rapidly overrun. He asked instead for a special study of bomber bases in Norway and Greenland. But the Joint Chiefs of Staff now looked with disfavor on the idea of bases in Norway.

> *... they were situated too close to enemy air bases and would be very vulnerable to attack. Any attempt to establish such bases before the outbreak of war might also provoke a Soviet invasion of the country. The strategic interest of the United States in Norway was to deny use of its territory by the Soviet Union rather than to use bases there for their own purposes.*[15]

Curiously enough, it was Denmark which, in 1947, initiated active military cooperation with its Nordic neighbors. The Danish navy, concerned as always about the entrances to the Baltic, was convinced that it could not by itself keep the narrows open if a major power demanded their closure. The Commander-in-Chief of the Danish navy, Admiral Vedel, launched conversations with his Swedish and Norwegian counterparts to enlist their cooperation. These conversations, although known to and unofficially approved by the Danish cabinet, dealt only with technical questions and were restricted to naval matters.

Contacts between Sweden and Norway, which shared the Scandinavian peninsula and had an obvious interest in working together on ground forces, were much slower to develop. But some Swedish officers were interested in closer contacts with the British on military and naval questions and London was eager to facilitate them. Consideration was thus given in 1947 to inviting senior Swedish military officers to attend the wedding of Princess

Elizabeth as a means of probing Swedish receptivity. The Foreign Office had reservations, however, because it was not yet clear how much aid the United States was prepared to extend to the Scandinavian countries, and it recommended against premature high-level talks with Sweden.

> *... if discussions are held with the Americans regarding security questions the talks will include Scandinavia. After talking to the Americans we are more likely to know where we stand in all these matters and by then our own planning and thinking will have further adapted itself to the new circumstances.*[16]

When the United States had made clear its renewed interest in Europe, Bevin launched his campaign for an association of Western democracies. There was no doubt in his mind that Denmark, Norway, and Sweden should be included in the future system, as reflected in his early January 1948 formulation of "The First Aim of British Foreign Policy."[17] They were not included in the public announcement of January 22, however, and were evidently bumped to the waiting list, along with Germany and Spain, because of Foreign Office fears that raising the possibility of Scandinavian participation might have counterproductive effects in the Nordic capitals.

The reaction in Sweden to Bevin's initiative was, as expected, largely negative. Although Sweden was Britain's most important trade outlet in 1947, and Foreign Minister Undén was becoming more wary of Soviet intentions, Stockholm was already concerned about how a more Western orientation on its part might affect Finland's relations with the USSR. Denmark was less negative but, in spite of parliamentary backing for rearmament, no agreement on defense strategy was apparent beyond a general wish for Scandinavian military cooperation, with some support from the United Kingdom. Danish Prime Minister Hans Hedtoft insisted that Denmark would not become a member of any bloc, stressing instead its membership in the United Nations and its duty there as a Nordic country. Foreign Minister Gustav Rasmussen, on the other hand, only twenty-four hours later was exploring the possibilities of an American military guarantee for his country.

Norway thus had to be the prime mover if Scandinavia was going to join the alliance train before it left the station. Until the

Soviet-engineered coup in Prague, Norwegians had tended to see themselves, like their Swedish neighbors, as bridge builders between the rival ideologies of East and West. There had even been an initial reluctance in Norway to accept Marshall Plan aid, amounting to some $350 million, as this seemed to be tantamount to taking the first step into a U.S.-led Western alliance. By 1948, however, Norway was insisting that a Scandinavian defense union could not be a satisfactory solution to its security problems unless it were linked to the broader security system of the proposed Atlantic Alliance. This was a dramatic turnaround from its inter-war attitude stressing "defense against our friends" to what has been termed a policy of "nailing the Anglo-Saxon allies" to their security responsibilities in the North.[18]

By early 1948, Swedish-Norwegian staff talks had begun in Oslo, reportedly at Swedish initiative, and hopes were expressed that a Scandinavian defense bloc might be formed within a few months. Discussions moved up to the cabinet level at the end of January when Danish Minister of Defense Rufus Hansen visited Oslo and Stockholm with the evident intention of acting as an intermediary between the conflicting views of the other two governments. This was evidently another reincarnation of the Scandinavians' recurrent hope of establishing a "third force" in Northern Europe, buttressed by British support. Not incidentally, Britain and the three Scandinavian states were headed at the time by Labor governments, which provided a measure of ideological or, as Bevin expressed it, spiritual solidarity.

The U.S. Department of State was not averse to development of a third force either. The chief of the European Office told the British Ambassador on January 21, 1948, that he envisaged "the creation of a third force which was not merely the extension of US influence but a real European organization strong enough to say 'no' both to the Soviet Union and to the United States, if our actions should seem so to require."[19]

When Soviet pressure on Finland became publicly known through the publication on February 28, 1948, of Stalin's letter to Paasikivi, concern mounted in all the other Nordic countries, especially Norway. When Finland signed a treaty with the USSR the following month, Norway became the only European nation sharing a frontier with the colossus of the Northeast which did not have a treaty of friendship, assistance, and consultation with

Moscow. Some of the concern was evidently stirred by a hint to Norwegian Ambassador Berg in Moscow from Alexandra Kollontay, a veteran of Soviet-Nordic diplomacy, that her government might be interested in a Soviet-Norwegian nonaggression treaty. The U.S. contemplated sending a naval force into the Norwegian Sea as a gesture of support, while the Soviet Union conveyed a different message by violating Danish air space around Bornholm.

Equally blunt hints were received from other sources, but no formal *démarche* was evidently made by the Soviet Government. Foreign Minister Lange reportedly deduced that the Soviet signals might be to designed provoke a statement from Oslo that Norway would not conclude any such treaty, thus effectively barring his country from adhering to a Western alliance. On March 8, he summoned the American and British Ambassadors to ask what assistance Norway could expect in case of aggression, making it clear to them that Norway was determined to turn down a possible Soviet invitation to negotiate a pact.[20]

At that time, from the Western point of view, there seemed to be a real possibility that the Italian Communist Party might gain a majority in the forthcoming elections and that their French comrades could gain decisive influence in France. Militarily weak Denmark and Norway could be regarded as liabilities to Western strategists as they strove to construct a defensive alliance; nevertheless, both London and Washington responded quickly and firmly to the Norwegian inquiry, with the United States in the lead as the British had hoped. The forthcoming Marshall Plan meeting in Paris was chosen as the venue for further discussions, as all the Nordic Foreign Ministers were to be present, in addition to Marshall, Bevin, and, of course, Bidault.

The three Nordic Ministers met in Copenhagen on their way to Paris, where they conferred separately with their Western counterparts. Bevin's meetings on March 15 and 16 with Lange and Rasmussen focused on political as well as security issues. He explained to them his ideas about three related security systems and also met with Sweden's Undén, warning him against Soviet pressure. The meetings with the Danes and Norwegians moved the discussions forward from mere declarations of sympathy to concrete security arrangements and held out the prospect of close cooperation with the United States and Britain in such arrangements. The Foreign Secretary's explanations to Lange included

Spitsbergen and, at least inferentially, all of northern Norway. For Denmark, the meeting signified that a decision at the political level was now urgent, while leaving to Sweden the task of demonstrating that a Scandinavian alliance would be more likely than an Atlantic one to keep its members out of future conflicts.

Sweden, however, was still committed to its ideal of neutrality. A government statement of February 4, 1948, explained its view:

> *If the new security organization [the UN] is undermined through the formation of political blocs or its capacity for action is paralyzed in some other way, our country must remain free to choose the path of neutrality. Whether a policy of neutrality would be possible in these circumstances would not depend on ourselves alone, and the prospects of being able to pursue such a policy cannot therefore be assessed in advance. But we do not want to deprive ourselves of the right and opportunity of remaining outside a new war by entering into any commitment at this stage.[21]*

In order to meet Norway's interest in more substantial security guarantees than those available from a divided United Nations, Sweden advanced the idea of a joint defense system with Denmark and Norway. Foreign Minister Undén traveled to Oslo on May 3, where he met with Norway's Prime Minister, Foreign Minister, and Defense Minister. All of the Norwegian leaders favored a Scandinavian union but continued to believe that it would not be credible without some kind of opening to the West. Undén was convinced that unconditional nonalignment was basic, in contrast to the Norwegian view that all options should be kept open.

It was not until the following September, at a meeting of Nordic Foreign Ministers, that an announcement was made that an inter-Nordic study would now be made even though "a certain difference prevails in the attitude toward problems of security policy."[22]

Between that date and February 1949, the British made two attempts to associate Scandinavia with the North Atlantic Pact, although with limited commitments. In the first, Robert Hankey of the Foreign Office held out the possibility of two separate pacts, one Nordic, one North Atlantic. Denmark and Norway would be members of both pacts, while Sweden would belong only to the

Nordic one. The proposed system of interlocking pacts would preserve Scandinavian unity but also imply certain Swedish commitments toward the other two nations, who would be members of NATO, albeit on a limited basis. Sweden would remain "non-belligerent" rather than neutral in the event that Denmark and Norway were drawn into a conflict by their NATO obligations and would take on military obligations only if its two neighbors were "actively attacked." If Sweden itself were attacked, it could count on the support not only of its Nordic allies but of the other NATO members.

In elaborating on the first Hankey plan, the United Kingdom made it clear that the three Nordics would not only have to agree to defend their own territory to the limit of their capabilities but also "to make available such facilities as are within their power, whenever required, in order to provide for the protection of the North Atlantic area." Hankey further explained that Sweden would be expected to cooperate in measures of economic warfare against Russia and would resist any attempt to prevent or dissuade her from trading with the Western powers (iron ore, ball bearings, timber, munitions).[23]

Neither of these points was congruent with basic Swedish neutrality policy. Moreover, the economic warfare proposals served to resurrect World War II antagonisms. As a result, Hankey's first proposal was virtually dead on arrival in Stockholm. Oslo, which was prepared to give the plan serious consideration, quickly saw that presenting it in Sweden would be counterproductive. Foreign Minister Lange and his colleagues continued to feel strongly that their country needed Swedish as well as Western support to ensure its security but concluded also that, if forced to choose between the two, Norway would have to side with the West.

In this delicate situation, Lange tried to come up with a compromise proposal, suggesting that Sweden might be willing to accept joint responsibility with Denmark and Norway for sealing off the Baltic and, concurrently, to accept a guarantee from the United States. There was considerable reluctance in Washington to accept such a solution, not only because of resentment over Sweden's "free ride" at U.S. expense, but also at its British provenance. But Secretary of State Marshall was prepared to listen. Lange had explained to him why he thought a Scandinavian union must have priority, and why such a union must have links with the West.

Under no circumstances, he indicated, could Norway defend both her coastline and her eastern frontier, so a neutral and friendly Sweden would be of fundamental importance.

In a conversation with Bevin on October 4, Marshall commented that "the critical point was the strait between Denmark and Sweden: if that could be made impassable in time of war then a Scandinavian *bloc* might not be too bad."[24] Only a few days later, Sweden's Undén personally disabused the Secretary of State of any idea that Sweden would accept such a solution.

Lange refused to give up hope although Undén had already made clear his view that a Scandinavian defense group could receive Western support without commitments or preparations in peacetime. In his opinion, military assistance would be forthcoming once the Scandinavian bloc had been established. The Norwegian cabinet leaned in this direction on October 18, 1948, when it reiterated its previous stand in favor of a Nordic defense union under the provisions of Articles 51–54 of the UN charter. Cabinet members hoped that this union would benefit from guarantees from the Western powers without automatic obligations on their own part. Only if a Western guarantee proved to be absolutely unobtainable on this basis would other solutions be considered.

The Committee on Scandinavian Defense, created in September 1948, noted on January 15, 1949, that Danish and Norwegian rearmament would depend largely on supplies from abroad, which they could afford only if the materiel were available on lenient financial terms. However, in the event of an attack, armed assistance would be needed immediately and, if no preparations had been made in advance, extensive assistance could not be expected for several months.

But Swedish members of the committee would not agree to a statement proposed by the other two participants that an agreement on a regional defense union must not exclude Scandinavia from receiving assistance "prepared in peace time." In response to this evidence of Sweden's adamant stand, Norway urgently requested information from Washington and London about progress so far in drafting a charter for the North Atlantic Alliance. Both allied capitals responded immediately, in messages reaching Oslo on New Year's Eve 1948.

Shortly thereafter, the Danish, Norwegian, and Swedish Prime Ministers, Foreign Ministers, and Defense Ministers met secretly in

Karlstad, Sweden, to review the situation. Sweden made what it considered a significant concession to the others by offering them an immediate alliance, in spite of their military shortcomings. However, the offer would not be open if Denmark and Norway formed an attachment to the West.

Although the British offered a modified version of an earlier proposal for interlocking Scandinavian and Atlantic Pacts, its chances of success were virtually nil. Despite a certain interest on the part of Sweden's military leadership, the Swedish Government was not prepared to abandon its sacred principles of neutrality. What the Norwegians viewed as Swedish doctrinal stubbornness had the beneficial effect, from the Danish point of view, of helping it to avoid a serious dilemma. As Nils Andrén has pointed out, "If Denmark had joined a completely neutral Scandinavian alliance, a quite different solution would have to be found for her strategically vital Arctic territory of Greenland."[25]

During an anticlimactic Nordic meeting in Copenhagen, January 22–24, it became clear that negotiations on a Scandinavian security pact had failed entirely. Denmark made a perfunctory inquiry about the possibility of a neutral Danish-Swedish alliance, but this was apparently not taken seriously by either side. In a communiqué of January 30, 1949, the three governments announced that there was not a sufficient foundation for a defense union. On February 9, 1949, Foreign Minister Undén explained to Parliament the government's approach to the controversy:

> *The Swedish Government was interested in the possibility that the three countries might form a defense union and act in relation to other states as an independent group untrammelled by alliance with any third party. We regarded the aim of a Scandinavian defense union as being to strengthen Scandinavia's ability to resist an attack on any of its three constituent states, to keep them outside any general war that might break out and in peacetime to remain aloof from other power blocs and thus to prevent to the greatest possible extent that our territories are drawn into the military calculations of the great powers.*[26]

Sweden then opted for a policy of strict neutrality. Foreign Minister Undén's statement of February 9 stressed that there was no entirely satisfactory solution to Sweden's security problems in the prevailing situation. Looking back to the beginnings of Sweden's neutrality policy under Karl Johan XIV, Undén made a strong defense of his government's policy.

> *The fact that Sweden has been able to remain at peace for 135 years has undoubtedly had a strong psychological effect on the attitude of the Swedish public towards the problem of security. During this long period Europe has been shaken by mighty conflicts but our country has never become involved. Whatever the explanation may be for our avoidance of war, our people cannot easily be convinced that their security now requires the abandonment of neutrality as an ineffective and out-of-date policy.*[27]

Finland was less inclined toward a philosophic justification for its stance of nuanced neutrality, continuing pragmatically to accept the limitations placed on its freedom of action by its exposed position along the western frontier of the Soviet Union.

In the aftermath of their failed effort at Scandinavian solidarity, Norway and Denmark joined NATO. As a condition of joining, however, they imposed restrictions on the emplacement of atomic weapons and the stationing of foreign forces on their soil. Unarmed Iceland, which had never been a party to the abortive negotiations for a Scandinavian pact, also joined NATO, with the understanding that it would not be required to provide military forces for the Alliance. As a poor country occupying an important strategic position, but with virtually no defense capability, membership in the North Atlantic Alliance appeared to be its only realistic option, in spite of widespread desire to preserve the nation's uniquely untrampled character.

Some surprise has been expressed that the other NATO countries were prepared to let the Scandinavians "dine *à la carte*" in this fashion, rather than accept the full range of Alliance responsibilities. But the United Kingdom and the United States were not inclined to make an issue of it, given their own inability in 1949 to provide significant military aid to their Nordic allies. Even more important, in return for the short-term military liabilities occasioned by the need to spread NATO'S slim defense capabilities so widely, the Allies acquired some extremely valuable real estate. Norway, Iceland, and Denmark's Greenland were prime candidates, in the era before development of intercontinental ballistic missiles, for the establishment of vitally important air bases and distant warning systems. All three were also key elements in NATO's potential antisubmarine defense system in the North Atlantic.

In spite of their decisions to go separate ways on the matter of defensive alignments, all five of the Nordic nations, including Iceland, resolved to continue their pattern of working intimately together on a wide range of issues. This pattern of cooperation has been institutionalized in a substantial bureaucracy and frequent meetings of the Nordic Council, as well as by regular consultations at ministerial level. The Council's charter, however, dating from 1952, carefully excludes defense and security matters from its agenda.

Notes — Chapter VIII

1. Gaddis, in Riste, ed., *Western Security*, 61.
2. John Spanier, *American Foreign Policy Since World War II* (New York: Holt, Rinehart and Winston, 1983), 72.
3. Riste, ed., *Western Security*, 14.
4. Timothy P. Ireland, *Creating the Entangling Alliance* (Westport, Conn.: Greenwood Press, 1981), 69.
5. Harry S. Truman, *Years of Trial and Hope* (Garden City, N.J.: Doubleday, 1956), 242.
6. Ireland, *Creating the Entangling Alliance*, 87-88.
7. Magne Skodvin, "Nordic or North Atlantic Alliance? The Postwar Scandinavian Security Debate" (unpublished paper) September, 1988, Woodrow Wilson Center, Washington, D.C.
8. Wahlbäck, *Roots of Swedish Neutrality*, 77.
9. Riste, ed., *Western Security*, 138.
10. Ibid., 132.
11. Ibid., 134.
12. Skodvin, "Nordic or North Atlantic Alliance?," 8.
13. Riste, ed., *Western Security*, 142.
14. Ibid., 143.
15. Ibid., 144.
16. Skodvin, *"Nordic or North Atlantic Alliance?*, 11.
17. Ibid., 12.
18. Riste, ed., *Western Security*, 147.
19. Skodvin, "Nordic or North Atlantic Alliance?," 22.
20. Ibid., 37.
21. Wahlbäck, *Roots of Swedish Neutrality*, 76-77.
22. Skodvin, "Nordic or North Atlantic Alliance?," 55.
23. Ibid., 58.
24. Ibid., 64.
25. Nils Andrén, "The Nordic Balance: An Overview," *The Washington Quarterly* (Summer 1979).
26. Wahlbäck, *Roots of Swedish Neutrality*, 79.
27. Ibid., 80.

IX

Stalin and the YYA

F inland's relationship with the USSR for forty-four years of the
postwar period was embodied in the 1948 Agreement of
Friendship, Co-operation and Mutual Assistance, known in Finland by its initials as the YYA agreement. Often misunderstood in
the West and frequently maligned, it accurately represented the
political and security realities governing Fenno-Soviet relations
until at least the end of the 1980s.

The subject of a possible treaty was broached even before the
end of World War II, after Finland had signed its separate peace
with the Soviet Union in September 1944. An Allied Control
Commission (ACC), which was established at that time, was
dominated by its Soviet representatives, with the West playing a
minor role. The British attitude was summed up in the instructions
from Foreign Minister Anthony Eden, dated August 9, 1944:

> *Although we shall no doubt hope that Finland be left*
> *some real degree of at least cultural and commercial inde-*
> *pendence and parliamentary regime, Russian influence will*
> *in any event be predominant in Finland and we shall not*
> *be able, nor would it serve any important British interest,*
> *to contest that influence.*[1]

Andrei Zhdanov, a veteran of the siege of Leningrad and an
experienced party leader not noted for his soft-heartedness, was
chairman of the ACC. Nevertheless, the commission was not as
demanding as many observers had expected. Heavy reparations
were exacted, as foreseen in the surrender terms, but Soviet representatives agreed to extend the payment schedule from six to eight
years and to reduce the total bill by the equivalent of some $73
million (1944 dollars) as a way of mitigating the burden. After the

USSR ratified the 1947 Paris Peace Agreement, some additional goodwill gestures were made, such as permitting Finnish trains to pass through the Porkkala area, although only with their windows closed.

In the early postwar years, the ACC also pressured Finns to put aside their normal legal procedures, resulting in the passage of emergency legislation which authorized the trial of the "war guilty." Under its provisions, eight Finnish leaders, including the wartime President Risto Ryti and two of his Prime Ministers, as well as Social Democratic leader Väinö Tanner, were sentenced to prison for their activities during the conflict. In addition, Finland's anti-communist laws had to be repealed, and the Finnish Communist Party finally became a legal organization.

Two thousand members of the newly recognized party met in October 1944 and elected a group of leaders who immediately entered into negotiations with some left-wing Socialists in preparation for the forthcoming national elections. On October 29, a new party was formed, known as the Finnish People's Democratic League. Other left-wing Socialists, who had been expelled from Väinö Tanner's Social Democrats, rallied to the new group as did some youth, student, and women's groups. The Communist Party remained predominant within the SKDL, however, and forty of the forty-nine seats won by the group in March 1945 went to Communists.

Many of the SKDL votes came at the expense of the Social Democrats, who fell in 1945 from their prewar total of eighty-five seats to only fifty. The former Old Finn, J.K. Paasikivi, then put together a coalition government which included the Social Democrats, with their fifty seats, plus the Agrarians and the SKDL, each with forty-nine. A Communist, Yrjö Leino, occupied the key post of Interior Minister, responsible for police and internal security matters, and he inevitably set out to place his comrades in important positions. However, the Communist Party soon experienced a decline in its influence among the electorate.

It was evidently Andrei Zhdanov himself who, in 1944 and 1945, raised the question of a mutual assistance and friendship pact. The idea was not entirely displeasing to many Finns, including a good many in the military services. Mannerheim, as President, apparently shared that view, reasoning that a treaty establishing limited military cooperation with the USSR might assuage the Soviet Union's genuine security concerns. By demonstrating their willingness to act as good neighbors, the Finns might thus be able to work toward some border adjustments favorable to themselves. A cooperative posture might also serve to calm any Soviet apprehensions about Finland's desire to retain a fairly substantial defense force.

Although Mannerheim sometimes felt that Paasikivi, who had become Prime Minister in September 1944, was too inclined to say yes to Soviet demands, the President himself evidently went beyond what was really necessary in proposing a text for an eventual treaty between the two countries. His draft would have called for both parties to aid each other in the northern Baltic and in the Finnish Gulf as well as on Finnish territory. Mannerheim's text would not, however, have included language requiring consultations in case of outside threats.[2]

By the autumn of 1945, Mannerheim's health had deteriorated, and he could no longer exercise a leadership role. He left Finland for a holiday in Portugal and, after the "war guilt" trial of his former associates, resigned. In March 1946, Paasikivi succeeded to the presidency.

The new President's foreign policy, later memorialized in the Soviet press as the "Paasikivi line," was firmly in the Compliant tradition. Essentially, he strove to maintain a real measure of Finnish national independence but in such a way as to avoid any suggestion of conflict with Soviet interests. He hoped thus to inspire confidence in the Soviet leadership that Finland would contribute to maintaining the security of both countries. Paasikivi, even in his most compliant mood, was not a naïve man. He was fully capable of standing up to foreign pressure, as he had done by resigning from the senate in 1909 in protest at Russia's illegal rule in Finland. A former ambassador in Moscow, he knew the Soviet leaders well, and they knew him, as he had met more than fifty times with Stalin and Molotov. In talks with his American counterpart during that period, Paasikivi observed that

> ... *he had learned that prestige meant more to them [the Soviet leaders] than anything else; that their invariable policy was to obtain what they could for as little as possible and then ask for more; that they never sacrificed immediate gains for considerations for the future; that they paid no*

*attention to what was said, but only to what was done; that
they endeavored to be paid a high price for what they must
do anyway; and that they were impervious to ethical and
humanitarian factors or those of abstract justice, being influenced exclusively by practical and realistic considerations.*[3]

The question of a "friendship" treaty took a back seat in the
early years after the war as the USSR proceeded rapidly to consol-
idate its position in central Europe. The German Democratic
Republic and Poland were brought completely under control, and
the Soviet grip tightened on Romania, Hungary, and Bulgaria. In
February 1948, the Czechoslovak Communists had fomented a
political crisis in that country and then took power on the strength
of their armed worker militias. Simultaneously, Soviet relations
with Tito's Yugoslavia were deteriorating, with Stalin and his
adherents among the southern Slavs trying to force the former
partisan leader from power.

In February 1948, Stalin wrote a letter to Paasikivi suggesting
a mutual assistance treaty "on the same basis as those recently
concluded between the U.S.S.R. and Hungary and Romania,
respectively, neighbors of the Soviet Union having fought against
the U.S.S.R. on the side of Germany."[4]

Stalin's letter, and particularly his reference to fighting on the
side of Germany, naturally provoked shudders among the Finnish
leaders. But Paasikivi and Foreign Minister Enckell could see some
advantages to a pact which would finally put an end to the
unwelcome presence of the Allied Control Commission. Fear
nevertheless remained that the Soviet leaders would try to impose
on Finland the kind of rigid domination they were exerting in
Central and Southeastern Europe. Such fears were not groundless,
as was shown by Zhdanov's speech to the founding Congress of
the Cominform in September 1947, when he had lumped Finland
with Hungary and Romania as a "new democracy" in the "anti-
fascist camp."

It was not revealed until much later that, in January 1948,
Stalin had confided to Yugoslav leader Milovan Djilas that "it was
a mistake that we did not occupy Finland." Given the thorny path
of Soviet relations with Belgrade at that time, however, it appears
likely that Stalin's ruminations had more relevance for the Yugoslav "comrades" than for the Finns. In Finland, further fuel was

added to the speculative fire when Hertta Kuusinen, leader of the country's Communists, former wife of Yrjö Leino, and daughter of one of Stalin's close associates, called for Finland to follow the road of Hungary and Romania.

According to Swedish diplomat Örjan Berner, "Mannerheim and Paasikivi talked gloomily in private about the likelihood of Finland becoming a Soviet satellite, or even, in due time, being incorporated in the Soviet Union."[5] There were, at the same time, clear differences between the Finnish situation and that of their neighbors to the South. In spite of losing the war to the USSR, Finland had not been occupied by Soviet troops, nor had Allied wartime agreements placed it within the Soviet sphere of influence. Most important of all, Finland's geographic position did not touch Soviet strategic nerve endings to the extent that, for example, Poland and Hungary did.

Moscow at the time saw the Marshall Plan as a U.S. effort to reinstall a capitalist system all over Europe, using NATO as its military arm to "roll back" the hard-earned gains of Soviet socialism. Finland's tactful refusal to participate in the Marshall Plan helped to defuse Soviet apprehensions about Finnish intentions in this regard. As a result, it appeared that the Soviet negotiators might be prepared to take a more relaxed attitude toward Helsinki than their colleagues had done with what Churchill had called the other "ancient capitals of Europe" now behind the Iron Curtain.

A high-level delegation, headed by Prime Minister Mauno Pekkala, was sent to Moscow to negotiate, accompanied by the Communist Minister of the Interior, Yrjö Leino. The delegation's instructions had been carefully drafted in Helsinki and, while conciliatory, set firm limits to what Finland was prepared to accept in agreement. Leino had fallen out of favor in Moscow by that time, but other members of the delegation were unaware of it. In any case, they had to assume that their "fall-back" positions could not realistically be kept secret from the Soviet side.

The Soviet delegation was also high-ranking, headed by Molotov and including Zhdanov and Anastas Mikoyan, both of whom reportedly showed themselves sympathetic to Finland's views. Both of them were interested in modernizing the Soviet Union's industrial structure and probably hoped to impart some of the Finnish work ethic to the USSR'S laboring masses. Zhdanov's influence was already on the wane, however, and he died somewhat mysteriously not long afterward. It quickly became clear, in any case, that Stalin himself was playing the lead role on the Soviet side.

At the first meeting of the negotiators, the Soviet Union, as the originator of the friendship treaty idea, presented a draft text based on its Hungarian–Romanian treaties. This Soviet draft proposed that any aggression be met jointly by Finnish and Soviet forces, signifying early and automatic intervention by the Red Army in any conflict. However, the Soviet side somewhat surprisingly agreed to work on the basis of a Finnish counterdraft, and the text eventually agreed upon differed in important respects from that of the treaties imposed on the Soviet satellites. In particular, it accepted Finland's phraseology that Soviet "assistance" could be given only after it became clear that Finland's own forces were unable to deal with the incident and only with Finland's agreement.

On a second issue, the Finnish draft was rather more forthcoming than the Soviet version. As Molotov pointed out, consultations under the Finnish text would not be limited to wartime only, as the Soviets had proposed, but could also extend to peacetime consultations about an outside threat. But the Finns confirmed their willingness to accept the broader phraseology on consultations and they offered compromise language on the first issue. This set forth Finland's obligation "as an independent state" to defend itself "within the frontiers of Finland ... if need be with the assistance and jointly with the U.S.S.R." The Soviet Union, for its part, undertook to give Finland the help required "subject to mutual agreement."[6]

There was apparently no serious difficulty on either side with the beginning of Article 1 of the treaty, which stipulated that it became operative only in the event of "Finland, or the Soviet Union through Finnish territory, becoming the object of an armed attack by Germany or any state allied with the latter."[7]

Although questions could later be raised about what countries might be considered as allied with Germany for purposes of the treaty, the text of that paragraph is pellucid in limiting Finnish action to its own territory. Equally clear is the phrase in the preamble which approvingly notes "Finland's desire to remain outside the conflicting interests of the Great Powers."[8]

The text of this short treaty, consisting of only eight paragraphs and a preamble, is contained as an annex to Fred Singleton's

A Short History of Finland.[9] Although his evaluation of the treaty ("It is based on a realistic assessment of mutual interest between two countries of unequal size and power, which in no way infringes the sovereignty of the smaller partner")[10] is indulgent, the language of the treaty is, in itself, quite anodyne. In this respect, as the Finnish negotiators understood quite well, no language on such "a scrap of paper" could prevent the Soviet leadership from meddling in Finnish external or internal affairs if they believed it were in their interest to do so. The Finns' preoccupation was, quite properly, to avoid giving the Soviet leadership any cover of legality for such interference, and they succeeded quite admirably in that limited endeavor.

Örjan Berner's evaluation of the treaty appears to be more balanced than that of Singleton and some official Finnish sources. "The treaty did not restrict Finnish independence any more than recent history, geography, and relationships of strength had done already."[11] The Finns were understandably relieved, while the Soviet leaders, including Stalin himself, also seemed pleased with the result.

The era of good feeling did not last very long because Soviet pressures on all of the Nordic countries intensified after the treaty's signature on April 6, 1948. The Finns and their fellow Nordics were soon accused by the Soviet media of trying to establish a Scandinavian defense alliance and later, when that option had been foreclosed, of trying to bring Finland into the Atlantic pact. Preparations were made for Soviet military exercises on the Finnish border, and it was suggested that the USSR would have to change its policy toward Finland if Sweden were to join NATO.

Soviet pressures were also felt on the Finnish domestic scene after a parliamentary enquiry commission reported that Yrjö Leino had abused his government position in 1945. The offenses for which he was censured included returning to the Soviet Union a group of émigré Russians who had been naturalized in Finland. Leino was also accused of trying to pack the police force, which was under his jurisdiction, with Communists or their sympathizers. The Communist-led unions had then called a general strike, with the apparent intent of provoking intervention by the Allied Control Commission.

Instead, President Paasikivi dismissed Leino from his post and called a general election, in which the SKDL suffered a substantial setback, falling from forty-nine to thirty-eight seats in the Eduskunta. The Social Democrats, on the other hand, registered a gain of four seats, for a total of fifty-four, and Social Democrat K.A. Fagerholm was invited to form a minority government. The conservative National Coalition Party and the Agrarians, led by Urho Kekkonen, also gained, while the SKDL, as a result of its defeat, was excluded from government office for eighteen years.

Fagerholm was subsequently subject to abuse in *Pravda* for advocating Nordic cooperation, especially as Denmark and Norway moved toward membership in NATO. But in spite of some angry criticism in the Soviet press about "the men of 1939, a reactionary force trying to lead Finland into catastrophic and senseless adventures," official relations were maintained on an even keel, and an important trade agreement between the two countries was signed later in 1948.

Clearly, serious complications were introduced in Soviet military planning by the creation first of the Western European Union and then of NATO. But in spite of Moscow's feverish press coverage in the early 1950s of the supposed threat to the Soviet Union posed by Scandinavian cooperation with "American-British warmongers," a concerted Soviet reaction to the problem was slow in coming. In the interim, Moscow's efforts to block the growing military consolidation of the United States with Western Europe by propaganda and political agitation failed. The USSR then moved to reinforce its hold over the military organizations of the satellite states, with its control eventually to be codified in the Warsaw Pact Treaty Organization, but not until 1955.

During that period, many significant trends became apparent. Rebuilding was well advanced in Western Europe, but America's worries about Soviet intentions and capabilities had been heightened appreciably by the Soviet nuclear explosion in the fall of 1949. Washington's attention was then drawn away from Europe by the exigencies of the Korean War. That three-year conflict added appreciably to the alarm, felt both in the United States and Europe, at the Soviet Union's perceived belligerence throughout the world. Encouraged by the international umbrella offered by United Nations endorsement, many U.S. allies provided assistance to the American-led resistance to Communist aggression. For example, Norway sent naval assistance, Denmark provided a hospital ship, and even neutral Sweden was represented by a hospital field unit.

As the hostilities in Korea dragged on, differences of opinion mounted between the United States and its European allies about the conduct of the war. The USSR was able to exploit some of this European discontent in its propaganda efforts. The Soviet hand was particularly apparent in the bogus Stockholm peace initiative, launched in 1950, during which hundreds of millions of people allegedly signed a plea calling for banning the atomic bomb. But the war was not an unalloyed benefit because an aroused public in the United States increased the challenge to the USSR by greatly escalating the share of the American budget devoted to defense.

The Korean War also galvanized some European governments into revamping their defense forces. Prior to the North Korean attack, most Europeans considered the Soviet threat to be largely a political one, based on intimidation and, possibly, Communist coups such as the Czech seizure of power in 1948. The apparent willingness of "international Communism" to use naked military force in Korea to achieve its objectives led many nations to give an ear to American calls for a military build-up in Europe.

The Norwegian Minister of Defense, Jens Christian Hauge, thus got the Storting to adopt a new definition of what was permissible under the country's "no foreign bases" policy. Allied forces were thereafter to be allowed more opportunities for maneuvers, during which Norwegian air and naval installations would be available to them. At the same time, the Norwegians, like the Danes, were anxious not to extend the responsibilities of the Alliance too far to the South. In July, 1951, they argued strenuously against bringing Greece and Turkey into NATO. Norwegian representatives suggested that the regional character of the Alliance be emphasized in order to avoid raising troublesome ideological questions. As an alternative to Greek and Turkish entry, they suggested the formation of a separate Mediterranean pact. But in spite of Norway's opposition, Greece and Turkey acceded to the North Atlantic Treaty in October 1951.

The Danish Government in 1950 also showed increasing receptivity to the idea of strengthening its military forces with the assistance of the U.S. military aid program. Still, as Danish Prime Minister Hans Hedtoft observed, his countrymen were most fearful of being occupied and liberated once again. In his view, the public was pacifist-minded but would fight without conviction. His hope was somehow to get Sweden into the North Atlantic Pact.

In 1951, NATO's "northern region" was designated part of Supreme Allied Command Atlantic (SACLANT), headquartered in Norfolk, Virginia. The region was defined as including Denmark, Norway, and Schleswig-Holstein, plus the Baltic Sea. The USSR reacted in a note of November 15, 1951, taking Oslo to task for "permitting Norwegian territory to be used by the armed forces of the aggressive Atlantic pact ... and putting Norwegian forces under the American military command which directs and plans military preparations in Norway." The Soviet Union further alleged that NATO had been allowed to set up headquarters for its Northern Command outside Oslo; that Norway had made preparations to receive foreign troops on its territory and was expanding naval and air bases, some of them close to Soviet territory; and that American and British air and navy units were conducting exercises in Norway. The Soviet note also specifically complained that Spitsbergen and Bear Island had been put under the authority of NATO naval forces, permitting them to conduct military maneuvers near those islands in direct violation of the 1920 Svalbard Treaty.[12]

The Norwegian Government responded that it was adhering scrupulously to the Svalbard Treaty, pointing out that no military fortifications or bases were being established there. It denied the Soviet allegation that Norway had aggressive intentions, either alone or as part of NATO. Oslo also cited Norway's own definition of its base policy, which permitted both Allied exercises and preparations to receive foreign troops. The exchange of diplomatic notes and public statements continued for some time, expanded by similar Soviet complaints about Danish policy. Moscow charged that anticipated military exercises in the Baltic (NATO's Operation Mainbrace) constituted a breach of Denmark's promise not to let foreign forces enter Bornholm.

The Soviets devoted special attention to Bornholm and to the purported German role in NATO'S "preparations for a new world war." The Polish Government added its voice, claiming that Bornholm was being prepared to become "the point of departure for the war preparations of the new Nazi Wehrmacht."[13] The Danish Government did not reply formally to the Soviet charges, but the Foreign Minister, in a conciliatory statement, asserted that, whatever might have been said about Bornholm in 1946, Denmark had in reality not permitted foreign troops to be stationed on the island and intended to maintain that policy.

Also in 1951, a NATO Supreme Allied Headquarters, Europe (SHAPE), was installed at Fontainebleau, near Paris, with General Dwight Eisenhower of the United States as its commander. At Rome, in November 1951, a special meeting of the NATO Military Committee recommended establishment of air bases in Denmark and Norway to deter and prevent a possible Soviet surprise attack on those virtually defenseless nations. Tirstrup and Vandel, on the Jutland peninsula, were proposed for Denmark, plus at least one major air base in southern Norway.

Very quickly, the North Atlantic Council, meeting in Lisbon in February 1952, accepted the inclusion of those bases in the organization's infrastructure program. This permitted the financing for the bases to come from general NATO funds rather than from national resources. It was estimated that 150 tactical aircraft would be established in Denmark, including fighter interceptors and light bombers. Norway was to receive three wings of seventy-five planes each, for a total of 225 aircraft.[14]

A Soviet Government declaration in October 1952 denounced Denmark's alleged intention to permit foreign armed forces to stay in Danish territory in peacetime. In Moscow's view, the Danes were thereby turning their country into a base for foreign troops and thus creating a threat to the USSR and other countries in the Baltic area. The Danish Government's reply denied any aggressive intent but refrained from commenting on the alleged plans.

In fact, Denmark's non-Socialist government did favor accepting the NATO air base offer, and construction, including extension of the existing runways at the two designated bases, commenced in September 1952. The Norwegian attitude was less clear. Although Oslo had been pressing the United States since mid-1950 to allocate forces to defend NATO's northern flank, no such forces were available. More important, perhaps, Norwegian public opinion was far from enthusiastic about welcoming United States units in apparent violation of the nation's 1949 declaration abjuring foreign bases. One Norwegian member of Parliament criticized the proposed deployment as the "maximum of provocation and the minimum of protection," i.e., a total reversal of existing national policy.

Urho Kekkonen, Prime Minister of Finland, added his voice to the growing controversy in a speech delivered on January 22, 1952: "An established and assured neutrality of the Scandinavian countries, such as that which Sweden has followed for nearly a century and a half, would therefore be in consonance with the interests of Finland."

Given the degree of Norwegian concern for the well-being of Finland, Kekkonen's interjection was bound to have an adverse effect on Norway's attitude toward deepening its military collaboration with the West. However, Norway's Trygvie Lie, who was now Secretary General of the United Nations, reportedly told his intimates that Kekkonen's so-called "pajama" speech (because he was ill in bed at the time) did not reflect the Prime Minister's real views. In Lie's account, the Finnish leader told him during a sauna conversation that Finland would be grateful when Norway received the American air wing.

Nevertheless, the Oslo independent daily newspaper, *Dagbladet*, probably spoke for many Norwegians when it editorialized on May 31, 1952, that an "absolute condition for Norway's participation in the North Atlantic Treaty was that no foreign forces should be stationed in Norway during peacetime unless Norway were attacked or threatened by attack." After noting that the Norwegian people agreed with this policy, *Dagbladet* added, "It is not politically possible to change it and it would be to the detriment of NATO in Norway if the Americans or any others made serious attempts to change it. Our special position in NATO has been recognized by the other members and we can veto any change. Against our will it cannot be amended and we will not amend it."

In London, British Foreign Secretary Anthony Eden suggested that Scotland could accommodate the air bases in question if Norway turned them down. Somewhat later, Field Marshal Montgomery complained that the Swedes were always putting pressure on Denmark and Norway not to have NATO air bases for fear the Soviets might demand similar bases in Finland. In fact, the Swedish Government was genuinely concerned that the presence of foreign troops in its western neighbors' territory would prompt Soviet demands to place its forces closer to Sweden.

In spite of Stockholm's attempts at conciliation, even Sweden was not immune from Soviet criticism and, in some cases, military action. Sweden, alone among the Nordics except for an obviously circumscribed Finland, recognized the incorporation of the three Baltic states in the USSR. In addition, in a move which generated a good deal of public criticism domestically, the Swedish Government at the end of the war turned over to the Soviet authorities several hundred refugee Baltic nationals. These men, who had arrived in Sweden wearing German military uniforms, were among the many Balts seeking refuge in Sweden at war's end.

Less friendly, in Soviet eyes, was the continued Swedish interest in the case of Raoul Wallenberg, a Swede who had been instrumental in saving thousands of Hungarian Jews from the Nazi death camps and who had disappeared in Budapest in 1945. Wallenberg's success in sheltering the Jews under the Swedish flag and forging Swedish work documents for them, sometimes pulling prisoners from the death trains, had captivated the hearts of many people of goodwill, and not just in Sweden. Moscow's refusal to admit fully the role of its former counterintelligence agency, *Smersh*, in his disappearance bedeviled Soviet relations with Sweden for decades. Not until 1957 did the Soviet Government admit that Wallenberg had been imprisoned in the USSR, and it continued for many years to insist that he died in the Lyubianka Prison in Moscow in 1947, in spite of many reports that he had been seen alive after that date.

In addition to the strong criticism in Soviet media of Stockholm's alleged nefarious intent to cooperate with NATO and particularly with Norway and Denmark, Soviet fighters in June 1952 shot down two Swedish reconnaissance aircraft over the Baltic. In this so-called Catalina Affair, the Swedish Government maintained that an unarmed military aircraft with a crew of eight was shot down over international waters by two Soviet MIG-15s on June 13. Three days later, another Swedish aircraft on a rescue mission was shot down by MIG-15s, again over international waters. Moscow's version of the incident insisted that the foreign planes had entered Soviet airspace and had been attacked after they had refused to land at a local airfield. The Soviet Government alleged that, in the second episode, the Swedish aircraft had been first to open fire. The Swedish Government proposed to refer to the matter to an international body such as the International Court, but the Soviet Government refused, claiming that "to defend the borders of the U.S.S.R. is the duty and obligation of the Soviet state."[15] The attacks on Swedish aircraft evidently represented an abrupt change in Soviet policy, as Moscow had previously tolerated Swedish reconnaissance flights near Soviet-controlled areas of the Baltic. According to Trygvie Lie, this accounted for the Swedish Government's reluctance to raise the matter in the United Nations.

Sweden also found itself in hot water with the Soviet leadership over its naval maneuvers in the Baltic, which coincided with NATO's Mainbrace exercises. Two years later, however, Sweden and the USSR signed an agreement providing for the rescue of endangered ships and aircraft, which preceded by some fifteen years the U.S.-USSR Agreement on the Prevention of Accidents at Sea. In spite of the relatively amicable conclusion to the Catalina Affair, the harsh Soviet reaction to the alleged intrusions conveyed a message to all comers that military reconnaissance flights in close proximity to the USSR could be hazardous to the health of aircrews.

The 1952 attack on Swedish aircraft was apparently at least partly successful in limiting NATO'S Nordic reconnaissance in the vicinity of Soviet installations. The same motivation may be seen in Norway's refusal to sanction naval or air activity by its allies east of the 24th meridian in the Norwegian Sea and Denmark's similar policy with regard to the area east of Bornholm in the Baltic. NATO concurrence in such limitations had to be conditioned on adequate reconnaissance and surveillance coverage of the proscribed areas by the Danes and Norwegians themselves. Both nations were, of course, vitally interested in potentially threatening Soviet military and naval activities near their own territory. The Kola Peninsula area bordering northern Norway was an especially difficult zone for Oslo, while Copenhagen's eyes were fixed on the amphibious units of the Soviet army and its Polish and East German counterparts in the Baltic, which were believed with good reason to be targeted on Denmark in case of war.

Domestic political problems continued to complicate execution of NATO's plans for air bases in Denmark and Norway. The Soviet attack on the Swedish aircraft had alarmed many Danes, and there was considerable press speculation that public opinion in Denmark was somewhat more amenable to accepting Allied air defense units. The press also reported that Danish air force crews had been told to defend themselves, if attacked over either Danish territorial waters or international waters, without awaiting further orders.

The Chief of Norway's Defense Staff, General Berg, when queried about similar measures for the Norwegian air force, responded, "We have no standing order to the effect that Norwegian military units shall fight if they are attacked outside Norwegian territory in time of peace ... the orders given comprise only the steps to be taken in the event of attack on Norwegian territory ... In north Norway where a foreign power is close to our border, definite regulations have been issued, but it is my impression that these instructions are observed in all details." General Berg did not, however, offer any information on what instructions were in force in the North.

Oslo's *Arbeiderbladet*, on June 19, 1952, reflected the views of many Norwegians when it editorialized: "The fear pervading some of the European nations causes many awkward situations. This fear is like a two-headed monster. It is exemplified by a desire to avoid provoking the Soviet Union, and it stimulates the need for close cooperation with the U.S.... Fortunately the U.S. has behaved tactfully in this case, which is both complicated and delicate." The editorial called for continued American forbearance and recognition that the stationing issue was an internal problem for the people concerned.

According to diplomatic reports, Norway's Prime Minister Oscar Torp and Foreign Minister Lange understood the need for the presence of foreign forces to strengthen Norwegian defenses. But their ability to implement a change of policy was limited by the fact that the former Prime Minister and current chairman of the Labor Party, Einar Gerhardsen, was convinced that changing the country's "no foreign bases" policy would jeopardize Norway's participation in NATO and could cause the party to lose control of the government in the 1953 elections. Torp and Lange may have feared that Gerhardsen could exploit the bases issue to restore himself to the position of Prime Minister. In view of the widespread public view that the imminence of war in Europe was now receding, Torp had no intention of giving his colleague and rival such an issue. The atmosphere was such that not one of Norway's political parties, with the possible exception of the Conservatives, favored a modification of the policy on bases.

Nevertheless, Norway did proceed with preparations for American use of Norwegian facilities in case of hostilities. In a secret but recently declassified *Luftforsvaret Overcommandoen* memorandum of October 18, 1952, Lieutenant General Finn Lambrechts, Commander-in-Chief of the Royal Norwegian Air Force, recognized that

> *As a result of the military planning pursuant to the North Atlantic Treaty, it has been established that there is a NATO requirement for immediate utilization in case of hostilities of the airfields at Sola and Gardermoen for deployment of U.S. Air Force units....*
>
> *The RNAF will take the necessary steps to permit the installations of technical equipment essential to the utilization during hostilities of Sola and Gardermoen airfields ... and the storing of reasonable quantities of supplies, technical equipment, and ammunition at these airfields for use during hostilities.*
>
> *It is understood that a limited number of technical and advisory U.S. personnel will assist the RNAF in facilitating the development of Sola and Gardermoen airfields and in taking care of maintenance, custody, and security matters insofar as these cannot be discharged by RNAF personnel. The total number at any time of such U.S. personnel and all other necessary arrangements will be determined by agreement with the competent Norwegian authorities.*

The inter-Allied negotiations for stationing U.S. Air Force units in Denmark finally broke down for good in 1953 when Denmark insisted on a veto over the use of the proposed U.S. forces. The Danes apparently had in mind a possible American desire to use their Danish-based aircraft in the case of "local wars," such as one between Turkey and Bulgaria or between East and West Germany. Danish representatives argued that Denmark had stipulated that its forces could be used only for the defense of Denmark. Why, then, could the United States not make the same statement with regard to its units to be stationed in Denmark? The Danes also insisted on the right of unilateral termination of the proposed agreement.Norway, too, refused to accept a United States Air Force wing, even on a rotational basis. Many Norwegians evidently believed that stationing American forces would encourage the USSR to invoke its Friendship Treaty with Finland and insist on stationing its forces there.

Along with Scandinavia's resurgent hopes for a lessening of East-West tensions in Europe, a growing concern surfaced over the inconclusive war in Korea. There was widespread apprehension that the Soviet Union might take advantage of America's preoccupation with that conflict to move against new targets in Europe. The Yugoslav leadership was apparently convinced that Moscow was preparing just such an adventure, and Finnish worries were mounting also. Tito and his colleagues became so concerned at one stage that they indicated their willingness to accept military aid from the West in case of war.

However much Stalin might have liked to erase an irritating competitor like Tito in the southern Balkans, he and his Politburo colleagues were more concerned with the deteriorating situation in central Europe. Signs were multiplying that West Germany was well on the way back to acceptance as a fully legitimate member of the European family and that its rearmament and incorporation in NATO would not be far behind. A treaty setting up a European Defense Community, which was to include the West Germany, had already been drafted when the Soviet Union played its best remaining card.

In a note of March 10, 1952, Moscow called for negotiations among the wartime Allies pointing toward a peace treaty with a unified Germany and the withdrawal of all occupation forces. The Soviet proposal also signified acceptance of German rearmament, provided the revived German state were committed to neutrality. How seriously this Soviet bid was intended may never be known because it foundered in a series of acrimonious notes between Moscow and Washington.

It is clear that the Soviet offer of a unified but neutral Germany served Soviet propaganda purposes admirably for a number of years, with echoes persisting up to the end of the 1980s. It is doubtful, however, that Stalin would have been prepared in 1952 to withdraw from the most precious portion of his new European defense in exchange for anything that the far from united Western Allies could agree upon. More than likely, the Soviet gambit was just another of the diversionary tactics so common in the annals of Stalinist diplomacy. In any case, Stalin himself was dead by the time the next episode began.

Notes — Chapter IX

1. Berner, *Soviet Policies Toward the Nordic Countries*, 42.
2. Ibid., 43.
3. Ibid., 41.
4. Ibid., 45.
5. Ibid., 45.
6. Singleton, *A Short History of Finland*, 189-91.
7. Ibid.
8. Ibid.
9. Ibid.
10. Ibid., 145.
11. Berner, *Soviet Policies Toward the Nordic countries*, 51.
12. Ibid., 76.
13. Ibid., 78.
14. Nils Ørvik, *Semialignment and Western Security* (New York: St. Martin's Press, 1986), 199.
15. Berner, *Soviet Policies Toward the Nordic Countries*, 80.

X

The Thaw

When Stalin died in March 1953, the reaction in Scandinavia, as well as most of the world, was a resurgence of hope in the possibility of genuine peace instead of continued Cold War. The death of the Georgian seminarian turned Great Russian nationalist appeared to open windows of opportunity in many areas. Perhaps new leadership in Moscow could reach an accommodation with the newly installed President of the United States, Dwight D. Eisenhower, and his dour but experienced foreign policy adviser, John Foster Dulles.

An amorphous collective leadership was proclaimed in Moscow, headed by a triumvirate of Georgi Malenkov, Lavrenti Beria, and Vyacheslav Molotov. Within a few days, however, it appeared that Prime Minister Malenkov, who had been a close associate of Stalin and second only to him on the Party Secretariat, had taken over at the head of the Soviet party-state apparatus. His early pronouncements about the need to produce more consumer goods, together with hints of a reduction in the tensions between the Soviet Union and the West, were encouraging. At the same time, Malenkov let it be known that the United States was not the only country to possess the hydrogen bomb.

Malenkov was soon obliged to give up his key position on the Secretariat, leaving the comparatively unknown Nikita Khrushchev as its ranking member. Khrushchev, who was the son of a peasant turned coal miner and had begun his own working life as a coal miner, was largely self-educated and considered somewhat crude by his colleagues. When the ambitious Beria tried to take advantage of his position as head of the People's Commissariat for Internal Affairs (NKVD) to advance to the top rung in the Soviet system, his colleagues quickly brought him down and had him killed. Malenkov's life was not shortened so brutally, but he was quickly pushed aside and eventually shipped off to run a power station in remote Ust-Kamenogorsk. As for Molotov, he continued as the top Kremlin authority on foreign policy until he overreached himself four years later as a member of what Khrushchev dubbed the "Anti-Party Group." Then he was sent into humiliating exile as Ambassador to Outer Mongolia, Moscow's most captive nation.

In the meantime, the attention of Kremlin policy makers had been seized by a series of disturbances in East Germany. After brutally suppressing the demonstrators, the Soviet régime moved to defuse the situation by accepting an end to East German reparations. The Moscow leaders also showed signs of a conciliatory attitude elsewhere, particularly with regard to their fallen-away comrade, Marshal Tito. During the same period, the USSR concurred in, and probably facilitated, a compromise settlement of the Korean War, leading to an armistice in July 1953.

Simultaneously, a perceptible thaw occurred within the Soviet Union itself as inmates of forced labor camps began to return from the Gulag Archipelago. A more relaxed Soviet leadership began to explore possible means of reducing the high level of tension in Europe. They were probably encouraged to pursue this course by the disquiet generated among America's allies by the American administration's unyielding stance on European security issues. Although it is difficult even today to quarrel with Secretary Dulles's critical interpretation of Soviet motives, his belligerent oratory about "massive retaliation" and "rollback" alienated important elements of European public opinion. Dulles genuinely believed that the neutralist and pacifist sentiments so close to the surface, especially in Scandinavia, were immoral, and he wished to give them no encouragement.

In 1954, after a four-year dispute, the French National Assembly voted down the proposed European Defense Community (EDC), which would have created a European army, with corps made up of units from different national armies. This was only the earliest in a series of ingenious, if impracticable, schemes to scramble national forces in such a way that they could never be unscrambled. The Allies recovered quickly from their momentary setback; West Germany soon became a full member of NATO and, together with Italy, also joined the Western European Union (WEU).

Membership in WEU was a critical part of the overall package permitting West German rearmament in spite of continuing reservations on the part of the French and other allies, especially the Scandinavians. The Union framework provided much the same guarantees against an independent German military role as had the EDC but in a much more practical way. Unlike each of its new allies, Germany would not have a national army because all of its troops would come under NATO command, headed by an American general. In joining the WEU, moreover, the West Germany obligated itself not to manufacture atomic, bacteriological, or chemical weapons without the concurrence of the Supreme Allied Commander and two-thirds of the Western European Union members.

The Soviet Government could only have been displeased at the prospect of seeing half a million armed Germans take the field again in Europe. On the other hand, the USSR by the mid-1950s was a superpower, enjoying a clear military superiority over any military machine the West Germans could possibly put together. A more realistic long-term danger to Soviet interests was that German rearmament, coupled with the security provided by the American military presence and increasing European economic integration, might constitute a potent economic and political threat to Soviet dominance in Eastern Europe. In 1954–55, therefore, the Soviet leaders mounted a series of attempts to turn aside or delay German rearmament. Clearly, however, Moscow was not prepared to pay a substantial price to block West German participation in Western defense. Its best offer was "to discuss" all-German elections as well as such questions as an Austrian peace treaty and atomic disarmament. The Soviet campaign generated a certain amount of interest in non-Communist Europe, but not enough to derail NATO's reinforcement by a new German army.

The USSR then convoked a Moscow Conference on European Security, which met in November 1954. This first Soviet attempt to organize an all-European forum was attended only by Soviet clients and sympathizers. Although the conference confined itself to ritualistic denunciations of German "revanchism," it did clear the ground for the formation in 1955 of the Warsaw Pact. This distorted mirror image of NATO, which included an East German military contribution, added little or nothing to Soviet control over the satellite military forces. The Warsaw Pact did, however, provide a degree of political cover for the continued presence of Soviet forces in Eastern Europe.[1]

Khrushchev and the new Soviet Prime Minister, Nikolai Bulganin, then made a dramatic pilgrimage to the Balkans for a visit with Marshal Tito in Belgrade. Although Yugoslavia remained formally "non-aligned," it had recently concluded an agreement with NATO members Greece and Turkey, drawing it somewhat in the direction of the Western camp. The two high-level Soviet emissaries assured Tito that the Soviet Union's previous hostility to his rule had all been the fault of Beria. Tito was prepared to play along with this line, at least temporarily, and there was a perceptible increase in consultations between the two capitals.

The international atmosphere had improved so much by 1955 that a Big Four summit conference was convened in Geneva in July. Conversations among the leaders were amiable for the most part, but little or no progress was registered on the problems dividing them. The Soviet delegates floated the idea of disbanding the Warsaw Pact Organization in return for the abandonment of NATO and the withdrawal of foreign troops from European countries. A variation on this theme would have provided for a general European security pact to replace both NATO and the Warsaw Pact and in which both parts of Germany would participate.

In fact, a number of proposals for demilitarizing Europe surfaced during 1955, sponsored by both Eastern and Western spokesmen. Foreign Secretary Eden, as well as Foreign Minister Molotov, proposed limits on troop levels and armaments in central Europe and advocated creation of a demilitarized zone there. British Labor Party leader Hugh Gaitskill called for the withdrawal of all foreign troops from both Germanies as well as from Poland, Czechoslovakia, and Hungary. George Kennan offered a similar proposal, adding the idea of reunifying and neutralizing Germany as well as a ban on nuclear weapons in Europe.

In January 1956, just before the expiration of President Paasikivi's second and final term, the USSR showed its endorsement of the "Paasikivi line" by returning the base area of Porkkala to Finland and also extended the Friendship Treaty (YYA) for twenty years. By the mid-1950s, it had become clear that the center of Soviet military activities was shifting away from the Gulf of Finland and Porkkala. In the North, interest was now concentrated around

Murmansk and the Kola Peninsula. At the same time, Moscow's holdings on the southern shore of the Baltic and concern about the threat from a renewed German navy impelled the move of Soviet naval headquarters eastward from Kronstadt to Kaliningrad (formerly Königsberg). Accordingly, as Khrushchev himself noted in 1957, Finland had lost much of its strategic importance for the USSR.

As a result, the Finns had a little more leeway to assert their neutrality, which received official Soviet sanction in 1956 when Khrushchev specifically named Finland among the neutral nations of Europe. Finland also became a member of the United Nations, and, as the USSR signaled that it no longer objected to Finnish participation in the Nordic Council, the last of the Nordic nations was able to join that organization also. All members of the Nordic Council were, of course, committed to exclude military and security questions from the council agenda. Although such limitations have not prevented proposals for a nuclear-free zone from being introduced to the Council, a majority of its members have barred them from consideration. Even more important than its recognition of Finland's neutrality, the USSR agreed to a peace treaty with Austria in May 1955 and withdrew its troops from that country. In return, Austria pledged itself to absolute neutrality and compensated the USSR liberally for allegedly "German-owned" properties the Soviet Union had seized during the occupation.

Still, the Soviet imprimatur on neutrality for Finland and Austria was clear, suggesting that the USSR was moving away from its conception of the world as divided into two warring camps. It now seemed possible for nations espousing an alternative view to have beneficial relations with the centers of both capitalism and communism without compromising their ties with either. "Neutrality," formerly a term of abuse, acquired a positive connotation in Soviet official parlance. Although the new Soviet lexicon had special resonance among the underdeveloped nations, it was also welcomed elsewhere, particularly in Scandinavia.

The credibility in the West of the new leadership in Moscow was significantly enhanced when, in February 1956, Khrushchev denounced Stalin and Stalinism in his famous "Secret Speech" at the Soviet Communist Party's Twentieth Congress. His remarks, however, also led to the subsequent disorders in Poland that summer and the Hungarian uprising in the autumn.

The Soviet effort to play down the impact in the West of the Hungarian crisis was made immeasurably easier by the almost simultaneous attempt by France, the United Kingdom, and Israel to reverse Colonel Gamal Abdel Nasser's seizure of the Suez Canal. This Western coup had to be abandoned in the face of strong American disapproval. The turmoil within the Alliance following the abortive Suez operation drew so much public attention in Europe that the Soviet action in Hungary failed to stimulate the condemnation it might otherwise have. In addition, the hollowness of Secretary Dulles's proclamations about "rollback" became evident to everyone, which further eroded the sense of a common Western purpose in the face of Soviet challenges.

Before the tragic events in Budapest, the USSR had taken advantage of reawakened Nordic receptivity to Soviet salesmanship by launching a concerted diplomatic offensive in the north, designed to transform the entire area into a "Zone of Peace." The Prime Ministers of Denmark, Norway, and Sweden were thus invited to Moscow, where they were wooed rather than pressured to cooperate in the reorientation of attitudes toward the USSR. Cultural and commercial contacts were much expanded and, for the first time since World War II, foreign warships (from Sweden) visited the port of Leningrad.

Sweden, together with the other European neutrals, Austria, Finland, and Switzerland, was praised in the Soviet press and urged to practice an even more "positive neutrality." In a joint communiqué at the conclusion of the Swedish Prime Minister's visit to Moscow early in 1956, the USSR "declared that the Soviet Union, as before, will respect this nonaligned and peaceful policy of Sweden."[2] At the same time, Moscow continued to insist that a really neutral policy had to be "active" by contributing to the peaceful resolution of international problems. One important objective, according to Denmark's Bent Jensen, was to draw the entire Nordic and Baltic region away from the influence of "imperialism."[3] The projected state visits to Scandinavian capitals scheduled for 1957 were evidently conceived as important steps in that campaign. In the aftermath of the Soviet army's brutal repression of the Hungarian uprising in the fall of 1956, however, all the Nordic states, except Finland, withdrew their invitations.

Reports that NATO was preparing to install nuclear weapons in Norway and Denmark compounded Soviet disappointment over the canceled visits, which was expressed in typically heavy-handed, counterproductive terms. In a letter to the Danish Prime Minister, Bulganin recited a long list of grievances, beginning with the alleged turnover of Greenland to the United States. Moreover, he continued:

> *The European part of Denmark is covered by a net of military airports and marine bases, built according to NATO military command plans, where American and British instructors are active. Thus no guarantee exists that foreign forces, called in by NATO command, would not appear on a few hours' notice on these Danish bases to be used against peace-loving countries.... NATO great powers can very well start military operations without giving their small allies any advance notice.*

Bulganin further warned that, in case of war, a Soviet nuclear attack would be directed against foreign bases in Denmark and Norway:

> *The Soviet people have no wish that the U.S.S.R., Denmark, or any other country be the target of an atomic bombardment or feel the effects of other modern weapons. But ... the Soviet Government would be remiss in its duty if it did not, in response to aggression, take immediate steps to direct a crushing blow against the aggressor and his whole net of military strongholds and bases established to attack the Soviet Union.... The devastating power of modern weapons is so great that in an atomic war, it would be tantamount to suicide for a country the size of Denmark to have given bases to foreign powers.*[4]

Bulganin also emphasized the responsibility Denmark had acquired because of its position at the intersection of important international waterways, and the Danes were cautioned to seek their security in international guarantees rather than a military alliance.[5]

In a commentary of April 9, 1957, *Pravda* repeated Bulganin's call for a Nordic Zone of Peace, which, it said, would be a big step in the direction of a common European security system. Clearly implicit was the suggestion that Denmark and Norway turn their backs on NATO and join in a new security system without an

American presence and thus open to Soviet domination. Neither Denmark nor Norway was persuaded. Khrushchev and Bulganin, during their June 1957 stay in Helsinki, again advocated turning the Baltic area into a neutral zone and pointed to Finland's relationship with the USSR as a model for other Nordic countries to follow. The Soviet position was again set forth in *Izvestia* on September 6, 1957, using words that revealed Moscow's apprehensions about the West Germany's incorporation in the Western alliance and the imminent creation of a West German navy.

> *The Baltic can and will finally become a sea of peace and benefit to all people living along its coasts. Four-fifths of the coastline lies in the zone of states that in one way or another are active for peaceful coexistence. Countries that belong to NATO, Denmark and West Germany, take up only a small part of the Baltic coast. Certainly if one or the other Baltic state decided to quit NATO it would simplify the efforts to turn that area into a sea of peace.*

In September 1957, East Germany followed the Soviet lead by calling for the transformation of the Baltic into a "sea of peace" as a fitting reply to West German "revanchism."

Early in 1957, after the NATO council had authorized its military authorities to develop plans for the early use of tactical nuclear weapons, the United States offered to equip Allied forces with both tactical nuclear weapons and dual-use, short-range missiles. Norway and Denmark were scheduled to receive one Nike (surface-to-air) missile battalion and one Honest John (surface-to-surface) missile battalion. Both kinds of missiles were to be capable of using either nuclear or conventional warheads. Later, in December of that year, Washington followed up with a proposal to establish NATO stockpiles of nuclear ammunition for tactical use in Europe and to provide medium-range ballistic missiles to the NATO Supreme Commander in Europe, who was, as always, an American general.

The Soviet Union predictably took strong exception to NATO's nuclear build-up, launching a propaganda campaign against it. Moscow also surfaced a number of proposals designed to blunt Western receptivity to the NATO proposals, such as a nuclear test ban and the creation of a nuclear-free zone in Central Europe. At the same time, in a typical example of Soviet "missile-rattling," directed at American allies in Europe, Bulganin wrote to British Prime Minister Harold Macmillan in December 1957:

> *How can such NATO measures as, for instance, the round-the-clock flights over the British Isles by British-based American bombers carrying atom and hydrogen bombs help to reassure people, to improve the situation? ... I say frankly that we find it difficult to understand what, in taking part in such a policy, guides the government of such a country as Great Britain, which is not only in an extremely vulnerable position by force of its geographical situation but which according to the admission of its official representatives has no effective means of defense against the effects of modern weapons. Nor can there, it is true, be any such defense.*[6]

NATO was also proceeding with plans to strengthen its northern defense region by establishing a subordinate Baltic naval command to direct the seaborne forces of Denmark and West Germany. Khrushchev, in his capacity as Secretary General of the CPSU, wrote a long letter of protest to his "counterpart," the head of the Danish Social Democrats, "comrade" H.C. Hansen. A few weeks later, there was an additional message from Bulganin addressed to Hansen as Danish Prime Minister, describing the plans as "measures which complicate the situation in the Baltic area and concern the security interest of other Baltic states."[7] In apparent deference to the Soviet *démarches*, implementation of the proposed command changes was postponed until the plans were made part of an overall reorganization two years later.

In his letter to Hansen, timed to arrive just before the December 1957 NATO ministerial meeting in Paris, Bulganin had also warned again of the disastrous consequences if Denmark were to receive nuclear weapons.[8] Although Hansen indicated that Denmark would accept the American offers of Nike and Honest John missiles, he declared at the NATO meeting that Denmark would not receive nuclear weapons "under present circumstances." In explanation, the Danish Government referred specifically to the Soviet *démarches* and to Denmark's wish not to act provocatively or to increase tension in the sensitive Nordic region. Similar Soviet messages to Norway produced similar responses. The Norwegian Prime Minister announced that his country "had no plans to let atomic stockpiles be established on

Norwegian territory or to construct launching sites for IRBMs [Intermediate Range Ballistic Missiles]."[9]

Apparently encouraged by the Danish and Norwegian display of reasonableness, Bulganin wrote again to Copenhagen in January 1958, expressing his satisfaction with Hansen's declaration, and suggested that favorable conditions now existed for declaring all of Northern Europe a nuclear-free zone. But Bulganin noted that airfields in both Denmark and Norway were being equipped to receive long-range bombers, which could carry nuclear weapons, and that both countries were preparing to receive short-range missiles which also had an atomic capability. Denmark could make a better contribution to peace and stability in the North if it took a position "which made it impossible for atomic weapons or missiles to be put on Danish territory." As for Norway, in a letter of January 8, 1958, to Prime Minister Gerhardsen, Bulganin first explicitly broached the idea of a Nordic nuclear-free zone, noting that Norwegian atomic self-denial would, because of the position of Finland and Sweden, create preconditions for making the whole of Northern Europe a zone free of atomic weapons, which would be an important guarantee for peace and stability in the area.[10]

It should be noted that both Denmark and Norway had addressed their policy declarations on atomic weapons either to their domestic or NATO audiences rather than to Moscow. They were thus able to keep open the option of reviewing their positions unilaterally, without giving the Soviet Union any pretense to invoke a *droit de regard* over the issue.[11]

This clearly was not the case in Finland, over which the Soviet Union continued to maintain a close watch. Soviet sensitivities were particularly apt to be aroused by Finland's Social Democrats, with Väinö Tanner as the chief villain. The secretary of the Social Democrats, Väinö Leskinen, was also something of a *bête noir* to many of the Soviet leaders. The antagonism between Tanner and Moscow's O.V. Kuusinen was of long standing, dating back to 1918. Tanner had been among those convicted of "war guilt" and imprisoned after the war, but in 1958 the Social Democratic Party elected him its leader. This precipitated a split in the party, leading to the formation of a new group known as the Social Democratic League, which later allied itself with the Communist-dominated SKDL.

K.A. Fagerholm, another Social Democratic Party leader, who had been named Prime Minister by Paasikivi in 1948, was only slightly more *persona grata* in Moscow than Tanner and Leskinen were. In 1948, as head of a minority Social Democratic administration, he had ejected the Communists from the key posts they occupied in the Finnish Government. In spite of Paasikivi's endorsement, moreover, the Soviet press accused him of advocating too much Nordic cooperation, especially after Denmark and Norway joined NATO.

Fagerholm ran unsuccessfully against the Agrarian leader Urho Kekkonen for the presidency vacated by Paasikivi in 1956, losing by only two seats in the electoral college. The new President adhered to his predecessor's careful approach to relations with the Soviet Union, leading Moscow to sanctify his policy direction as the "Paasikivi-Kekkonen line." However, in 1958, with a magnanimity Soviet politicians found difficult to comprehend, Kekkonen asked Fagerholm to be Prime Minister again. The USSR made its displeasure clear in what became known as the "night frosts" crisis by withdrawing its ambassador without appointing a successor and suspending a number of bilateral negotiations.

Fagerholm's government, which was a broad coalition including all the parties except the SKDL and its left-wing Socialist allies, was forced to resign late in 1958. Khrushchev subsequently assured Kekkonen that Moscow had reacted strongly solely because of the presence of persons behind Prime Minister Fagerholm (Tanner and Leskinen) who were "well known for their hostility toward the Soviet Union."[12] Nevertheless, the short-lived crisis revealed a continued Soviet preoccupation with Finland's internal affairs. More surprisingly, it reflected an unusually muted reaction from Finnish political leaders, perhaps because some of them stood to gain from Fagerholm's ouster.

The stern face of Soviet policy was also reflected by a renewed squeeze on the advanced Western position in Berlin. In November 1958, a Soviet note announced that the USSR would allow the Western Allies six months in which to agree to its proposal to make West Berlin a free, demilitarized city. If not, the note indicated, the area would be turned over to the East Germans, and the West would then have to negotiate with that "government" if they wanted to maintain access to the city. When the West held firm, however, Khrushchev agreed to a foreign ministers' meeting in

Geneva to discuss the matter, and the ultimatum was repeatedly extended.

In the interim, at Eisenhower's invitation, Khrushchev made his triumphal 1959 tour of the United States. He was by that time the unchallenged leader of the USSR, and his visit persuaded many Americans that this straight-talking, if uncouth, Russian was a man worthy of serious attention. Meeting together at the President's retreat at Camp David, the two leaders appeared to make progress in resolving differences, and Eisenhower even hinted that changes might be warranted in the West Berlin situation. Speaking to the United Nations General Assembly, the Soviet leader presented a plan for general and complete disarmament which was to prove a staple item in Soviet propaganda for decades thereafter.

The proper role of nuclear weapons continued to be a sensitive issue throughout Europe, opening the way for renewed Soviet attempts at "wedge-driving" in the Alliance. In a flurry of proposals, Khrushchev advocated the creation of nuclear-free zones in the Balkans, the Adriatic, and Central Europe, as well as in the Far East, and held out the possibility of security guarantees to participants by the nuclear-weapons states. All of these areas were to be "parts of a broad zone of peace which would separate the armed forces of NATO and the Warsaw Pact." As for Northern Europe, he proposed that the USSR, together with the Western powers, agree "to regard these countries as being out of bounds for rockets and atomic weapons and to respect the status quo in the area."

In June 1959, East Germany joined the USSR in presenting a proposal to all the Baltic Sea countries, urging them to make the Baltic Sea a "sea of peace," i.e., a zone free of nuclear weapons and missiles, and barring the presence of military bases of other nations. Speaking in Riga during the summer of 1959, Khrushchev again invited Denmark and Norway to follow the example of Finland by entering into a nuclear-free zone of peace covering the Scandinavian peninsula and the Baltic region. In his view, the entry of Denmark and Norway into NATO was due to a misunderstanding, and he called on them to evaluate the situation more "correctly." Without mentioning the recent "night frosts" crisis with Finland, Khrushchev stressed how the Finns had formed a "correct" estimate many years before, when they "realized the necessity of living in peace and friendship with the Soviet people."[13]

When NATO'S Scandinavian members failed to respond favorably to Khrushchev's Riga initiative, Moscow canceled a projected state visit later in 1959 to Copenhagen and Oslo. The General Secretary expressed his frustration in a speech in Stettin:

> *But how the Danes, Norwegians and politicians in other countries involved ... could react unfavorably to peace-wishing proposals, obvious to anyone, for the formation of a zone of peace — this we simply cannot understand. Should war erupt in this area, it will be swept from the face of the earth, many millions of the people of those countries will be destroyed.*[14]

The Soviet Government's official organ, *Izvestia*, made its position clear in August via an authoritative "Observer" article. According to *Izvestia*, the establishment of a nuclear-free zone in Scandinavia and in the Baltic could be the "first stage in the transition of all the Nordic countries to a neutral position."[15] The Soviet appeal failed to generate much interest in the target areas of Denmark and Norway as public opinion in both countries continued to support NATO membership.

Khrushchev's hopes for a breakthrough with the American President on Berlin and other issues, in the "spirit of Camp David," were dashed when an American U-2 reconnaissance aircraft was shot down over the Soviet Union late in 1959. The fact that the downed U-2, which had taken off from Turkey, was to land at Bodö, Norway, was a considerable embarrassment to the Norwegian government and weighed against a recommendation by the Norwegian military authorities that tactical nuclear weapons should be stockpiled in Norway during peacetime. The government decided that although such weapons could well be introduced into the country by its allies in wartime, they should not be stationed there in time of peace.

When the new American President, John F. Kennedy, met Khrushchev in Vienna in June 1961, Khrushchev strove repeatedly to bully the young American leader on Berlin and other issues, insisting that there was a new relationship of forces in the world. When Kennedy asked whether Khrushchev believed it to be impossible to find anyone who would be neutral both to the United States and the USSR, the General Secretary replied affirmatively. Khrushchev devoted most of his attention to Berlin and

Germany, noting that delay in signing a peace treaty would benefit only West German militarists and could not be justified. President Kennedy noted that the United States was not in Berlin because of anyone's sufferance, certainly not that of the East Germans. America had fought its way there, he pointed out, and a peace treaty denying the United States its contractual rights would be a belligerent act. The General Secretary concluded that the calamities of war would be shared equally. It was up to the United States to decide whether there would be war or peace.

Kennedy drew the appropriate conclusion from the discussions in Vienna that "It will be a long, cold winter" and returned to Washington determined to take the steps necessary to face up to the Soviet challenge. Some American reservists were called up and military appropriations were increased. The war of nerves continued for some months afterwards. In August, facing a continuing hemorrhage of skilled manpower pouring into West Berlin, the USSR and its German allies built a wall to separate the two parts of the city. Two weeks later, the Soviet Union announced its resumption of nuclear tests, culminating in the explosion of the most powerful weapon yet produced by any nation.

The unpredictable Soviet leader zigzagged once again in October 1961 by proclaiming at the Twenty-Second Soviet Party Congress that he would not insist on an early resolution of the West Berlin problem. Khrushchev's new and remarkably conciliatory stance appears to have been dictated by an imminent crisis in Soviet relations with China, although this was not apparent in the West. It is also likely that dividing the two sections of Berlin by the "wall of shame" had eased the problem there sufficiently that Moscow no longer felt urgency in dealing with it.

The Nordic nations were unable to take much solace from Khrushchev's change of mood over Berlin because a new crisis suddenly loomed over Finland, known as the "note crisis" of 1961. Although the exact relationship of events is not clear, Khrushchev may have wished by raising the stakes in Helsinki to maintain some pressure on the West, particularly West Germany, while stepping back from the confrontation over Berlin. There is also evidence that internal divisions at the Soviet Party Congress, perhaps between military and civilian leaders, led to the escalation of tensions in the Baltic.

The timing of the Soviet initiative was particularly surprising because during a visit to Finland only a month earlier, Soviet President Leonid Brezhnev had praised "the peaceful foreign policy which has been consistently followed by President Kekkonen and Finland's Government." Nevertheless, in a note of October 30, 1961, the USSR requested consultations with Finland under the provisions of their 1948 Treaty, which was keyed to threats from "Germany or countries allied with Germany." The note pointed to what it termed the dangerous situation prevailing in the Baltic caused by increased West German influence in Norway and Denmark, as well as to Sweden's "tendency to underestimate the danger of [West German] military preparations in Northern Europe and willingness to cooperate with that country."[16]

Shortly before the Soviet note was delivered, an article in the Soviet periodical *International Affairs* criticized plans for joint military exercises by German, Danish, and Norwegian troops, as well as the increase in the strength of West German naval forces in the Baltic, citing rumors that those forces might be equipped with Polaris missiles. But the particular target of the article, like the note, was NATO's plan for a joint Danish-German military command in Denmark, Schleswig-Holstein, and the Baltic.[17] (This was the same plan shelved two years before in the wake of earlier Soviet protests.)

In its note, the USSR raised no complaint about Finnish behavior but claimed that recent events had demonstrated West Germany's intention of dominating the western Baltic and therefore posed a "threat of military aggression" as set forth in the Friendship Treaty. The note did, however, reflect the USSR's concern over the alleged contrast between the policy of the Finnish Government and "certain circles in Finland [which] actively support the dangerous military preparations of the member states of NATO and contribute ... to the dissemination of war psychosis."[18]

Only a few days later, on November 6, 1961, the Soviet press agency TASS pursued a similar line with regard to Sweden. In TASS's interpretation, while Sweden's policy of non-alignment could promote peace in Europe, some Swedish political circles were sympathetic to West Germany's nefarious plans, especially in the Baltic. As for Norway and Denmark, although they themselves had no aggressive plans, TASS said, their encouragement of the

West German military threatened the peaceful frontier between the USSR and Finland.

The sudden Soviet pressure prompted uneasiness throughout Scandinavia and the Western world. President Kekkonen tried to play down the crisis, noting that consultations had to be agreed to by both sides, not merely imposed by the USSR. The Finnish Foreign Minister was then dispatched to Moscow to meet with Andrei Gromyko, who, in a change of emphasis, stressed Finland's internal situation as a cause of concern. According to a Finnish Government communiqué of November 14, 1961, the Soviet Union asserted:

> *The political situation in Finland has become unstable and there is in Finland a certain political grouping whose purpose is to prevent the continuation of the present foreign policy orientation.... The Soviet Government is willing to accept immediate assurances that Finland's present foreign policy orientation will continue and that nothing will prevent the development of friendly relations between Finland and the Soviet Union. If this kind of certainty can be obtained very soon, military consultations can perhaps be avoided.*[19]

In explaining Soviet concerns, Gromyko commented to his Finnish counterpart that the Soviet military were eager to have consultations. There was little surprise, therefore, when Gromyko's softer line lasted only a few days, after which the Soviet Government resumed its earlier approach, asking that consultations begin as soon as possible. In a conversation with the Finnish Ambassador in Moscow, Gromyko's deputy gave three principal reasons for concern: 1) a visit to Norway by West German Defense Minister Franz Josef Strauss, 2) NATO naval exercises in the Baltic, and 3) establishment of the unitary Baltic Command.

Kekkonen determined that the situation was serious enough to warrant direct discussions with Khrushchev, so he hastened to Novosibirsk, in Siberia, to meet him. During their meeting, on November 24, Kekkonen reportedly argued that consultations under the treaty would very probably cause a war panic throughout Scandinavia, which would have negative effects for all concerned. In effect, he seemed to be saying, if Moscow places new obligations on Finland, the three Nordic members of NATO would come under strong pressure to take countermeasures, perhaps including the stationing of foreign troops on their territory. Kekkonen's arguments may have been especially telling because they were similar to those Khrushchev had heard only a few days before from the Norwegian Foreign Minister, who had invoked the possibility of changes in Norway's nuclear or base policies if the Soviet pressures on Finland continued. Presented with the threat of upsetting the Nordic equilibrium, Khrushchev evidently blinked, and the crisis came to an end as quickly as it had begun, ironically at the same time as the Danish Parliament confirmed the new Baltic Approaches (BALTAP) Command.

Although the Soviet Government had succeeded in reminding the Scandinavian states that "Big Brother" was watching, their gains from the note exercise were very limited. If anything, the Danes and Norwegians drew closer to NATO. Sweden expressed its concerns by emphasizing the assumption that Moscow would do nothing to change Finland's neutral status. Stockholm's policy, explained Prime Minister Tage Erlander, would be "not to compromise our neutrality in any way and not to do anything that can injure Finland's interests."[20]

In return for dropping the request for consultations, Khrushchev asked that Finland follow events in Northern Europe closely and, if necessary, express its views on measures to promote peace in that area. His request implied rather than stated that Finnish security interests often ran parallel to those of the Soviet Union. Kekkonen, on the other hand, continued to stress that Finland had primary responsibility for requesting consultations if its government believed them necessary. Moreover, Khrushchev warned, "the action of rightist and Tannerist groups in Finland, aiming to destroy the friendship between the Soviet Union and Finland and to break the Paasikivi-Kekkonen line, causes serious uneasiness with us."[21] This reference to the Finnish presidential elections, scheduled for 1962, drew the desired response from the Finns. The Social Democratic candidate for president, Olavi Honka, withdrew, and Kekkonen was subsequently reelected. There has been speculation that Honka's candidacy was the real cause of the crisis, and that Kekkonen himself may have encouraged Soviet concern in order to buttress his domestic political position. Neither allegation is very persuasive, however, because the Social Democratic candidate was not widely considered to constitute a genuine electoral threat to Kekkonen.

The Soviet KGB defector, Oleg Gordievsky, claimed that his superiors in Moscow regarded Kekkonen as their "highest-ranking agent during and beyond the Cold War." He evidently had regular meetings with a Soviet case officer, and "there was high excitement in the Center in 1956 when Kekkonen became President of Finland, a post he was to hold for the next twenty-five years." According to Gordievsky, Viktor Vladimirov, a KGB *Rezident* in Helsinki, was promoted to General for handling the Finnish President. Gordievsky, however, saw Kekkonen as a Finnish patriot, one of the many Finnish politicians who looked on private Soviet contacts as a prudent adjunct to their careers, (known in Finland as *Kotiryssa*, or "house Russians" by analogy with *Kotikissa*, a pet cat.) Kekkonen, according to Gordievsky, was careful not to compromise Finnish independence, and any official whom he suspected of doing so was quietly sidelined when a suitable opportunity arose. At the same time, "in private as well as in public Kekkonen was always careful to show himself a dependable friend of the Soviet Union. He sometimes agreed to include in his speeches 'theses' prepared by the International Department of the Central Committee and handed to him by the resident."[22]

Kekkonen did not follow up publicly on Khrushchev's invitation to observe and comment on events in Northern Europe until May 28, 1963, when he proposed an agreement to make the whole Nordic region into a nuclear-free zone. Whether or not this was one of the "theses" suggested by the Soviet *Rezident*, such an agreement would have clear benefits for Finland since it could eliminate the chance that the USSR might again invoke the Friendship Treaty if Denmark or Norway became more closely associated with nuclear weapons. Helsinki would also find its position enhanced if an accord helped to stabilize the Finnish border with Norway, again removing any pretext for Soviet concern over that issue. More generally, the neutralization of all Scandinavia would allow Finland to draw closer to its Nordic neighbors and, indirectly, to the West, where its economic interests were increasingly centered.

Kekkonen denied that he had either asked or informed the Soviet government of his Nordic nuclear-free zone (NNFZ) proposal beforehand, but Moscow's attitude was already well known to be favorable. The Soviet hand in the NNFZ proposal may also be seen in the fact that, as Bent Jensen has noted, Soviet spokesmen have linked Kekkonen's 1963 initiative directly to the note crisis in 1961. Certainly, most Scandinavians believed that while the voice was the voice of Kekkonen, the hands were those of Moscow.

The Swedish reaction to the original Soviet proposal in the late 1950s had been that they had no objection to a nuclear-free zone if the only nuclear power in the area (the USSR itself) would remove its nuclear weapons. In 1961, Sweden's Foreign Minister Undén had himself suggested creating nuclear-free zones in all of Europe, with the same proviso as to participation, an initiative specifically cited in Kekkonen's 1963 proposal. Similarly, Per Haekkerup, then Danish Foreign Minister, helped to pour cold water on the Kekkonen proposal by observing in February 1964 that "the Nordic countries already are a non-nuclear region. None of the countries have atomic weapons, and none of these countries plan to get them." Accordingly, such an agreement was not necessary. "If Denmark should bind itself in its future policy, a necessary condition would be that we knew the future circumstances. An agreement on the Nordic region as a permanent nuclear-free region is therefore only conceivable as part of a general European arrangement."[23]

In spite of the calculated coolness throughout Scandinavia to a nuclear-free zone in the North, Khrushchev continued to show great interest in the Nordic area and, just before his fall from power in 1964, he made his often postponed return trip to the northern capitals. The atmosphere was not propitious because, among other things, of the continuing anti-Soviet repercussions from the Colonel Stig Wennerstrom spy case in Sweden. However, because of the embarrassment for all concerned if a third postponement had to be announced, the visit was allowed to proceed as planned.

While in Oslo, the Soviet leader expounded on his ideas for the Nordic area, sounding the same ominous theme he had used so often before:

> *From our point of view, countries like Norway, Denmark, Sweden and Finland could best guarantee their security by adopting a policy of neutrality recognized by both parties — the Western powers as well as the socialist*

countries. Such a policy would guarantee that these coun-
tries, in case of military conflict, would be protected from
the devastating effects of modern weapons.[24]

Only a few months later, in October 1964, the ebullient
Soviet leader was deposed by his Politburo colleagues. Although
Khrushchev had given them offense on a number of occasions, the
event which triggered his abrupt removal was reportedly a renewed
attempt on his part to come to grips with his major European
problems, specifically West Berlin and its place in a divided
Germany. According to this plausible scenario, Khrushchev decided to test the reaction in West Germany to a broad compromise
agreement on the future of Europe, built perhaps around a revised
proposal for a nonaggression pact between NATO and the Warsaw
Pact. Accordingly, he dispatched a trusted intermediary, his son-
in-law, Alexei Adzhubei, to explore the possibilities in Bonn. In an
account published in Moscow in October 1989, Khrushchev's
son, Sergei, accused KGB chief Vladmir Semichastny of using his
agency's reports to portray Adzhubei's activities in Germany in a
bad light.[25]

Consternation over the implications of such a dramatic
change of policy regarding Europe may well have played a pivotal
role in persuading Brezhnev and the other Politburo members to
take advantage of Khrushchev's temporary absence in the Crimea
to remove him from office. His downfall marked the end of the
second major period in Soviet postwar policy in Europe. The
oligarchy which replaced him, headed by Leonid Brezhnev, attempted to maintain the general policy direction charted by its
predecessors. However, changes in the international environment
and, above all, the need for broader interaction with the economically vigorous countries of Western Europe, impelled them to
steer a more flexible course. That course, contrary to Lenin's
dictum that the road to Paris led through Peking, headed north
— to Helsinki.

Notes — Chapter X

1. Ulam, *Expansion and Coexistence*, p. 560.
2. Berner, *Soviet Policies Toward the Nordic Countries*, 83.
3. Bent Jensen, "The Soviet Union and Denmark/Scandinavia: Perception and Policy — Pressure and Promises," *Nordic Journal of Soviet and East European Studies*, 3 (3-4) (1986), 47.
4. Berner, *Soviet Policies Toward the Nordic Countries*, 92.
5. Jensen, "The Soviet Union and Denmark/Scandinavia," 62.
6. Ulam, *Expansion and Coexistence*, 609-10.
7. Berner, *Soviet Policies Toward the Nordic Countries*, 86.
8. Jensen, "The Soviet Union and Denmark/Scandinavia," 63.
9. Berner, *Soviet Policies Toward the Nordic Countries*, 93-94.
10. Ibid.
11. Ibid., 94.
12. Ibid., 97.
13. Jensen, "The Soviet Union and Denmark/Scandinavia," 64.
14. Osmo Apunen, *A Nuclear-Free Zone and Nordic Security* (Helsinki: Finnish Institute of International Affairs, 1975), 18.
15. Jensen, "The Soviet Union and Denmark/Scandinavia," 64.
16. Berner, *Soviet Policies Toward Nordic Countries*, 99-100.
17. Ibid.
18. Ibid.
19. Ibid., 100-1.
20. Ibid., 103.
21. Ibid., 102.
22. Christopher Andrew and Oleg Gordievsky, *KGB* (New York: Harper Collins, 1990), 433-34.
23. Jensen, "The Soviet Union and Denmark/Scandinavia," 66.
24. Berner, *Soviet Policies Toward the Nordic Countries*, 104.
26. *Ogonek*, #43, October 1989.

XI

To The Helsinki Station

I n spite of their reservations about Khrushchev's apparent willingness to strike a bargain with the Federal Republic of Germany, his successors soon found themselves pursuing a similar tack, encouraged by limited improvements in relations between the superpowers. Already in July 1963, for example, the United States and the Soviet Union had joined with Great Britain in signing the Limited Test Ban Treaty, agreeing not to test nuclear weapons in the atmosphere, in outer space, or under water. Neither France nor China signed the treaty, but both German states did.

Soviet eagerness to conclude the Limited Test Ban Treaty may have been increased by Moscow's concern over American plans to create a nuclear Multilateral Force in NATO. This complex scheme would have installed nuclear-tipped missiles on a number of surface vessels manned by NATO multi-national crews. In a note of April 8, 1963, to Bonn, the USSR specifically linked the proposed force to the Baltic region. Moscow's concern was not only that West Germany might possibly acquire nuclear weapons but also that the Baltic might become a base area for the Multilateral Force fleet or for U.S. submarines armed with nuclear weapons.

Western theorists, on the other hand, hoped that a Multilateral Force would satisfy the incipient French and German interest in possessing nuclear weapons without permitting either of them control over their use. Never popular among the smaller nations of the Alliance, particularly in Scandinavia, what came to be called derisively the "Multilateral Farce" had to be abandoned in the face of France's marked dissatisfaction with it.

By the spring of 1966, Gromyko was signaling Moscow's continued interest in "the German option" by calling for a European Security Conference. In the Soviet optic, such a conference could, among other things, permit the normalization and improvement of Soviet relations with West Germany. Bonn, not wishing to be left behind in the general enthusiasm for détente, sent a "peace note" in March 1966 to all governments except the East German, offering to exchange pledges not to use force in settling international disputes. The proposal was not accepted by the Warsaw Pact countries, but over the next few years Bonn gradually abandoned its policy, known as the Hallstein Doctrine, of refusing recognition to any state which recognized East Germany.

The Danes were already on record as favoring a "properly prepared" security conference and, in June 1966, suggested to their NATO partners that such a conference could be useful if the United States and Canada participated, but this received a cool welcome at the Ministerial meeting. Even before that time, the Danes (and the Belgians) had been active as members of the so-called Group of Nine in furthering contacts and discussions with members of the Warsaw Pact and Europe's non-aligned states. (The group consisted of the two NATO countries, three members of the Warsaw Pact, of which Poland was the most active, and four non-aligned states.)

French President Charles de Gaulle, as always eager to demonstrate France's independent and important role, visited Moscow in June 1966. There, and during subsequent visits to Poland and Romania, he reiterated his view that the unsatisfactory state of East-West relations in Europe was "a European question" which could not be settled on a bloc-to-bloc basis. Strongly implied was the notion that the "Anglo-Saxons" would not necessarily be invited to participate in resolving the "European question." As if on cue, the Warsaw Pact's Political Consultative Committee, at a heads of government and party meeting in Bucharest in July 1966, issued a formal Declaration on Strengthening Peace and Security in Europe. This Bucharest Declaration called for a European conference on "questions of European security and cooperation," implicitly excluding the United States. During 1966 also, the French President made his policy clear in a more tangible way by announcing France's withdrawal from NATO's integrated military organization, although not from the Atlantic Alliance itself. The Soviet leaders were naturally happy to encourage de Gaulle if it would help to undermine NATO's position, but they did not appear to take his claims to leadership in Europe very seriously.

Similar views prevailed in Denmark and Norway, where opinion leaders were not likely to see de Gaulle's France as the solution to their security problems, although his stance did awaken their long-standing uneasiness about belonging to one of the "blocs." During the following decade, the doctrine of the Nordic Balance began to take on an almost theological intensity in Scandinavia, as some people strove valiantly, they thought, to pluck the petal of peace from the nettle of threatened nuclear war. "Peace ethics" became the subject of broad interest, stimulated by scholars such as the Norwegian sociologist Johan Galtung. By the beginning of the 1970s, much of the intensity of the discussion was being fueled by the perception, gained largely from American television coverage of the Vietnam war, that the United States was prepared to destroy South Vietnamese villages in order to "save" them. How then, Scandinavians asked, would the fate of the Nordic nations differ from that of South Vietnam in the case of a full-scale nuclear war between the superpowers? In Denmark, particularly, some suggested that Nordic participation in the North Atlantic Alliance should be allowed to expire when its initial twenty-year term had passed. In December 1966, the Alliance approved a proposal by Belgian Foreign Minister Pierre Harmel to establish a study group to report on "the future tasks of the Alliance."

The resulting "Harmel Report," written largely in the Belgian Foreign Ministry but heavily influenced by a Norwegian-Danish draft, was approved by all the Allies one year later. It called attention to the fact that "the political tasks of the alliance have assumed a new dimension." Accordingly, while maintaining its deterrent and defensive role, the report recommended that NATO simultaneously pursue a more stable relationship by working to "further a détente in East-West relations." In a phrase that was to have particular resonance in Scandinavia, the report proclaimed that "military security and a policy of detente are not contradictory but complementary."[1]

President Kekkonen tried to counter the Harmel Report's effect on his Nordic neighbors in September 1967 when he declared that there was no longer need for Denmark and Norway to be members of NATO because the world situation was quite different from that in 1949 when they joined the Alliance. At the same time, he made it clear that a Scandinavian defense alliance replacing the NATO ties was no more acceptable in the 1960s than it had been twenty years earlier. Finland still could not participate in such an organization because of the conflicting obligations of its 1948 treaty with the USSR. For its part, Moscow emphasized that a Scandinavian defense union would undermine Swedish neutrality because it would necessarily lead to Sweden's integration in the Western Alliance.

Also in 1967, the Conference of European Communist and Workers' Parties, meeting at Karlovy Vary in Czechoslovakia, repeated its 1966 proposal for a European security conference. It denounced President Lyndon Johnson's policy of "bridge-building" with the countries of Eastern Europe as subversive and called for the abandonment of NATO when its initial term expired in 1969. NATO concentrated on gearing up for the impending struggle for the hearts, minds, and pocketbooks of its member nations. The Alliance illustrated the Harmel Report's conclusion that defense and détente were complementary by showing its willingness to explore arms control issues. During their June 1968 ministerial meeting in Reykjavik, the Allies declared that a process leading to mutual force reductions should be initiated.

NATO was not the only "bloc" to experience centrifugal forces during the mid-1960s. Similar symptoms of polycentrism appeared within the Soviet sphere as well, with Romania's Nicolae Ceausescu the principal culprit. In 1967, Bucharest broke ranks with its allies by recognizing West Germany. Romania also refused to sign a proclamation on nuclear nonproliferation, to cooperate in strengthening the Warsaw Pact's military command, or to join in Pact denunciations of the course of events in Czechoslovakia. Moscow was irritated but not particularly concerned, even when the Romanians stubbornly refused to follow Soviet guidance on important issues. Few Russians, it appears, took the Romanians seriously.

The Prague Spring of 1968, with its aim of establishing a new Communism "with a human face," however, was profoundly disturbing to the Soviet leadership, already under strain from a festering dispute with China. They soon came to regard the new Czechoslovak Government's policies as a threat to Moscow's hegemony throughout Eastern Europe. In a pattern reminiscent of its response to the Hungarian crisis twelve years earlier, the Soviet leaders alternately threatened and cajoled Alexander Dubcek and his colleagues. Finally, impelled by worry that the infection might spread into other portions of the Soviet empire, or even within the USSR itself, and under pressure from hard-line leaders in Berlin and Warsaw, they sent in the tanks.

The shock to Western public opinion proved to be remarkably short-lived, although the United States abruptly canceled an imminent summit meeting between President Lyndon Johnson and Brezhnev, which had been expected to launch the Strategic Arms Limitation Talks (SALT). That meeting would also have provided an American seal of approval for the growing sentiment in Western Europe in favor of détente.

Some of the strongest reactions came from within the already fragmented Communist movement. Tito and Ceaucescu had good reason to be concerned and conferred together urgently. China, while making it clear it disapproved of Czechoslovak revisionism, gloated at this latest example of Soviet imperialism. The Italian and French Communist Parties trod the uncertain path toward Eurocommunism by condemning the invasion. In Helsinki, the Communist Party protested events in Prague by abruptly cancelling its fifty-year anniversary celebration. Chairman Aarne Saarinen, who sympathized with Alexander Dubcek, complained that TASS was also interfering in the internal disputes of the SKP. Taisto Sinisalo's "Opposition Wing," on the other hand, strongly approved of the Soviet intervention.

Soviet President Alexei Kosygin, who had replaced Khrushchev as Moscow's principal contact with Kekkonen, made a special journey to Helsinki aboard a Soviet cruiser in October 1968 in an attempt to explain why the USSR had been obliged to invade Czechoslovakia. While in Finland, Kosygin evidently attempted without success to reconcile the two hostile factions of the Communist Party, but he did manage to quiet Saarinen's outspoken criticism of Soviet policy. Finland's President reportedly took the occasion to point out that the Soviet Union obviously had much more trouble with its Communist allies than it had with neutral, friendly, and capitalist Finland. The Finns and their fellow Nordics could once again take comfort in the realization that Finland had never become a member of the "Socialist camp." The Finns were thus not subject to the strictures of the Brezhnev Doctrine, under which territory once made "Socialist" could not revert to a "non-Socialist" pattern.

But relations between the USSR and Finland were not to be entirely tranquil during the 1970s. The USSR prevented Finland's Ambassador to the United Nations, Max Jakobson, who had been helpful in negotiating the Nuclear Non-Proliferation Treaty, from becoming U Thant's successor as UN Secretary General. There was also a return in Moscow to statements stressing the provisions on military cooperation in the 1948 Fenno-Soviet Treaty on Friendship and Cooperation. This represented a palpable step back from Khrushchev's favorable reference to Finland's "neutrality" in 1956 during a statement to the Twentieth Party Congress.

Some apparently authoritative Soviet press articles questioned the so-called neutrality clause in the treaty's preamble, in which Finland expressed its desire to keep out of conflicts between the great powers. They reasoned instead that the treaty's text on military cooperation gave it "the character of a treaty of joint guarantees of security on a bilateral basis." According to some articles, such clauses would come into force if there were a danger of a military offensive against the USSR, even if Germany were not the main instigator.

By 1971, Soviet representatives were insisting during official visits that the joint Soviet-Finnish communiqués issued at the conclusion of each of them include a lengthy definition of Finnish foreign policy, the wording of which was as follows:

> *Resting on the Treaty of Friendship, Cooperation and Mutual Assistance between the Soviet Union and Finland, the foreign policy of Finland, the Paasikivi-Kekkonen line, guarantees the unflagging development of friendship with the Soviet Union, and expresses Finland's striving to exercise a peaceloving neutral policy in the interests of international peace and security and of maintaining friendly relations with all countries.*[2]

Finland, in August 1973, agreed to the text of a joint declaration with the USSR, saying that it could not be neutral in matters of war and peace but was "for peace" and "against war." In Bent Jensen's view, this was an example of the USSR's attempt to move Finland from the "zone of peace" into the "camp of peace," i.e., into the Soviet sphere of influence. More troublesome than such legalisms, perhaps, but based on the same preoccupations, were Moscow's recurrent efforts to keep Finland from participating in

Western-oriented trade organizations. It was not until 1965 that the Finns had been able to join the Organisation for European Cooperation and Development (OECD) and, when the European Free Trade Association (EFTA) was formed in 1969, the USSR mounted a propaganda attack against it. According to the Soviet press, EFTA was bound to be dominated by the United Kingdom, and membership in such an organization, which discriminated against the Socialist states, would be incompatible with a policy of neutrality. Sweden was in a position flatly to reject the Soviet allegations, but Finland had to proceed more cautiously. It finally worked out a special agreement with EFTA which took into account not only the Finns' desire for economic ties with its members but also their need to maintain their position in the Soviet market. Finland did not feel free to become a full member of EFTA until 1985.

During the 1970s, as some of the seven members of EFTA began seriously to contemplate abandoning that organization and entering the European Economic Community (EEC) instead, Helsinki's position again became difficult. As part of the resulting ferment, the creation of a Nordic economic cooperation scheme, NORDEK, was proposed. Although designed to serve as a Nordic customs union, it was also seen as providing some negotiating advantage in the forthcoming approach to the EEC.

Moscow took strong exception to the NORDEK concept, however, viewing it as an important step toward Finland's incorporation in the Western European framework. Faced by Soviet objections, the Finnish Government concluded it could not participate in the proposed NORDEK institution, although the Finns still hoped to benefit from some of the trade measures associated with it. But, without Finland, the idea had little attraction to the other Scandinavians.

In 1973, after NORDEK had faded from view, Denmark decided to apply for membership in the EEC, while Norway voted in a referendum against entry. Norway, instead, negotiated a free-trade agreement with the EEC, as did Sweden. Finland subsequently followed the lead of Norway and Sweden, while concurrently reaching an agreement with COMECON, the Soviet bloc economic coordination organization.

Soviet trade with Finland expanded greatly during the 1970s, but this had little to do with the COMECON link. The rapid increase in the price of oil during that period forced Finland to pay more for its supplies of Soviet oil and to expand its shipments to the USSR in recompense. Although the USSR remained Finland's largest single customer, its share of Finnish trade had declined steadily. In 1989, the last normal year before the shattering of the former Soviet Empire, the Soviet Union took only 15 percent of Finland's exports, compared to 14 percent for Sweden, 12 percent for the United Kingdom, and 10 percent for West Germany.

The other Scandinavian states also came under pressure from the Soviet Union during the 1970s. The USSR embarked on a major naval build-up in the Far North, where it carried on a number of ambitious exercises in the seas around the North Cape area of Norway. During the spring of 1975, the Soviet Northern Fleet deployed about 220 ships in the Norwegian Sea in an exercise which simulated attacks on Western reinforcements to northern Norway.

Less alarming perhaps, but of considerable economic and defense interest, has been the long drawn-out dispute with the USSR over territorial delimitation in the Barents Sea. Negotiations on this issue began in 1974 but quickly ran into trouble, partly because of the changes in international law introduced as a result of the Law of the Sea Conference. The area in dispute is a huge one, amounting to 155,000 square kilometers. As a temporary measure, the two sides agreed in 1978 on a "Grey Zone," designed principally to protect cod and other fish stocks. Some observers, such as the Danish scholar Erling Bjøl, have interpreted that agreement as a concession to Norwegian fisherman at the expense of Norway's long-term security interests in the North. The Norwegian Government later also concluded that this agreement favors the Soviet Union and demanded that it be changed before further progress on other bilateral matters could be achieved.

Moscow has made it clear that it would like to have a kind of Norwegian-Soviet condominium over Svalbard and much of the Barents Sea. As early as 1944, Foreign Minister Molotov told his Norwegian counterpart, Trygvie Lie, that the Soviet Union wanted the Spitsbergen treaty revoked and the area ruled through a condominium of their two countries. In the face of Norwegian refusal to agree to such a Soviet voice in the development of the region's economic resources, including the petroleum deposits on the continental shelf, Russia is not likely to agree to modify the current Grey Zone arrangements. Historically minded Norwegians point out that it took Norway 300 years to obtain the Tsar's agreement to a fixed land border in the North, which was not achieved until 1826.

In the mid-1970s, Oslo also found itself in a series of mini-crises involving the military forces of its giant neighbor. Soviet troops shot missiles into the Barents Sea in violation of international understandings, and Soviet reconnaissance jets frequently intruded into the Norwegian security zone. Soviet submarines were reportedly observed in Norwegian fjords, and several instances of Soviet espionage in Norway were also uncovered about the same time. In April 1978, two large Soviet helicopters landed at a national park on Spitsbergen without permission from the Norwegian authorities or even information about their flight plans. When the Soviet side refused to recognize the Norwegian protest, Oslo was reduced to complaining that they "ought to" have requested permission.

Within a few weeks, the mini-crisis atmosphere grew as, on eleven occasions in the course of one month, Soviet ships anchored illegally off the coast of Finnmark. All of the ships stopped in the Barents Sea off the Varanger and Nordkyn peninsulas, a particularly sensitive area because of the submarine monitoring links maintained by the Allies in that vicinity. Norway's Defense Chief, Sverre Hamre, called the boat episodes "gunboat diplomacy," while Foreign Minister Knut Frydenlund said he hoped it was merely coincidence but feared a comprehensive pattern. When Soviet authorities finally offered an "explanation," however, the Minister declared himself satisfied and asked that the press guard against overdramatization of the episodes. Reports also appeared in the Norwegian press about a new Soviet radar station on Svalbard, which had been erected without permission from the Norwegian authorities. Norwegian officials indicated that this action was in clear violation of their regulations but that if the Soviets had sought permission to expand their base at Kapp Heer, it would have been granted.

There were additional incidents that same summer. One involved the crash of a Soviet military plane on the island of Hopen, part of the Svalbard archipelago. This proved to be a light bomber of the TU-16 Badger type carrying arms and ammunition and manned by a crew of seven, all of whom were killed in the crash. The investigation by a Norwegian civilian commission was hampered by protests from the Soviet representatives who had been invited as observers. Soviet ships, including a *Kresta*-class cruiser, anchored only seven nautical miles off Hopen. A long struggle for possession of the aircraft's "black box" then ensued, during which Moscow bombarded the Norwegian Government with protests, at one point describing its decisions as "unfriendly action."

Official Norwegian visits to the USSR and new talks on the Grey Zone near Svalbard were postponed, as was a meeting of the Norwegian-Soviet Fisheries Commission. The mini-crisis then continued as Soviet vessels stopped and inspected three British trawlers which were fishing in the Grey Zone with Norwegian licenses. Finally, the TU-16's "black box" was opened by the Norwegians, who put out the word that rust had destroyed the instrument. When the flight recorder was returned to the Soviet Union on November 15, there was a noticeable thaw in Soviet attitudes, and the Deputy Foreign Minister was invited to Moscow on an official visit. Foreign Minister Frydenlund, in an address to the Storting, emphasized his desire to avoid similar episodes in order to maintain neighborly relations with the USSR but warned that "we must be mentally and practically prepared for new episodes that can occur."[4]

Sweden's relations with the USSR were less troubled during this period. In spite of some Soviet criticism of the magnitude of Swedish defense spending, cordial exchanges between the armed forces of both countries became commonplace. A group of Soviet MIG-21 fighters flew to Sweden in 1967, marking the first time a Soviet military air unit had visited a Western nation. Later, there were several exchanges of naval visits to Leningrad and Stockholm, the last of which featured the presence of Admiral S.G. Gorshkov, the Commander-in-Chief of the Soviet navy. The Soviet Union warmly welcomed Swedish criticism of American policy in Vietnam, which blistered Stockholm's relations with Washington for more than a decade. It was considerably less pleased when Stockholm turned its oratorical guns in the direction of Moscow after the Soviet invasion of Czechoslovakia, but did not react very strongly, probably relieved that the damage to its international prestige had been fairly limited. After a short cooling-off period, the Soviet and Swedish Defense Ministers exchanged official visits.

Moscow bridled somewhat when Prime Minister Olaf Palme began to speak out critically on the dangers of superpower collusion, a message which was warmly received in the underdeveloped world. But, for the most part, the Soviet press maintained a discreet silence, even when Sweden tried to sell its Viggen aircraft to NATO countries with a government guarantee that spare parts would be available even in wartime.

Denmark's problems with defense during this period were sometimes more concerned with its domestic than its international implications. The "1969 problem" of renewing membership in NATO never posed a serious alternative to Danish participation in the Alliance. Still, it took the combined effect on the Danish public of the Harmel Report and the invasion of Czechoslovakia to put an end to any possibility that Denmark would withdraw. The palpable shift in public opinion following the Prague events probably contributed to the formation in January 1968 of a bourgeois coalition including the Radicals. This pacifist-minded party explicitly agreed that there would be no change in Alliance policy for the duration of the coalition, that is, beyond the 1969 deadline. In the interpretation of Martin Heisler of the University of Maryland, "A nondecision was reached. Denmark chose not to exercise the treaty's provision for opting out — but the choice was made, to some extent, for want of an acceptable alternative master security policy."[5] In a fairly typical Danish (and Nordic) political maneuver, the entire question was buried in a study commission.

Formal government-to-government relations with the USSR were marked by a high degree of cordiality. Prime Minister Anker Jørgensen, who had succeeded in making himself *persona non grata* in Washington because of his criticism of U.S. policy in Vietnam, was a welcome guest in Moscow in 1973, and Foreign Minister Gromyko came to Copenhagen the following year. In an even more impressive gesture of mutual amity, Queen Margrethe and Prince Henrik visited the Soviet Union in 1975. In 1976, the USSR put six nuclear armed submarines on station in the Baltic, thus ending its *de facto* status as a nonnuclear sea, but continued to call for the conversion of the Baltic into a zone of peace by eliminating Atlanticist influence.

Iceland's defense problems during this period were not unlike those of Denmark, although the island nation had to cope with a domestic Communist movement far more influential than Denmark's. Iceland has neither an army nor a navy, so its defense has been entrusted to the Iceland Defense Force, composed of about

3,000 U.S. Navy and Air Force personnel, most of them stationed at Keflavik airport. In addition to AWACs and ASW aircraft, the base has been home to a squadron of modern jet fighters. In 1956, differences over NATO and the U.S. presence broke up the governing moderate coalition and briefly installed a new coalition opposed to the U.S. military base. Pacifist sentiment had been encouraged by the Soviet Union's return of Porkkala to Finland but was restrained by Soviet suppression of the Hungarian uprising in 1956.

From 1959 to 1971, Iceland was governed by a coalition of the Social Democratic and Independence Parties, but in June 1971, the general election showed a pronounced swing to the left. The new government called for the defense agreement with the United States to be reviewed or terminated, with an early departure for the defense force. Somewhat surprisingly, however, a petition urging the government not to terminate the agreement prematurely was signed by 50 percent of the electorate. Before any effective steps could be taken, a new election in June 1974 reflected a swing back to the right, and pro- and anti-NATO sentiment continued to fluctuate for much of the succeeding decade.

Because of the almost total dependence of Iceland's economy on fishing, the electorate has usually been preoccupied with protecting its fishing grounds from excessive exploitation by foreign fleets. Although Iceland maintains no military capability, it has provided itself with a Coast Guard, comprising about 120 officers and enlisted men, with three armed fishery protection vessels, one patrol airplane, and two helicopters. In line with national priorities, the Icelandic Government has led the way in extending territorial waters to twelve nautical miles in 1964 and to fifty nautical miles in 1972. The United Kingdom opposed those extensions, which led to two so-called "cod wars," but without causing major damage to Iceland's overall relations with its allies.

In October 1975, however, Iceland unilaterally introduced a fishing limit of 200 miles, and its 1973 agreement with the United Kingdom on fishing limits expired the following month. When the two countries were unable to reach a new agreement, a third and much more serious "cod war" erupted, leading to armed clashes at sea and several casualties. In February 1976, Iceland broke diplomatic relations with the United Kingdom, the first time a diplomatic rupture had occurred between two members of the Alliance. Meanwhile, the Icelandic Government tried to exploit U.S. and Allied interest in maintaining the Keflavik base to put pressure on the British.

Although NATO was at pains to avoid taking sides between the United Kingdom and Iceland, the Allies did strive to help the two antagonists to reach a settlement. Not until June 1976 was an agreement reached, after which the British trawlers withdrew from Icelandic waters. The Oslo Agreement of 1976 establishing a 200-mile economic zone probably confirmed Rekjavik's view that the NATO base is a useful negotiating asset in the protection of its vital fishing interests.

Less than a year after the brutal suppression of the Prague Spring, détentist sentiment resurfaced in force throughout Western Europe. By March 17, 1969, therefore, the Warsaw Pact Political Consultative Committee, meeting in Budapest, advanced a new appeal for a meeting of "all European countries," again excluding the United States. But Ambassador Anatoliy Dobrynin in Washington informed Henry Kissinger, then President Richard Nixon's adviser on national security affairs, that the Soviet Union would not object to U.S. participation. Kissinger was not attracted to the proposal, regarding it as "the maximum Soviet program for Europe, put forward in the name of enhancing European security."[6]

Most of America's allies, especially Norway and Denmark, were more enthusiastic, particularly when Finland also proposed a conference on European security and cooperation, although there was some pique among the Nordics because Helsinki had not consulted them in advance. The adroit Finnish move to curry favor with its powerful Soviet neighbor while also strengthening ties with Western Europe eventually gained it the honor of hosting the conference, although that was still some years away. The conference initiatives were cautiously welcomed by NATO during its spring 1969 ministerial meeting.

The major thrust toward détente was provided by the election that fall of Willy Brandt as the new West German Chancellor. He forced the government in Bonn to rethink its policy of attempting to work around the East German régime and, in the face of Soviet resistance, to broaden West German ties with Eastern Europe. Brandt and his foreign affairs adviser, Egon Bahr, then launched their *Östpolitik*, which focused instead on eliminating obstacles to a broad-ranging détente in Europe. Over the course of the next two years, West Germany moved steadily ahead on that course, fully accepting the territorial consequences of World War II.

Henry Kissinger summarized his qualms about the new German policy trend in his memoirs:

> *Brandt's new Östpolitik, which looked to many like a progressive policy of quest for detente, could in less scrupulous hands turn into a new form of classic German nationalism. From Bismarck to Rapallo it was the essence of Germany's nationalist foreign policy to maneuver freely between East and West. By contrast, American (and German) policy since the 1940s had been to ground the Federal Republic firmly in the West, in the Atlantic Alliance and then the European Community.*[7]

Sentiment in Scandinavia was much more favorable to Willy Brandt, whose personal prestige was high because of his anti-Nazi past. As a Social Democrat, moreover, the views of Germany's new chancellor were seen to be in harmony with majority sentiment in the North. He had spent the war years there and spoke Norwegian and Swedish fluently so that he was able to communicate directly with Scandinavia's public via frequent appearances on television. In fact, Brandt, who was married to a Norwegian, seemed to embody all the desirable traits Scandinavians hoped to find in the postwar generation of Germans.

Kissinger and President Nixon recognized that the renewed Soviet overtures to the Western Allies were an attempt to practice selective détente and thus to divide the United States from the Europeans. They realized, in addition, that turning down the security conference idea flat would leave the United States isolated in the Alliance. They resolved therefore to support Brandt's *Östpolitik* but to link it closely to the Alliance as a whole. Accordingly, the U.S. made agreement on a European Security Conference dependent on progress on Berlin and other German issues. The Allies concurred and, at its December 1969 ministerial meeting, the Alliance stressed the need for careful advance preparation and the prospect of "concrete results." It also recalled the earlier Reykjavik proposal on mutual and balanced force reductions.

As it turned out, progress was possible on the German issues. Early in 1970, West Germany and the USSR concluded a major economic agreement, and later that year the two sides agreed to a nonaggression pact, which asserted that neither of them had territorial claims against anyone. They also agreed to consider inviolable the frontiers of all states in Europe, "including the Oder-Neisse line which forms the western frontier of the Peoples' Republic of Poland," as well as the frontier between East and West Germany. Bonn then entered negotiations with Poland, Czecho-slovakia, and East Germany, leading to the signature of parallel treaties with those countries. The United States, Great Britain, and France signed a quadripartite agreement with the Soviet Union on Berlin, which regularized the status of West Berlin and provided guarantees for Western access to the city.

In such an atmosphere, the momentum toward a European Security Conference mounted to the point where it could no longer be denied. Increasing dissent within the United States itself over Vietnam, coupled with rising European concern about a possible American retreat into isolationism, combined to make the idea of force reductions attractive to allies on both sides of the Atlantic. In June 1970, a Warsaw Pact meeting in Budapest moved in the direction of reality by including the United States and Canada in its renewed call for a European Security Confer-ence. The Pact allies also apparently put some pressure on the East Germans to adopt a less rigid diplomatic line and the dour Walter Ulbricht was gradually eased out of his position as head of the East German Communist organization, known as the Socialist Unity Party.

The Soviet campaign for a European conference, and the reciprocal demand on the part of the West for mutual and bal-anced force reductions, merged in a surprising way in the spring of 1971. In the U.S. Congress, Senator Mike Mansfield was making his annual plea that U.S. forces in Europe be reduced substantially. Just days before the Mansfield Amendment seemed certain of adoption, however, Leonid Brezhnev called for the beginning of negotiations on arms reductions in Europe. This undercut Mansfield's position, and the amendment was defeated overwhelmingly, sixty-one to thirty-six.

Henry Kissinger has argued that this episode was merely one more instance of Moscow's inability to adjust to a rapidly changing situation. In retrospect, however, it seems likely that Brezhnev and his Politburo colleagues weighed the alternatives carefully before opening the door to what were certain to be long, drawn-out negotiations. They may simply have wanted to avoid disturbing the improving prospects for an early breakthrough on SALT. Whatever the rationale, they evidently decided against pushing for an early American pullback from Europe, preferring the stability a substantial U.S. presence could offer. Once again, Soviet fears that West Germany might gain access to nuclear weapons seem to have played an important role in the evolution of Soviet policy.

In June 1971, NATO made an abortive attempt to send Secretary General Manlio Brosio on an exploratory mission to East Europe to look into the prospects for force reductions, but the Warsaw Pact countries were unresponsive. Nevertheless, the NATO Ministerial Communiqué in December 1971 affirmed the Alliance's willingness to move ahead with force reductions, as well as a European security conference. The Warsaw Pact responded positively but with reservations.

Finally, at their May 1972 summit meeting, Brezhnev and Nixon decided to proceed with both negotiations more or less simultaneously. The multilateral conference to prepare for the Conference on Security and Cooperation in Europe then opened in Helsinki on November 22, 1972, followed in January 1973 by explanatory talks in Vienna on force reductions which came to be known as Mutual and Balanced Force Reductions (MBFR). Before the drama of Watergate brought President Gerald Ford into office, the Vietnam War had been concluded and a good beginning had been made in negotiating a strategic arms limitation agreement. Kissinger's ambitious plans to enmesh the Soviet Union in a web of mutually reinforcing ties with the West (the "Lilliput strategy"), which had showed some early promise, suffered greatly from the debacle of Nixon's downfall.

Nevertheless, the slowly grinding diplomatic mills finally produced an agreement at the Conference on Security and Cooperation in Europe (CSCE) which was endorsed by the leaders of thirty-five nations at Helsinki on August 1, 1975. For Soviet leaders, the Helsinki Final Act served as a surrogate peace treaty "drawing a line under World War II" and thus provided an aura of legitimacy to their rule. That did not last, however, and we can see now that the "Helsinki Process," by illuminating the Soviet régime's essential illegitimacy, eventually served to bring down the structure of Soviet control everywhere in Eastern Europe and to undermine it fatally at home.

Notes — Chapter XI

1. The North Atlantic Treaty Association, *Facts & Figures* (Brussels: NATO Information Service, 1989), 402-04.

2. Bo Petersson, "From Avoiding the Subject to Outright Criticism: Soviet Commentators and the Vexing Case of Finnish Neutrality," in *Nordic Journal of Soviet and East European Studies*, 4(1)(1987), 56.

3. Bent Jensen, "The Soviet Union and Scandinavia: Status Quo or Revision — 'Nordic Balance' or 'Nordic Peace Zone?'" in *Nordic Journal of Soviet and East European Studies*, 4(1)(1987) 10.

4. Kirsten Amundsen, *Norway, NATO, and the Forgotten Soviet Challenge*, (Berkeley: Institute of International Studies, 1981), 29.

5. Martin Heisler, "Denmark's Quest for Security," in *NATO's Northern Allies*, ed. Gregory Flynn (Totowa, N.J.: Rowman & Allanhead, 1985), 58.

6. Henry Kissinger, *The White House Years* (Boston: Little, Brown, 1979), 414.

7. Ibid., 409.

XII

End of an Era

The Helsinki Final Act of 1975, the result of over two years of CSCE negotiations, runs to some 40,000 words, representing a series of hard-fought compromises between Eastern and Western delegates. Their debates were often illuminated, and sometimes moderated, by comments from representatives of the "neutral and non-aligned" countries. The most prominent and active of these states were Austria, Switzerland, Sweden, and Finland. The last two, because of their close ties with the Nordic members of NATO and their ability to work constructively with the Soviet representatives, were especially influential in the drive for a mutually acceptable agreement.

The Final Act is divided into three broad sections. The first deals with security matters — in CSCE parlance, the first *panier* (or basket) issues. It begins with a lengthy section titled "Declaration on Principles Guiding Relations Between Participating States" that contains language designed to satisfy nearly all contending views. It covers such matters as sovereignty, the nonuse of force, nonintervention in internal affairs, human rights in general, and cooperation among states. The first basket also includes provisions dealing with confidence-building measures, such as advance notification of military maneuvers and the exchange of observers.

The second basket, dear to the hearts of all Eastern European and some Western delegates, groups a number of provisions designed to expand cooperation in commerce, industry, science, technology, and the environment. The third basket, particularly important to the United States, deals with human rights issues.

The Helsinki Final Act was sometimes disparaged in the United States by those pundits impatient for more rapid progress toward its proclaimed objectives. In their view, the West at Helsinki granted recognition to the territorial gains registered by the USSR as a result of World War II in return for only token gestures by the Soviet Government in the field of emigration and human rights. The Final Act did, in fact, endorse the inviolability of national boundaries and guarantee signatories against any assaults on those boundaries. The most important of those boundaries had, however, already been accepted by West Germany in a series of bilateral treaties with the Soviet Union and its Eastern European allies. Moreover, one of the Act's seven principles specifically provides that frontiers can be changed by peaceful means and by agreement. This provision was especially important to West Germany because it kept open the possibility of Germany's eventual reunification. As for Latvia, Lithuania, and Estonia, President Gerald Ford, at the signing of the Final Act, made it clear that the United States had not changed its position on the status of the Baltic States, i.e., nonrecognition of their forcible incorporation in the USSR.

Brezhnev and his colleagues, it is clear, failed to appreciate the extent to which the Helsinki Final Act sanctioned the subsurface yearning throughout Eastern and Central Europe for a more humane society. By the time they and their successors realized the danger, it was too late. The tide of revolt mounted steadily throughout the following decade, and even the Kremlin's most strenuous efforts could not prevent it from breaching the barriers erected by Stalin and his avatars.

When the Soviet Government and the leaders of the Warsaw Pact published the text of the Helsinki Final Act, they anticipated that their subjects would finally accept Communist rule as a *fait accompli*. Instead, many of their citizens were encouraged to use its language against their oppressors. This was the time of the Charter 77 movement in Czechoslovakia, associated with Vaclav Havel, and the rise in Poland of Solidarity, under the leadership of Lech Walesa. Simultaneously, Helsinki monitor groups were created in the USSR, mostly in the larger cities such as Moscow, Leningrad, and Kiev, but also in the Baltic Republics. The leading role of the Soviet Union's most eminent scientist and dissident, Andrei Sakharov, in this movement led to his citation by the Nobel Peace Prize committee as "the conscience of mankind." The Soviet Government's inability to isolate him or to suppress an increasingly vocal dissent showed that the Kremlin's control over its people was no longer ironclad.

The CSCE "process," rather than the agreement, has reflected the changing European scene for nearly two decades. Helsinki 1975 can also be seen as a watershed in the history of the postwar world, not only as a gauge of progress but as a catalyst for political change. The Helsinki Final Act played a major role in this area by calling for follow-up conferences at which compliance with its various provisions could be assessed. These meetings may be the ultimate basis for a judgment of the "Helsinki process" as a whole.

The first CSCE Review Conference, in Belgrade in 1977, quickly bogged down in a confrontation between the U.S. and Soviet delegations and concluded without significant result. The next meeting, which began in Madrid in 1980, opened in spite of the Soviet invasion of Afghanistan, which was not part of the CSCE area, but under its shadow. When the Polish Government in December 1981, under obvious Soviet pressure, instituted martial law in an attempt to clamp down on rising discontent, Western Foreign Ministers came to Madrid *en masse* to denounce the action. The conference then recessed until the end of 1982, at which time tempers were only slightly cooled. Nevertheless, over the course of the next ten months, with considerable assistance from the group of neutral and non-aligned countries, all thirty-five participants managed to reach agreement on a comprehensive and substantial concluding document. In addition to separate chapters on security, economic, and human rights issues, the Madrid concluding document provided for a number of subsequent conferences on a variety of specialized topics. As usual, the Nordic countries, whether in the NATO or the neutral and non-aligned grouping, were energetic and resourceful in reducing tensions in Europe.

By this time, the Soviet military in Eastern Europe and the Western Military Districts of the USSR had for several years been equipping their forces with a sophisticated new missile, the SS-20, which generated great concern in the Western Alliance. The three-warhead SS-20 was a mobile missile, difficult for NATO reconnaissance to track and almost impossible to target. It was, therefore, a potent threat to military installations and cities throughout Europe, to which Western forces had no counterpart. The military challenge to the Alliance was therefore serious. However, as Norway's Johan Jørgen Holst pointed out, the SS-20s posed an even more important challenge to the balance of the political order in Europe because the new missiles exceeded the framework of a negotiated balance between the United States and the Soviet Union. Moreover, in his view, it was a challenge not to the nuclear weapon states among the Allies but rather to the major nonnuclear weapon states.[1]

As the number of deployed SS-20s grew during the late 1970s, so did concern in NATO circles. That concern was highlighted in October 1977 by West German Chancellor Helmut Schmidt in a dramatic speech to the International Institute for Strategic Studies in London. The Chancellor pointed out that

> *SALT codifies the nuclear strategic balance between the Soviet Union and the United States. To put it another way: SALT neutralizes their strategic nuclear capabilities. In Europe this magnifies the significance of the disparities between East and West in nuclear tactical and conventional weapons....*
>
> *Strategic arms limitations confined to the United States and the Soviet Union will inevitably impair the security of the West European members of the Alliance vis-à-vis Soviet military superiority in Europe if we do not succeed in removing the disparities of military power in Europe parallel to the SALT negotiations. So long as this is not the case we must maintain the balance of the full range of deterrence strategy. **The Alliance must, therefore, be ready to make available the means to support its present strategy,** which is still the right one, and to prevent any developments that could undermine the basis of this strategy.[2] (emphasis added).*

Finland's President Kekkonen responded to Schmidt during a speech in May 1978 at the Swedish Institute of International Affairs, focusing on new developments in military technology, such as mini-nukes, precision-guided munitions, the neutron bomb, and, especially, cruise missiles.

> *In the event of a conflict situation in Europe, what would it mean to the small Nordic countries if, for example, great-power missiles equipped with nuclear warheads flew over their air-space at the altitudes of a few hundred meters on their way to targets on the other side? ... The practical conclusion from the Finnish — and, I venture to*

presume from the Swedish — point of view is an earnest
appeal to the great powers that they at the earliest opportu-
nity, as part of their SALT talks, seek an agreement on
banning cruise missiles, on freezing their development, or
at least on substantially limiting their range…. The objec-
tive would be a separate treaty arrangement covering the
Nordic countries which would isolate them from the effects
of nuclear strategy in general and new nuclear weapons
technology in particular.[3]

Kekkonen's attempt to isolate the Nordic countries from the evils of advanced military technology was naturally well received in those countries, but it generated a warm response also among "peace activists" outside Scandinavia. Nevertheless, after stormy debate, NATO ministers on December 12, 1979, agreed to meet the Soviet challenge by deploying a new generation of American ground-launched missile systems. When fully deployed, the Alliance planned to have 108 Pershing II ballistic missile launchers and 464 ground-launched cruise missiles, all with single warheads. At the same time, in a gesture directly descended from the Harmel exercise twelve years earlier, the Allies resolved, in a "double track decision," to launch a simultaneous effort to negotiate a complementary arms control effort which could obviate the necessity for NATO to deploy the new nuclear munitions.

This decision to install U.S. intermediate-range nuclear forces (INF) served to catalyze a wide-ranging debate on the essentials of nuclear deterrence, but nowhere was the decision to add to the number of nuclear weapons in Europe more controversial than among the Nordic members of the Alliance. Although no consideration was ever given to installing the missiles on their territories, their governments did agree to fund the new installations as part of normal NATO infrastructure expenditures, which would involve a modest financial contribution on their part, in accordance with the normal budgetary process.

Even this limited participation in INF was not satisfactory to many Nordic parliamentarians, who fought vigorously to prevent the spread of such weapons. The Norwegian Labor (Social Democratic) Party had been forced from office in the elections of September 1981, when a Conservative government took over for the first time in fifty years. A divided Labor Party then struggled to postpone a decision on INF funding. In June 1982, thirty-one of the thirty-two Storting votes cast against the INF infrastructure program came from Labor Party members. In what has been termed the most serious cleavage on security policy since 1949, the Storting decided in November 1982, with only a one-vote majority and after prolonged debate, to provide Norway's 1983 contribution of 11 million kroner for INF infrastructure.

Denmark's Social Democrats, like their Norwegian brethren under pressure from their left-leaning members and the Left Socialist Party and also recently excluded from the government, were more successful in affecting national policy. In the fall of 1982, Poul Schlüter became Denmark's first Conservative Prime Minister since 1894, heading a government whose center-right coalition (including Liberals, Center Democrats, and the Christian People's Party as well as his own party) held only 66 of the Folketing's 179 seats. In December 1982, the Social Democratic Party, which was still the country's largest single party, pushed the minority coalition government into insisting at the NATO ministerial meeting that the INF deployment be delayed until some agreement could be reached at Geneva between the United States and the Soviet Union. If adopted by the rest of the Alliance, such a stand would have given the USSR a permanent veto over NATO's deployment of the missiles. A year later, because the Danish Government could find no majority in Parliament for continuing its contribution, it was compelled to renege on paying the balance of Denmark's share in the infrastructure funding.

The Soviet Union was understandably reluctant to bargain away its edge in theater-range missiles, but following a visit to Moscow by Chancellor Schmidt in July 1980, it agreed to negotiations. Although preliminary discussions began in the fall of 1980, they made little progress on substantive issues. By then, some 200 SS-20s had been deployed, with a total of 600 warheads, while Soviet spokesmen continued to insist on maintaining "the balance which now exists." At the May 1981 NATO ministerial meeting in Rome, the Allied foreign ministers emphasized their continued willingness to negotiate on INF but not to accept the latest Soviet proposal for a moratorium on deployments which would freeze NATO in a position of permanent inferiority. The Allies also signaled their determination by confirming their 1977 goal of increasing defense expenditures about 3 percent annually. This was a pledge that some NATO parliaments were politically unable to meet. However, concerted pressure from their allies did manage to prevent even Denmark from decreasing its military budget significantly.

Regular negotiations on INF between the United States and the Soviet Union began on November 30, 1981, accompanied by frequent inter-Allied consultations in NATO. The Soviet side attempted to include French and British nuclear forces in an eventual ceiling of 300 "medium-range" missiles and nuclear-capable aircraft in Europe, a proposal which was promptly rejected by the West. The two sides then exchanged a series of proposals, none of which were mutually acceptable. Impatience with the lack of progress on the negotiating track led to growing receptivity in Scandinavia to the notion of a nuclear "freeze." There was also a renewed interest in President Kekkonen's proposal for a Nordic nuclear-free zone. Kekkonen's ideas had been welcomed in Moscow but attracted little attention in Scandinavia, partly because of the Soviet interpretation by a senior Soviet official in the Finnish magazine *Kanava*.

> *It should be borne in mind that the Soviet Union is a nuclear power and therefore neither can its territory nor any part thereof be included in a nuclear-weapon-free zone or in a so-called 'security belt' adjacent to the nuclear-free zone; nor can the stipulations of the nuclear-free zone be an obstacle to navigation by Soviet vessels in the straits of the Baltic Sea, regardless of the type of weapons they carry.*[4]

In June 1980, President Brezhnev had offered to consider some vague "measures" in unspecified areas adjacent to a nuclear-free zone, stimulating some enthusiasm among Scandinavia's campaigners against nuclear weapons. Scandinavia's governments, on the other hand, insisted instead on a tangible *quid pro quo* from the Soviet side. Sweden was naturally interested in Soviet concessions in the Baltic; Norway stressed the importance of Soviet concessions in the Far North. The 1982 Palme Commission advocated the elimination of battlefield nuclear weapons within a 150-kilometer wide belt on each side of the Iron Curtain and helped to focus public attention on INF. The spread of such ideas was considerably facilitated by discussions within an international social democratic forum, dubbed Scandilux, which included representatives from

Norway, Denmark, the Bénélux countries, the United Kingdom, and West Germany.

In November 1983, deliveries of the first ground-launched cruise missiles began in the United Kingdom and West Germany. Although the anti-nuclear movements had mobilized hundreds of thousands of supporters, they were unable to block INF deployment. In December, the USSR broke off MBFR negotiations and adjourned the START talks in Geneva without setting a date for their resumption. In May 1984, Moscow announced the deployment of additional missile complexes in East Germany.

The deadlock on the INF front thus appeared to be total. Almost at the same time, however, a new venue for discussions opened its doors in the North, a Conference on Confidence and Security Building Measures and Disarmament in Europe (CDE). After a short preparatory session in Helsinki, the CDE convened in Stockholm early in 1984, just one month after the Soviet delegations had abandoned all the other disarmament fora. In September 1986, the Stockholm meeting brought forth an accord which enhanced measures for advance notification of military maneuvers, invited observers to them, and made such measures obligatory. Also, the zone of confidence-building measures was broadened to cover all of the Soviet Union's European territory, reflecting de Gaulle's old vision of a Europe "from the Atlantic to the Urals."

By early 1985, the Soviets had resumed negotiations in Geneva, undoubtedly reflecting in part Moscow's growing concern over President Reagan's Strategic Defense Initiative (SDI). Soviet concern over SDI was almost matched in NATO capitals; President Reagan had announced his initiative on March 23, 1983, immediately after a NATO Nuclear Planning Group meeting but without consulting the Allies. SDI's ultimate aim was ostensibly to replace the doctrine of mutual assured destruction by a more moral strategy for mutual survival, but it was seen in Europe as undermining NATO's basic premise of nuclear deterrence.

NATO and Nordic leaders were concerned that SDI could "de-couple" the United States from Europe by permitting the Americans to erect a nuclear sanctuary for themselves, leaving the Allies alone to cope with Soviet pressures. Usually unstated, a desire to see the United States share a mutual vulnerability with them was a primary national interest for most European states, including the Scandinavian. In this case, Denmark's characteristic allergy to nuclear involvement was echoed in distant Greenland, where it was presumed some SDI installations would be located. In November 1984, the island's Landsting passed a resolution banning the storage, use, or transit of nuclear weapons on Greenland or its waters in peace or wartime.

European nervousness about SDI was heightened by the continuing controversy over the installation of American intermediate-range missiles in Europe and by the Reykjavik summit in 1986, which seemed to demonstrate what Stuart Croft termed "a disturbing lack of American sensitivity to the concerns and interests of their European allies."[5] As François de Rose, France's former Ambassador to the Atlantic Alliance, put it, "Reykjavik seemed to indicate that the bedrock of deterrence was really negotiable." France, West Germany, and the United Kingdom immediately stepped up their defense consultations, and members of the nearly moribund Western European Union decided to breathe new life into that organization. In October 1987, the group agreed on a "platform on security interests," emphasizing the importance of nuclear weapons to European defense. The WEU's membership was broadened by the inclusion of Spain and Portugal and, in 1989, Greece and Turkey were accorded consultative status. At the 1991 Rome summit meeting, the Allies agreed that the WEU should function simultaneously as the defense arm of the European Community and the European pillar of NATO. Given their domestic political complexities, neither Norway nor Denmark was tempted to join WEU, but in 1991 Norway, although not a member of the EC, applied for and was granted consultative status with the organization.

In the wake of the successful installation of American intermediate-range nuclear missiles in a number of NATO countries, the Soviets were obliged to negotiate seriously with the U.S. An agreement on intermediate- and short-range missiles, the first arms control agreement to provide for the destruction rather than merely the limitation of nuclear weapons, was reached in December 1987.

Notes — Chapter XII

1. Johan Jørgen Holst, "Lilliputs and Gulliver: Small States in a Great-power Alliance," in Flynn, ed. *NATO's Northern Allies*, 269.
2. Helmut Schmidt, *Survival* (London: IISS, Jan/Feb 1978), 4.
3. *Yearbook of Finnish Foreign Policy* (Helsinki: 1978), 65.
4. Bjøl, "Nordic Security," 28.
5. Stuart Croft, *The Impact of Strategic Defenses* (London: IISS Adelphi Paper 238, Spring 1989), 12.

XIII

Gorbachev in the Balance

When Mikhail Gorbachev came to power in March 1985 following the brief interregnums under Andropov and Konstantin Chernenko, his highest priority was to stabilize the Soviet position at home and abroad. In foreign affairs, Gorbachev picked up anew on Brezhnev's repeatedly frustrated quest for international respectability. Taken together, the internal and external campaigns signaled that the heirs of the October Revolution were still seeking that elusive legitimacy which alone could justify the existence of their régime at home as well as abroad.

In pursuit of this goal, Gorbachev had considerably more success abroad than at home in the Soviet Union, where his efforts were often met with protests and derision. But he showed considerable finesse in his manipulation of the Western media and public opinion. For example, a June 1989 poll in West Germany indicated that a record 90 percent of respondents answered "yes" when asked whether Gorbachev was a man they could trust. And that was before the fall of the Berlin Wall later that year and the historic retreat of Soviet occupation forces from Eastern Europe. He coined the evocative phrase "Europe — Our Common House" in a speech to the House of Commons in December 1984, even before he had become General Secretary. On October 1, 1987, speaking in Murmansk, Gorbachev launched an ambitious attempt to bring the Nordic area more fully into his campaign for a common European home. He later described this as an attempt to construct what he called "the Northern wall and roof of the common European home." As Robert Janes has pointed out, this was like building the roof for the house first, since it seemed easiest, while continuing to work on the blueprint for the rest of the edifice.[1]

The Murmansk speech built upon an earlier address Gorbachev made in Vladivostok in 1986, which focused on naval armaments, particularly in the Pacific. But the 1987 proposals expanded on the original theme by including limitations on submarine activities and, while directed primarily at the USSR's northern flank in Europe, were much broader in concept and application.

Gorbachev's focus on the northern seas was hardly unexpected, given the concern with which the USSR had been viewing the U.S. Navy's ambitious new strategy in that area. In January 1986, then Chief of Naval Operations Admiral James D. Watkins had publicly lifted the veil on what had previously been a top secret strategy, saying, "We will wage an aggressive campaign against all Soviet submarines, including ballistic missile submarines." Secretary of the Navy John F. Lehman dramatized the issue by predicting that U.S. nuclear-powered attack submarines would attack Soviet ballistic missile submarines "in the first five minutes of the war."[2]

The Soviet president spoke in Murmansk of "the freezing breath" of the Pentagon's "Arctic strategy" and pointed to the threat this posed of an increased militarization of the area.[3] Only a week later, during a luncheon speech in Moscow honoring visiting Finnish President Mauno Koivisto, Gorbachev returned to the same idea. Not only did the NATO countries wish to maintain a high level of military confrontation, he charged, but "the waters and airspace of the North Atlantic and the adjoining seas are being chosen as a sphere for such confrontation."[4]

In Murmansk, Gorbachev offered a kind of package deal, tying together proposals on economic and environmental issues as well as security matters. As in Vladivostok, also a major base for the Soviet navy, the Soviet President called for limitations on the size of naval forces and restrictions on their maneuvers. The specifically military aspects of his speech had been foreshadowed by Yegor Ligachev during a press conference in Helsinki in November 1986. Ligachev stressed at that time that the USSR had already dismantled its medium-range missile launchers on the Kola Peninsula together with the bulk of such launchers in the Leningrad and Baltic military districts. In addition, some short-range and theater-range missiles had been removed from those districts. He also raised the possibility of eliminating the Soviet Union's six ballistic missile submarines in the Baltic if agreement could be reached on a nonnuclear status for that area. In conclusion, the leader of the Soviet Communist Party's hard-line faction pointed out that the entire European part of the USSR, including the Kola Peninsula, would be included in the confidence-building measures agreed upon at the recently concluded CDE Conference in Stockholm.

Gorbachev's remarks at Murmansk the following year were broader in scope and directed to NATO as a whole, including the United States, thus going beyond a purely regional approach to Nordic security matters. In addition to reiterating the Soviet call for a Nordic nuclear-free zone, he proposed a reduction of naval and aircraft activity in the Baltic, North, Norwegian, and Greenland Seas and asked for a total ban on naval activities in certain international straits and sea routes, the specifics of which were to be agreed upon.

Gorbachev proposed that large air and naval maneuvers be limited to one every other year and prohibited entirely in sea areas with heavy merchant traffic. These would be complemented by seasonal bans on exercises in fishing regions. He also proposed extending Confidence Building Measures on land-based maneuvers agreed at the 1984 Stockholm Conference to include large naval and air maneuvers and to provide for attendance at them by invited observers. The U.S. Navy, however, remained adamantly opposed to any constraints on its activities on the high seas.

Gorbachev's comprehensive Murmansk address was particularly notable for introducing economic and environmental themes, both of which evoke strong feelings in Scandinavia. He called for an "Arctic Zone of Peace" and, in addition to the security measures cited above, proposed peaceful cooperation in exploiting the resources of the North and the Arctic. Under this heading, the USSR would team up with its neighbors in extracting oil and gas, as well as other resources, from the North, including the Kola Peninsula. He also proposed that a total energy plan be formulated for Northern Europe. The Murmansk proposals also offered cooperation in exploration and scientific research in the Arctic, joint action on environmental protection, and opening up the northern sea route from Europe to the Far East to foreign vessels with the assistance of Soviet icebreakers.

Although many Western observers felt at the time, and some still feel, that Gorbachev's proposals were limited to advancing the

Soviet Union's security interests in a one-sided manner, some Soviet scholars such as Raphael Vartanov and Alexei Roginko claimed that "more has been done by the Soviet Union to develop Arctic cooperation since the Murmansk speech than during the previous seventy years."[5] Writing in 1990, these scholars pointed to a number of bilateral agreements on Arctic issues the USSR had recently concluded with the United States, Canada, Norway, and Finland, as well as the International Conference on Research in the Arctic, held in Leningrad in December 1988, as evidence of an improved political atmosphere. There had also been a start toward developing cultural links among the Arctic peoples of all the countries concerned. This was highlighted by the inauguration of airline service between Alaska and Siberia, which facilitated visits between the Inuits on both sides of the Bering Straits.

At the end of 1986, Gorbachev had assured Norwegian Prime Minister Gro Harlem Brundtland that the USSR "had no malicious intentions with regard to Norway and that we in the Soviet Union have long-standing friendly feelings toward your people."[6] This conversation proved to be the start of a three-year period during which Sweden and Finland, as well as Norway, became the targets of intensified Soviet diplomatic activity.

Gorbachev's Murmansk speech, amplified somewhat by Prime Minister Nikolai Ryzhkov during his visits to Stockholm and Oslo in January 1988, provided the talking points used by Soviet representatives during that period. What might be termed the Ryzhkov corollary suggested that NATO and the Warsaw Pact strive to reach an agreement on areas in the North and West Atlantic where anti-submarine activities should be banned, a suggestion to which the U.S. Navy was bound to be strongly opposed. He further antagonized U.S. admirals by proposing that concentrations of naval forces not be allowed in international straits or entrances to them, including "the Baltic straits, the Skagerrak, the Danish Sound, the English Channel and the area around Iceland, the Faroe Islands and Scandinavia." Moreover, Ryzhkov added the Barents Sea to the area designated for Confidence Building Measures.

Ryzhkov did his best to sweeten the pill for his hosts in both Oslo and Stockholm at the beginning of 1988 by hinting at a shift in the Soviet position on the demarcation of the Barents and Baltic Seas. However, his suggestion in the Norwegian capital that the disputed area in the Barents Sea be made a joint partnership zone, with both countries contributing to cooperative ventures on a fifty-fifty basis, failed to attract much enthusiasm there. The Norwegian Government took the proposal under consideration but continued to call for further negotiations on the delimitation issue.

Ryzkov was more successful in Stockholm. A major dispute there, which had bedeviled relations between the two countries for two decades, concerned the line to be drawn between Sweden and the coast of Lithuania delimiting their respective zones of economic interest. Both sides agreed that the division should follow a median line equidistant from each other's coasts. But the Soviet-proposed line ignored Gotland, a large Swedish island with a population of 55,000. Once Ryzhkov had agreed in principle to a compromise settlement, negotiating an agreement became easy. The compromise agreement, which gave the Swedes 75 percent of the disputed area but provided special privileges for Soviet fishermen for twenty years, was signed in April 1988.

While in Stockholm, Ryzhkov showed some understanding of Swedish concern over the fate of Raoul Wallenberg, who had disappeared while in Soviet custody at the end of World War II. But it was several years before even limited progress was made on clarifying Wallenberg's fate. In August 1989, the KGB invited some of Wallenberg's friends and relatives to Moscow, where they were given some of the missing man's personal effects and documents. The documents, including his Swedish diplomatic passport, had been found "by chance," it was said, in the course of a project investigating repression under Stalin. Later, after the failure of the 1991 coup, the new head of the KGB, Vadim V. Bakatin, turned additional documents over to the Swedish Government and a joint Soviet-Swedish commission was established to investigate the matter.

The joint commission met in Stockholm in December 1991 to review the documents, which support Andrei Gromyko's February 1957 statement that Wallenberg had died of a heart attack in prison in Moscow on July 17, 1947, two and half years after he was seized by Soviet forces in Budapest. The Swedish diplomat was evidently charged with spying on the USSR for the Germans. He may also have been suspected of working with American intelligence on the basis of his contacts in Stockholm with an officer of the American Embassy there. Some of the newly released documents had evidently been inked over to conceal references to Wallenberg, at the instigation of Viktor S. Abakumov, the notorious head of the Soviet Union's wartime counterintelligence unit and later Minister of State Security. Abakumov was arrested after Stalin's death and executed in 1954. A memorandum to Abakumov from the prison doctor, A.L. Smoltsov, reported the prisoner's death, and a handwritten note from the doctor indicated that Abakumov had ordered Wallenberg's body cremated without an autopsy. However, a Moscow newspaper speculated late in 1991 that the Smoltsov letter was a fake. Moreover, the Moscow authorities did not explain to the satisfaction of Wallenberg's family numerous reports that he was seen alive well after 1947, and some of his relatives continued their inquiries into the case.[7]

The USSR made its first unilateral troop reductions in Eastern Europe during April 1989. In May, Gorbachev followed up by announcing the unilateral withdrawal of 500 short-range nuclear weapons from Europe. Gorbachev did not focus on the Nordic area again until October 1989, when his remarks had great relevance to the rapidly deteriorating situation on the southern shore of the Baltic.

Speaking on October 26, at Finlandia Hall in Helsinki, the site of the 1975 CSCE Agreement, the USSR President updated his Murmansk proposals by announcing plans to destroy four Soviet nuclear missile submarines in the Baltic. Two other submarines of the six originally deployed in 1976 had reportedly been withdrawn from the area earlier in 1989. Gorbachev pledged that the remaining four Golf-class vessels and their payloads would be destroyed by the end of 1990 and not replaced. Repeating earlier statements, he asserted, "As of now, we have no medium- or shorter-range missiles on operational status in areas adjacent to the north of Europe.... Soviet tactical nuclear systems are now deployed in areas from which they cannot reach northern Europe from any given site in Soviet territory."[8]

Gorbachev made the usual ritualistic Soviet call for a Nordic nuclear-free zone but appeared resigned to continued U.S. rejection of the idea. The White House did not fail to respond as expected. Its spokesman, Marlin Fitzwater, said that "we do not believe nuclear-free zones contribute to security in Europe. Most of these proposals have been designed to affect NATO deterrence capability while leaving Soviet nuclear weapons intact." Raymond

L. Garthoff observed, "Gorbachev is seeking to gain political advantage from a cutback that the Soviets were engaged in anyway.... It's a favorable development, but does not represent a substantial step or a big concession."[9] Former Secretary of the Navy Lehman chimed in that Soviet admirals had wanted for years to retire the Golf-class submarines because they were "ancient, rickety machines that add almost nothing to the military equation and are very expensive to maintain."

Gorbachev also proposed that a parliamentary group of Nordic countries, including the USSR, meet to discuss all problems of the region, "ranging from security to human rights." This proposal envisaged contacts between the Nordic Council and the Supreme Soviet of the Soviet Union, as well as regional Soviets "situated in the northern part of the USSR." The suggestion for parliamentary contacts was welcomed by the Presidium of the Nordic Council, and a number of meetings subsequently took place between Soviet and Nordic parliamentarians.

A more overtly political move in the Finlandia Hall speech, and one with considerably greater effect, was Gorbachev's statement that the Soviet Union "unconditionally recognizes Finland's neutral status and shall continue to do so in the future." This was a palpable change from the standard Soviet phraseology since Khrushchev's time, which stressed Finland's obligations under the Friendship and Mutual Assistance Treaty and spoke only of Finland's "aspirations to neutrality." In contrast, Gorbachev emphasized that Finnish neutrality complemented rather than contradicted the treaty. The Finns, of course, were gratified. Some Finnish observers suggested, prematurely, that Gorbachev's new and enlightened stance signified his approval for a pan-European reorientation on the part of the Nordic nations, including Finland. If so, they speculated, Moscow might even be prepared to drop its objections to Finnish membership in the European Community.

More important than such speculative nuances, Gorbachev's remarks, coming as they did during a period of growing political turmoil in Eastern Europe, could be read as a signal to the rebellious countries of that region that "Finlandization" was an acceptable goal for them in the years to come. Asked by reporters during his visit if Finland could be a model for Eastern Europe, Gorbachev replied, "To me, Finland is a model of relations between a big country and a small country, a model of relations between states with different social systems, a model of relations between neighbors."

Gorbachev had already in March told Karoly Grosz, General Secretary of the Hungarian Communist Party, that he was not prepared to use armed force to maintain his party or other similar parties in power. His Helsinki remarks seemed to confirm that the countries of Eastern Europe could go their own way internally as long as they did not threaten Soviet strategic interests. Further evidence of this policy shift was provided when Gorbachev and Koivisto signed a joint declaration of principles in which they endorsed "absolute respect for the principle of the freedom of social and political choice, de-ideologization and humanization of the relations between states, adherence to international law in foreign policy activities, and giving priority to human interests and values."

In a dramatic repudiation of the "Brezhnev doctrine," the two leaders also agreed that "the use of force of any kind cannot be justified: neither against another alliance, nor within these alliances, nor against neutral countries from any quarter." On the same occasion, Gorbachev and Koivisto also signed a series of more prosaic agreements looking toward greater cooperation in protecting the environment, developing the economy of the Kola Peninsula, and resolving trade difficulties. Particularly important to the Finns was an agreement sharply to reduce sulfur emissions from two Soviet nickel smelters near their border which had been poisoning Finland's forests.

President Koivisto, in a demonstration of Finnish deference to Moscow's sensitivity about the USSR's internal empire, went out of his way publicly to emphasize his country's lack of support for separatist movements within the borders of its giant neighbor. Although tensions were now erupting in the Soviet Union, he said, "underneath the surface, there is every reason for confidence in the ability of this community of peoples to solve its problems in a way that enables the distinctiveness of the parts to be increased while strengthening the whole."

A good measure of agreement among the Nordic neutrals was then reflected in remarks made the following month by Swedish Foreign Minister Sten Andersson during a visit to Estonia. In order not to hamper *perestroika's* prospects, he said, "the expansion of the Baltic republics' independence must take place within the framework of the Soviet Union." This was, of course, fully consistent with Swedish policy since the 1940s, when Sweden was the only Nordic country to recognize the Soviet annexation of the Baltic nations. Although in March 1988, Carl Bildt, leader of the opposition Moderate Party in the Swedish Parliament, had called for Nordic initiatives to bolster the emerging Baltic independence movement, in November 1989, Andersson confirmed again the Swedish Government's position that the USSR was not an occupier in the Baltic states.

At that time, it still appeared premature to envisage an early break-up of the Warsaw Pact, particularly in the light of Foreign Minister Shevardnadze's remark in October that the new political situation in Eastern Europe did not mean that "these states stop being our neighbors, allies or friends." But Gorbachev's address, taken with Shevardnadze's assurances that Moscow accepted political pluralism in Eastern Europe and that all countries had "an absolute freedom of choice," appeared to point to a continued erosion of Pact cohesion. This impression was reinforced by Press Spokesman Gennadi Gerasimov's flippant comment that the USSR had adopted a "Frank Sinatra doctrine," under which all nations could say "I did it my way." He then added, "I think the Brezhnev doctrine is dead."

The Soviet Union's interest in improving its image in Northern Europe and the rest of the Western world, in order to secure the economic and political benefits of *détente*, was also clear elsewhere. An important stage in the USSR's continued search for international legitimacy was reflected in the course of the third CSCE follow-up meeting, which convened in Vienna in November 1986. Soviet positions on a number of humanitarian issues softened significantly during the two years of the negotiations, which concluded in January 1989.

In his speech to the closing CSCE session, U.S. Secretary of State George Shultz could point to a number of improvements on the European scene. While noting that dark areas still remained, particularly in the East Germany, Czechoslovakia, Romania, and Bulgaria, he was able to observe that "the picture in the Soviet Union and some countries of Eastern Europe has brightened in significant respects." Specifically, he noted that the jamming of radio broadcasts had stopped, prison gates in the USSR had opened for more than 600 prisoners of conscience, including the remaining Helsinki monitors, and there was greater freedom of expression and assembly in countries where those basic rights had long been denied.

As a result, the mood at the conclusion of the Vienna review session was quite different from that at the Madrid conference in 1983, which had been dominated by the USSR's shooting down of a Korean airliner over Sakhalin Island. Even so, speaking in Vienna at the beginning of 1989, neither Secretary Shultz nor anyone else was able to foresee the tumultuous events which were to occur later that same year throughout Eastern Europe.

Nevertheless, the cumulative effect of the "Helsinki process" was clearly evident in what became the *annus mirabilis* of 1989. The Hungarian Government's public justification for its willingness during that summer to permit thousands of East Germans to flee to West Germany through Hungary and Austria, in spite of East German objections, focused on the obligations accepted in the Helsinki Final Act. By opening the floodgates to emigration, the Hungarian stand cleared the way for the rapid collapse of the régimes imposed on the peoples of Eastern Europe during the 1940s. As William Hyland has pointed out, "If it can be said that there was one point when the Soviet empire finally began to crack, it was at Helsinki."[10] It is ironic that some of the CSCE's most fervent supporters since then have been Russian nationalists seeking to invoke the Final Act's human rights provisions to protect ethnic Russians living outside the Russian Federation in former republics of the USSR, including the Baltic states.

The Nordic governments rushed to offer friendship and economic aid to the new régimes in the developing democracies of Eastern Europe. Scandinavian attention soon passed, however, from the death rattle in the Soviet Union's former satellites to the convulsions in its internal empire, particularly their close neighbors on the southern shore of the Baltic.

Visitors to the Baltic Republics of the USSR ever since they were opened to visitors from the outside world in the late 1950s had had ample opportunities to observe the determination of the local populations to maintain their separate identities. In August 1988, that determination became manifest in officially condoned public demonstrations during which thousands of Estonians, Latvians, and Lithuanians challenged Moscow's rule and its interpretation of history. Despite the U.S. Department of State's release in 1948 of captured German documents setting forth details of the deal, USSR authorities insisted there was no conclusive evidence that Stalin and Hitler had secretly agreed in 1939 to Soviet annexation of the Baltic states.

By permitting the demonstrations on the anniversary of the Ribbentrop-Molotov Pact, Gorbachev and his advisers evidently hoped, in line with their general policy line of *perestroika* and *glasnost*, that giving the Balts a modicum of freedom would encourage them to take the lead in restructuring the entire Soviet economy. As Janis Peters, the head of the Latvian Writers Union, observed, Gorbachev seemed to have singled out the Baltics as a kind of laboratory.[11]

Similar official thinking was apparently behind the willingness of the authorities, announced during the summer, to grant official status to the flags which had flown over the Baltic states before their incorporation in the USSR. Those who displayed such national flags would therefore no longer be subject to prosecution. In October, shortly after Pope John Paul II named Vincentas Sladkevicius the first Lithuanian cardinal in 300 years, the Catholic cathedrals in Vilnius and Klaipeda were returned to church control. When that happened, according to the *New York Times*, "word went out in churches around the republic to pray for Gorbachev."

Soviet reformers had reason to be encouraged by the enthusiasm with which people in the Baltic republics had supported *perestroika*. The Soviet press, in what Western reporters considered to be a gross underestimate, said that 100,000 people, or about one-sixth of the city's population, had turned out in the Lithuanian capital of Vilnius. Soviet media did not carry Western news reports that policemen had shoved and beaten some people attending the rally. However, TASS, in welcoming the rallies in the Baltic Republics, introduced a strong note of caution: "At the same time, one cannot fail to notice destructive nationalist sentiments that benefit only forces opposed to the campaign for perestroika." In Riga, Latvia, where demonstrators and the police had clashed the previous year, a crowd of 20,000 assembled to chant slogans of independence. Banners declared implicit solidarity with the other "captive nations" of the Eastern bloc by listing the dates of Soviet interventions: "1956-Hungary, 1968-Czechoslovakia, 1979-Poland."

Still, at that time, Western newsmen reported that few Balts believed that secession from the Soviet Union was a realistic possibility, and far fewer publicly advocated such a course. The limit of their intentions seemed to be reflected in the action of the Estonian Parliament, which asked the USSR Parliament to draft a new treaty defining the respective roles of the republics and the central government.

Although there was great ferment in other Soviet republics such as Armenia, Moldavia, and Ukraine, the three Baltic states were consistently in the forefront of those demanding greater freedom from dictation by the center. The "Singing Revolution," which featured mass performances of once outlawed patriotic anthems, swept through the region. By the fall of 1988, popular fronts had been formed in Estonia and Latvia, while the Lithuanian Movement for Support of Perestroika, usually known as "the Movement," or *Sajudis*, was holding an organizational congress.

In October 1988, Alexander Yakovlev, then believed to be Gorbachev's closest adviser, told the *New York Times* that the grassroots political movements in the Baltic republics had legitimate grievances and should, in general, be encouraged. But, he added, some of their ideas were "out of touch with reality" and any expectation that the republics could regain the independent status they had before 1940 was "simply unrealistic." Pointing as an example to the demand by *Sajudis* for a separate Lithuanian currency, he scoffed, "How can they have their own currency? … California doesn't have its own currency."[12]

In October also, the Kremlin completed a clear sweep of the top party leaders in the Baltic republics by replacing the First Secretary of the Lithuanian Communist Party, Ringaudas Songaila, with Algirdas Brazauskas, reputed to be a reformer and sympathetic to *Sajudis*. This followed shortly after the replacement of Karl Väino by Väino Valjas in Estonia and Boris Pugo by Jan Vagris in Latvia. Pugo had been transferred to Moscow to assume more important responsibilities, eventually becoming head of the Ministry of Internal Affairs.

Although nationalist sentiment is common to all three Baltic states, their demographics are substantially different, complicating efforts to coordinate their drive for independence. Their economic situations, while not identical, are less divergent, reflecting a comparative prosperity by Soviet standards. At the equivalent of $6,740 per person (1990), Latvia had the highest per capita gross national product in the Baltics and in the USSR. (The average for the USSR as a whole was about $5,000.) Because of heavy immigration to

Latvia by Russians and other Soviet nationalities since 1945, that republic's population of 2.7 million had become roughly half non-Latvian. To Moscow's chagrin, nearly half the republic's non-Latvian residents apparently favored independence. The basic split in opinion seemed to stem more from political convictions, either democratic or conservative/authoritarian, than from ethnic differences. But some ethnic predilections persisted, as reflected in the split within the Latvian Communist Party in the spring of 1990. The old-line residue of that party turned out to be largely Russian in origin.

Estonia occupied the middle of the Baltic spectrum, with a gross national product of $6,240 (dollar equivalent) in 1990 and a majority of native Estonians in a total population of 1.6 million. That majority had eroded sharply since World War II, however, slipping from 88 percent in 1940 to 77 percent in 1959, and to about 60 percent in 1990, due largely to immigration from other Soviet republics. But it was also partly the result of the higher birth rate among the Slavs compared to the Estonians.

The nationalist drive developed most clearly in Lithuania, which had a per capita gross national product of $5,880 in 1990. In spite of its larger population of 3.7 million, it was less urbanized than the other two Baltic states and had attracted far fewer Slavs. The 20 percent non-Lithuanian population was heavily concentrated in the larger cities and towns. Like their Polish neighbors, the Lithuanians remain fiercely attached to the Catholic Church as an integral part of their national patrimony. The most important division of opinion in Lithuania was described as "orthodox nationalists versus realist nationalists."

On October 22, 1988, the founding congress of *Sajudis* began in Vilnius, where 1,021 delegates (980 of whom were Lithuanians) endorsed resolutions to sever most of the republic's political and economic links with the USSR. Only after a last-minute appeal by the new Communist Party leader, Brazauskas, did the congress step back from calling for full independence. "Let us listen to Cardinal Sladkevicius, who said, 'Let us learn to wait,'" he pleaded. Brazauskas also told the meeting that "The goals of *Sajudis* reflect the interests of all peoples residing in Lithuania." He said that Gorbachev wished to extend greetings to the gathering, relating that the General Secretary told him that he saw in *Sajudis* the "driving force of reform capable of strengthening the authority of Lithuania."[13]

Disturbed by indications that discontent was rising in the Baltics and that local Communist Party leaders were joining in the protests, the Kremlin, in mid-November, dispatched a trio of Politburo members as a kind of "truth squad" to all three capitals. Viktor M. Chebrikov, until recently head of the KGB, went to Estonia, while Vadim A. Medvedev spent the day in Latvia, and Nikolai N. Slyunkov visited Lithuania. All members of the squad emphasized the importance to the republics of their economic ties with the rest of the USSR, implying that further pressures for independence could lead to a withdrawal of vital supplies of energy.

In November 1988, the Estonian Supreme Soviet, under pressure from the new Popular Front, invoked the text of the USSR Constitution, which described the republics as "sovereign socialist states," and declared Estonia sovereign. Henceforth, it decreed, Soviet laws would not enter into force in Estonia without ratification by Estonia's own Parliament. Moscow immediately, if unconvincingly, pronounced the move invalid. In January 1989, the Estonian Parliament adopted a law making Estonian the sole official language.

Simultaneously, Lithuanian Communist Party Chief Brazauskas, who was facing a tough election battle in March for a seat in the new USSR Parliament, revealed plans for a new constitution for the republic. The draft document asserted the republic's sovereignty and its right to dispose of its own national resources, as well as declaring Lithuanian the official language. Article 70 of the new draft constitution provided that Soviet laws would take effect in Lithuania only if they "do not interfere with the sovereign rights of the republic." Reminded that Gorbachev had declared such changes "unacceptable" in Estonia, Brazauskas commented that "Perestroika is a very complicated process.... What was unacceptable previously can become acceptable later. Everything can be discussed."[14]

Pravda was not so sanguine. On February 22, it ran an article deploring what it said was the collaboration of some Lithuanian party members in actions hostile to Soviet Lithuania. This it termed the tactic of "trying to have it both ways." Part of *Sajudis* "has drawn openly closer to the slogans of the clearly anti-socialist (Lithuanian Freedom) League and the so-called Party of Lithuanian Democrats." Still, polls had shown that "one-third of Communists and Young Communist League members are guided by

Sajudis support groups in making political decisions." *Pravda* then added, "Democracy and glasnost are a mighty bell.... It is being furiously rung by bellringers who have latched onto restructuring but are very far removed from its true aims."[15]

The March 1989 elections for the new Soviet Parliament turned up significant majorities for the new Popular Front candidates, who drubbed their Communist Party rivals. Their margin of victory was most impressive in Lithuania, where thirty-six of the forty-two deputies elected were members of *Sajudis*. Although some of the winners were simultaneously members of *Sajudis* and the Communist Party, they ran on the independence platform rather than that of the Communist Party. Algirdas Brazauskas won a parliamentary seat, but only after *Sajudis*, for tactical reasons, decided not to enter a candidate against him.

On May 18, 1989, the Lithuanian legislature crossed the Rubicon, declaring by a vote of 291 to 8 that the republic wanted independence. Although calls for independence had previously been made by political and social groups throughout the Baltics, this was the first time that an official governmental organ had added its voice to the demand. The legislators also voted unanimously for a constitutional amendment granting the republic the right to veto Soviet laws and to control migration to the republic. This amendment was similar to one passed by the Estonian Supreme Soviet in November 1988 but rejected, under strong pressure from Moscow, by the Lithuanian and Latvian legislatures.

The bold Lithuanian move came only a few days after the leaders of popular movements in the three Baltic republics met in Tallinn as a Baltic Assembly to organize a united fight for their independence. Spokesmen in Tallinn called on the United Nations to help them become independent, emphasizing that they intended to pursue that goal through legal and political means rather than by civil disobedience. Asked for the stand of the U.S. Government on independence for the Baltics, a State Department spokesman replied, "We strongly support the peaceful efforts of the people in the Baltic states to regain control over their own destiny. The pace, direction and final objectives of those efforts are up to the Baltic people themselves to determine."[16]

By August 1989, the fiftieth anniversary of the Ribbentrop-Molotov agreement, Moscow was finally willing to admit the existence of its secret protocol on the Baltic states. But Alexander

Yakovlev, who had chaired a government commission on the subject, continued to deny that the pact resulted in an illegitimate annexation of the Baltics. Yakovlev insisted in an interview that "it is far-fetched to seek some kind of inter-relation between the present status of the three republics and the (1939) non-aggression treaty."[17] Two co-chairman of the Yakovlev Commission immediately told the press that the conclusions Yakovlev expressed in the interview "to a significant degree did not coincide with the opinion of the overwhelming majority of members." Nonetheless, the official Soviet position remained that the three Baltic legislatures had overwhelmingly voted to join the USSR, and *Pravda* published the texts of their original "appeals" to do so.

On August 22, 1989, a commission of the Lithuanian Parliament declared that Moscow's annexation of the republic in 1940 was invalid. The commission charged that Stalinism and Hitlerism had destroyed independent states by secret deals and, in language later approved unanimously by the entire legislature, stated, "The independence of many of these states has been restored, but Lithuania, Latvia and Estonia still have not reacquired their independence."[18]

Mass rallies throughout the Baltic republics on August 23, 1989, were dramatized by hundreds of thousands of Estonians, Latvians, and Lithuanians linking hands across the 400 miles from Tallinn to Vilnius. A statement issued by the rally leaders, including some government officials and Communist Party officials, said that the Soviet Union had "infringed on the historical right of the Baltic nations to self-determination, presented ruthless ultimatums to the Baltic republics, occupied them with overwhelming military force, and under conditions of military occupation and heavy political terror carried out their violent annexations."[19]

This provoked an angry response from Moscow, whose willingness to use military force against unarmed demonstrators had been demonstrated in the Soviet republic of Georgia in April. Invoking the possibility of "impending disaster," the Soviet Party's Central Committee declared that a "nationalist hysteria" had infected the Baltics like a "virus" and that the fate of the Baltic peoples was in serious danger. Moscow took particular umbrage because, it charged, "nationalist leaders contacted foreign organizations and centers, seeking to involve them in what was in fact the internal affairs of their republics and treating them as consultants and advisers, as if people in the West were better aware of the actual needs of the Baltic nations."[20]

Aside from the activities of some residents and citizens of the United States who had gone to the Baltic states to assist their compatriots as advisers, the chief targets of this Soviet broadside were obviously the Nordic nations. Governments and individuals throughout Scandinavia had taken leading roles in furthering the spread of democratic ideas and methods in the Baltics with material assistance as well as advice.

Russians and other non-Baltic ethnic groups in the Baltic states were incensed, particularly about the new language laws which discriminated against the use of Russian, the USSR's *lingua franca*. Feelings were intensified, moreover, when the Estonian Parliament passed a law in August decreeing rigid residence requirements for voting in local elections or standing for local office. It was estimated that the new legislation could disenfranchise up to 100,000 Slavs living in Estonia. The Presidium of the USSR Supreme Soviet quickly declared the election law unconstitutional.

When some 40,000 Slavs went on strike to protest the linguistic laws, the Estonian Government banned strikes, but without effect. In a conciliatory gesture, the Estonian Communist Party chief, Väino Valjas, called on the strikers to help negotiate a compromise of their grievances, but indicated that the Estonian authorities had no intention of rescinding the new legislation.

The leaders of the Communist Parties in the other two Baltic republics then joined in the move toward conciliation. In separate but similar statements, all three sought to appease the central authorities while going along with the momentum for change in their area. Nationalist leaders showed a similar inclination to lower the temperature a bit by meeting with Party officials and agreeing to postpone some of their political demands until the situation had calmed down. Vytautas Landsbergis, the musicologist who had become chairman of *Sajudis*, warned the group's governing council against inflammatory statements or slurs against Russians or others as they might become a pretext for a crackdown.

Brazauskas, head of the Lithuanian Communist Party, suggested on September 5 that the Balts should not push so hard for independence that they provoked Moscow to use military force.

He also said that Lithuania was not economically prepared to stand alone, and that attempts to disassemble the Soviet federation would endanger the stability of Europe. "There is a balance of political forces — Western countries, NATO, the Warsaw Pact. Everything is in balance now. That creates good conditions for normal relations between states, between different systems. Hardly anyone is very interested in upsetting this balance."[21]

In mid-September 1989, also, Gorbachev met with the Party leaders of Estonia, Latvia, and Lithuania in an effort to lower tensions. Noting that "we have grown up together," the General Secretary urged a "reasonable compromise" and warned against the "ruinous" step of attempting separate Communist movements. According to TASS, Gorbachev agreed that "there's a need to grant the parties of the constituent republics greater independence." In almost the same breath, however, he said, "The idea of federalism in the Party's structure would be a death blow to its unity."

In November, the USSR legislature by a vote of 296 to 67, with 37 abstentions, gave Gorbachev's soothing words more credibility by enacting a bill to grant the Baltic republics a large measure of economic autonomy, to take effect on January 1, 1990. It provided for the three republics to gain control over factories and other state-run enterprises. But Moscow would retain authority over the armed forces stationed in the area as well as oil and gas lines, together with "other facilities that have national importance." Commenting on the new legislation, Leonid Abalkin, a key economic adviser and Deputy Prime Minister, made it clear that Moscow still hoped to use the Baltics as a testing ground for *perestroika*. In his view, the new law would "ease the transition to economic autonomy for all fifteen republics and help establish a rational relationship between them and the union."[22]

The response from the Baltic was not long in coming and could not have been encouraging to Abalkin and his colleagues. On December 7, 1989, Lithuania defied President Gorbachev by ending the Communist Party's monopoly of power in the republic. A few days later, local elections in Latvia and Estonia reinforced the message by delivering majorities for their respective National Fronts, both of which were pledged to work for independence.

Also during December, it became known that representatives of the three Baltic popular movements had been meeting discreetly and "unofficially" with officials from the office of UN Secretary Perez de Cuellar. In addition, meetings were held late in 1989 with officials of the Norwegian, British, and Belgian missions to the United Nations. Baltic representatives also continued their regular informal meetings with State Department officials in Washington and Canadian officials in Ottawa.

On December 24, 1989, the Soviet Congress of Peoples' Deputies, or Parliament, declared by a vote of 1,432 to 252, with 264 abstentions, that Stalin and Hitler had illegally conspired in 1939 to divide Eastern Europe into spheres of influence. Consequently, it found that the secret agreement between the two leaders had violated "the sovereignty and independence" of other nations. Nevertheless, Gorbachev rebuked nationalists seeking secession from the Soviet Union for endangering the country through their calls for independence.

On May 18, 1989, the Lithuanian Parliament had unambiguously called for national independence; in August, Lithuania's annexation by the USSR was declared invalid, and in December, the Communist Party was deprived of its monopoly on political power. The Lithuanian legislature also campaigned to permit military recruits to do their military service in their home republics. All four of those departures from Soviet orthodoxy were bound to be regarded as cardinal sins in the Kremlin. When, at the end of 1989, the Lithuanian Communist Party collapsed, the focus of the struggle between the Balts and Moscow came to center on Lithuania.

Notes — Chapter XIII

1. Robert W. Janes, "The Soviet Union and Northern Europe," *Annals of the AAPSS* (November 1990), 171.

2. "No Quarter for Their Boomers," *U.S. Naval Institute Proceedings* (April 1989), 45.

3. *Pravda*, October 2, 1987.

4. *Pravda*, October 7, 1987.

5. Raphael V. Vartanov, and Alexei Yu Roginko, "New Dimensions of Soviet Arctic Policy: Views from the Soviet Union," *Annals of the AAPSS* (November 1990), 71.

6. *New York Times*, December 29, 1986.

7. *New York Times*, December 28, 1989.

8. *New York Times*, October 27, 1989.

9. Ibid.

10. William Hyland, *Mortal Rivals* (New York: Random House, 1987), 128.

11. *New York Times*, August 25, 1988.

12. *New York Times*, October 28, 1988.

13. *New York Times*, October 24, 1988.

14. *Washington Post*, January 19, 1989.

15. *Pravda*, February 26, 1989.

16. *New York Times*, May 19, 1989.

17. *Washington Post*, August 19, 1989.

18. *New York Times*, August 23, 1989.

19. *New York Times*, August 24, 1989.

20. *New York Times*, August 27, 1989.

21. *New York Times*, September 6, 1989.

22. *Washington Post*, November 28, 1989.

XIV

Focus on the Baltics

The year 1990 has been identified as the first year of the post-Cold War era. But residues of the Cold War persisted, not least in the Baltic states. There, history seemed to be squeezing the universe into a ball, rolling it, in T.S. Eliot's phrase, toward an overwhelming question. The Baltic peoples, unwilling participants in a fading multinational state ruled from Moscow, appeared to be lurching toward a major international crisis. However, as the poet had said, there would be time "to murder and create" and "time yet for a hundred indecisions, and for a hundred visions and revisions."[1]

At the end of December 1989, the Communist Party of Lithuania had broken with the all-union party and formed a new group, the Independent Lithuanian Communist Party (ILCP), described as almost Social Democratic in orientation. Gorbachev hastily called a meeting of the CPSU Central Committee and summoned ILCP leader Algirdas Brazauskas to the Kremlin to explain himself.

Brazauskas, a veteran politician who had had enough personal support at home to survive the Party's crushing electoral defeat in March 1989, tried to justify the split with Moscow by the need to avoid complete disaster in the impending local elections. Unpersuaded, the CPSU Central Committee sent a delegation to Lithuania to emphasize that developments in that republic were going too far, too fast. Gorbachev then personally carried the argument into Lithuania via a three-day barnstorming visit, the bristly atmosphere for which was set by *Sajudis* leader Vytautas Landsbergis, who welcomed him to Vilnius as "the leader of a friendly neighboring country." In response, Gorbachev hammered at the adverse economic consequences of Baltic separatism.

While millions of incredulous television viewers throughout the USSR watched, Gorbachev, President of the Soviet Union and General Secretary of the Communist Party, pleaded that if pressures for secession continued, his future as well as theirs would be in doubt. Lithuanians, many of whom argued with him in the streets of Vilnius, were not impressed. But Gorbachev himself seemed to learn from the encounter as he realized, perhaps for the first time, the emotional depth of nationalist resentment.

The Kremlin warnings succeeded in getting the attention of the restless Communist Parties in Estonia and Latvia, which adopted a more circumspect line than their Lithuanian comrades, saying merely that they wanted to refine their links with the CPSU. The United Nations Secretariat also got the message of Moscow's displeasure. A senior UN official announced that the Secretariat had suspended its informal meetings with Baltic representatives, accusing Baltic nationalist leaders of exploiting their contacts with the United Nations and indicating that "they really embarrassed the Secretary General."[2]

The local elections in Lithuania on February 24, 1990, proved to be just as humiliating for the Communists as Brazauskas had feared. *Sajudis* captured 72 of the 90 seats decided in the first round, enough for a clear majority in the 141-seat local parliament. Coupled with its victories in the second round, *Sajudis*-backed candidates captured two thirds of the legislature's seats. Brazauskas' Independent Communists came in second in the balloting, followed by representatives of the old pan-Soviet Lithuanian Communist Party.

In official Washington, fears were growing that Soviet repression of its Baltic citizens could imperil important U.S.-Soviet ties, including the projected Washington summit meeting. The administration drew a sharp distinction between the case of the Baltic states, whose incorporation in the USSR had never been recognized, and the crisis situation in Armenia and Azerbaijan, where people were not pressing for peaceful political change but were instead "revisiting old ethnic hatreds."[3]

The seriousness of the Baltic challenge to Soviet cohesion was illustrated by the abundant growth of new parties and movements. Latvia alone could count about thirty political parties, while Estonia had sixteen. An Estonian Citizens' Committee also organized the election of a new Congress of Estonia. Early in March, more than half a million Estonians reportedly took part in the election, open only to those who could trace their family's citizenship to the period of independence between the two world wars. It was not clear how the new body would relate to the regular Supreme Soviet of the Estonian Republic, to be elected on March 18.

On March 11, the Lithuanian Supreme Council, or Parliament, declared the restoration of the nation's independence. The far-reaching declaration was carried by a vote of 124 to 0, with 6 abstentions. The legislators emphasized, however, that the they wanted "permanent good political and economic relations" with the USSR, adding a call "to begin negotiations to settle all the issues connected with the restoration of an independent state of Lithuania, which has already been accomplished."[4]

The Parliament also, by a two-thirds majority, elected as President the non-Communist Landsbergis, a kind of modern-day Constitutionalist, together with two more Compliant figures, the former Communist Kazimiera Prunskiene as Prime Minister and Brazauskas as Deputy Prime Minister. Foreign Ministry spokesman Gerasimov, in Moscow, warned other nations not to support the attempted breakaway: "Whoever tries officially to dictate to us is guilty of involvement in internal Soviet affairs."

The United States Government responded cautiously to what it called the "ongoing Baltic dilemma." White House spokesman Marlin Fitzwater urged the Soviet Union to "respect the will" of Lithuanian citizens and enter into "immediate constructive negotiations" with the republic. The spokesman's written statement also said the administration "expects the government of Lithuania to consider the rights of its minority population."[5]

The Soviet Congress of Peoples' Deputies pronounced Lithuania's declaration of independence invalid and instructed President Gorbachev to "guarantee the protection of the legal rights of every person living on Lithuanian territory as well as the rights of the union and other republics." Gorbachev adopted a more moderate line, stressing his offer of a new union treaty. But he added that secession could only come at the end of a lengthy bargaining process. Meanwhile, the new (alternative) Estonian Congress met in Tallinn and demanded an exact deadline for ending what it termed the occupation and illegal annexation of the Republic of Estonia. The March elections for the Supreme Soviets in Estonia and Latvia showed sizable majorities for the Popular Fronts in both countries.

On March 21, Gorbachev ordered civilians in Lithuania to surrender their private firearms to the central government and put stricter controls on the travel of foreigners to that republic. Prime Minister Prunskiene condemned the new restrictions as violations of the republic's sovereignty. Landsbergis also denounced the Gorbachev decree, adding, "The ghost of Stalinism is walking in the Kremlin and the shadow of it lies far to the West."[6]

A few days later, Soviet tanks rolled through the streets of Vilnius, while paratroopers raided hospitals in a brutal roundup of Lithuanians who had fled the ranks of the Red Army. Communist Party members loyal to Moscow also seized control of the Party's headquarters. President George Bush warned that "any attempt to coerce or intimidate or forcibly intervene against the Lithuanian people is bound to backfire." During a press conference, he repeatedly asserted Washington's refusal to recognize that Lithuania was part of the USSR. "However," he noted, "there are certain realities in life. The Lithuanians are well aware of them."[7]

Other foreign governments maintained a discreet silence for the most part, but the Baltic states themselves refused to be intimidated. Meeting in Vilnius in the framework of the interwar Baltic Council, Estonian and Latvian representatives expressed full support for Lithuania and accused Soviet officials of waging a "war of nerves." Two weeks later, the three republics announced plans to form their own "common market" in order to work toward greater economic independence.

On March 27, Soviet troops forcibly seized many Lithuanian deserters from the Red Army, some of whom had sought shelter in the city's psychiatric ward. An emotional Landsbergis pleaded again for international support and denounced the U.S. administration, which he said had "sold us out." He charged that the U.S. Government, via an exchange of secret telegrams between U.S. Secretary of State Baker and Soviet Foreign Minister Shevardnadze, had accepted the use of force against the republic.

The Lithuanian President's attempts to embarrass Gorbachev's Western supporters seemed to backfire as the U.S. administration made clear its unwillingness to take the republic's side against Moscow. Policy makers in Washington had evidently concluded that the continued Soviet withdrawal from Eastern Europe and Moscow's cooperation on German unification were too important to be jeopardized by a rupture over Lithuanian independence. Some U.S. politicians, such as Senators Jesse Helms and Alphonse D'Amato, denounced the administration for its failure to support the breakaway republic more effectively. The Republican whip in the House of Representatives, Newt Gingrich, indicated that he was brought to support the administration's position only after he had been "educated" by the President. But the Democratic Speaker of the House, Thomas S. Foley, evidently needed little persuasion, commenting, "I don't criticize the President [Bush] at this moment in recognizing that circumstances are very delicate, very serious, and I think he should be given the benefit of the doubt as he deals with this."[8] President Bush appealed for a peaceful end to the secession crisis but assured Gorbachev in a letter that the United States was not seeking to make things difficult for the Kremlin.[9]

French President François Mitterrand praised Gorbachev's efforts to democratize the Soviet Union and observed, with regard to Lithuania, "Our role is not to pour oil on the fire.... I can imagine the terrible problem that this poses to the Soviet leadership." British Prime Minister Thatcher told the House of Commons that Britain regarded the Soviet annexation of Lithuania in 1940 as illegal but said that it "was recognized as fact in the Helsinki Treaty of 1975." Only Norway denounced the Soviet actions clearly, calling the storming of the hospitals where army deserters had taken shelter "brutal and unwise." Sweden's Foreign Minister Sten Andersson, in contrast, said the Soviet leadership was "behaving responsibly toward Lithuania."

Meanwhile, on March 30, the Estonian Supreme Soviet took a less confrontational line than the Lithuanians. It did not proclaim immediate independence but announced only the beginning of a transition period leading to restoration of the constitutional organs of state power in their republic. The Latvian Supreme Soviet adopted a similar declaration on May 4.

The Soviet Union's super-Parliament, the Congress of Peoples' Deputies, granted extensive new presidential powers to Gorbachev with the avowed purpose of averting the danger of civil war. It moved toward adoption of new legislation which would permit independence only if two-thirds of a republic's total electorate voted in favor. The bill would also require the agreement of the

Congress of Peoples' Deputies itself and a five-year cooling-off period before the independence option could be exercised.

By the end of March, some signs of give began to appear in the Lithuanian position. Landsbergis pleaded for a response from Gorbachev to earlier calls for "negotiations." The latter responded by offering to open a discussion with the Lithuanian leaders immediately if they repealed their declaration of independence. In a separate message "to the Lithuanian people," Gorbachev noted, "People in Byelorussia and the Kaliningrad region are raising the issue of returning territories transferred to Lithuania after it joined the USSR."[10] Indeed, Byelorussia had announced that if Lithuania seceded, it would lay claim to Vilnius and six other districts, saying that it had ceded the territories in question to Lithuania in 1940. Vilnius is located just eighteen miles from the Byelorussian frontier and had been occupied by Poland between the wars, but it belonged to Byelorussia for only a brief period at the onset of World War II.

Landsbergis denounced Gorbachev's "threats" but added that "the day after tomorrow, the Lithuanian Parliament will resume its work and on its agenda it will consider this unexpected statement of President Gorbachev." As a column of Soviet armed personnel carriers rumbled through the Lithuanian capital on April 1, officials there stressed that while a retreat from independence was out of the question, all other issues were open for negotiation. At the same time, a resolution of the Lithuanian Parliament's Presidium tactfully praised Gorbachev's strong leadership in encouraging political freedom and expressed admiration for his commitment to law. It "respectfully reminded" him that Lithuania stood by its March 11 renunciation of Soviet authority but invited him to send a representative to hear the case for independence.[11]

After vigorous debate, the Estonian Supreme Soviet passed, seventy-one to twenty-two, a resolution supporting Lithuania's struggle. In Riga, the Latvian Communist Party split as nearly one-third of the 792 delegates to its Party Congress walked out when Conservatives tried to postpone discussion of the republic's independence.

After several unsuccessful attempts to meet with senior Soviet leaders, a group of Lithuanian representatives led by a Deputy Prime Minister, Romualdas Ozolas, was received in Moscow on April 3 by Gorbachev adviser Yakovlev. Yakovlev told the Lithuanian representatives that the March 11 declaration was a blow directed against *perestroika*, but he asserted that "a normal dialogue on all issues of mutual interest was possible on the basis of the situation that existed before March 10."[12]

On April 7, more than 200,000 Lithuanians gathered in Vilnius to back the Parliament's defiance of Moscow. Repeating the words of Lithuania's fourteenth-century national hero, Duke Gediminas, Landsbergis told the chanting crowd that there would be no retreat from the March 11 declaration, saying, "Iron will melt to wax and water will turn to stone before we will retreat."[13]

On April 8, Gorbachev and his new Presidential Council decided to take "additional economic, political and other measures" against Lithuania. Gorbachev followed up on April 10 by describing Lithuania's declaration of independence an "an adventure" and an "overnight coup." He reiterated his call for Lithuania to hold a referendum on independence and indicated that he had not ruled out the possibility of imposing direct presidential rule on the rebellious republic "if the situation there developed into a civil conflict."[14] Gorbachev's spokesman, Arkady Maslennikov, added that the Soviet leadership would not necessarily insist that Lithuania repeal its independence proclamation but that it must at least declare a "moratorium or freeze" on passing laws that conflicted with the Soviet Constitution. In Maslennikov's estimation, loss of Soviet subsidies on oil, gas, and other supplies would cost Lithuania the equivalent of $6 billion per year.

On April 13, Gorbachev issued a forty-eight-hour ultimatum to the Lithuanian leaders: if Vilnius did not rescind new laws establishing citizen identity cards, challenging the Communist Party's right to certain properties, and rejecting the Soviet military draft, he would instruct other republics to stop supplying "those categories of products that are sold on external markets for freely convertible currency."[15] Lithuanian officials, led by President Landsbergis, were unyielding, saying that if Moscow tried to apply economic pressure, they would appeal to the United States and other democracies for supplies. They protested that Gorbachev's ultimatum had been issued on Good Friday and ran through the Easter weekend, when their government would be at a standstill. President Bush and Prime Minister Thatcher, who were meeting in Bermuda, showed some irritation at the Soviet move. However, neither would say what they would or could do if Gorbachev carried out his threat.

Soviet officials informed their Lithuanian counterparts on April 17 that crude oil supplies to the republic would be halted and the flow of natural gas sharply restricted. Lithuania, which normally consumed 18 million cubic meters of gas a day, would be limited to 3.5 million cubic meters per day. Even that rate of flow was later to be reduced substantially.

The Lithuanian Parliament reassembled after the Easter weekend and heard a variety of suggestions. Prime Minister Prunskiene seemed to sum it up for her colleagues when she said, "There is a growing sense in the Parliament that we have to be very clever in our dealings with Moscow, that we have to be the conciliatory party now. But there has been no call whatsoever to revoke the declaration of independence. I think everyone regards this as non-negotiable."[16]

Clearly, Lithuania was highly vulnerable to cuts in its fuel supply. Some 97 percent of the fuel used to heat the republic's homes and run its factories needs to be imported, and virtually all had come from other Soviet republics. It had very little hard currency (about $500,000) to pay foreign suppliers, whose bills could run to $5 million a day, and no assurance that the Soviet navy would permit any non-Soviet tankers to reach Lithuanian ports. Moreover, although the implicit annual subsidy to Lithuania from receiving oil and gas at Soviet internal prices might be much less than the $5.9 billion claimed by the central government, it was certainly substantial. In addition, Western experts pointed out, the cutoff would have been a financial windfall for the USSR, thus strengthening its bargaining position.

Prunskiene and her Foreign Minister, Algirdas Saudargas, began a visit to three Nordic capitals on April 18, hoping to find help for the endangered republic from foreign investors or their governments. The Norwegian Government indicated that Lithuania was free to buy its oil, but the state oil company, Statoil, said that such sales could only be at market prices and for foreign currency. The Lithuanian delegation then went on to Copenhagen for talks with officials there, receiving a similar friendly but cautious welcome in the Danish capital.

During the final leg of her journey, in Stockholm, where she also failed to garner concrete promises of aid, Prunskiene declared that Lithuania was more in need of moral support than of material deliveries. Announcing the opening, at the initiative of the Swedish Center Party, of an international bank account to collect funds in support of Lithuanian independence, the visiting Prime Minister indicated that the choice of Stockholm was an expression of her nation's faith in Sweden. In a mordant aside, however, she added the hope that the money collected would not suffer the same fate as Lithuanian gold stocks did during the last war.[17]

Gorbachev again tried to balance the stick he was brandishing in Lithuania with some carrots for the other Baltic republics. On April 19, he met with representatives from Estonia and Latvia and proposed a new confederation of the fifteen Soviet republics. He reportedly told the Latvians that if they wanted to secede, they could do so, following the new parliamentary procedures. In such a case, the USSR would withdraw all its military bases from Latvia. If they decided to stay, on the other hand, which he hoped they would do, Latvia would receive some kind of unspecified special status within the new confederation. Meeting with the Estonian President, Gorbachev demanded that Estonia revoke its March 30 declaration of a gradual transition to independence. The Estonian delegation agreed to put Gorbachev's proposal to their parliament for its consideration.

Once the threatened cuts in fuel supplies to Lithuania had begun, the response in Washington and other capitals was much more nuanced than earlier statements by Bush and Thatcher seemed to foreshadow. Bush warned Moscow that the United States would retaliate for a cut in fuel shipments to Lithuania, but the White House made it clear it was not prepared to cancel the summit meeting with President Gorbachev, scheduled to begin on May 30. Administration officials explained that the President wanted, if possible, to avoid punishing Moscow for its conduct in Lithuania so as not to oblige the United States to respond to every tactical move in what would probably be a long struggle between the Baltic republics and the Kremlin. Secretary Baker received strong congressional support for that policy on April 18 when he appeared before the House Ways and Means Committee.

A meeting between Presidents Bush and Mitterrand in Florida on April 19 showed that neither chief executive was willing to risk improved relations with Moscow in order to push for an early resolution of the Lithuanian crisis. Bush was encouraged to maintain his "hands-off" policy in the confrontation between Vilnius and Moscow by the results of a poll published in the *Wall Street Journal* on the same date. It showed that 61 percent of the

American public thought close links to Gorbachev were more important than support for Lithuanian independence. Even if the Soviet Government were to use force to block Lithuanian independence, nearly two-thirds of those polled favored going ahead with the forthcoming Bush-Gorbachev summit meeting.[18]

In response to a Moscow suggestion that Lithuania suspend its declaration of statehood for two years, President Landsbergis indicated that Vilnius was prepared to consider a moratorium on full independence. Fortunately, a *deus ex machina* soon appeared which would ease the way toward at least a temporary resolution of the crisis. On April 26, President Mitterrand and German Chancellor Helmut Kohl sent a joint letter to President Landsbergis urging his government to suspend "for a time the effects of the decisions taken by your parliament, which would lose none of their value since they are based on a universally accepted principle: the principle of self-determination of peoples."[19] Landsbergis promised to study their proposal attentively. Under questioning by Washington journalists, the White House reversed an original statement that it had not been involved in the Mitterrand-Kohl initiative and conceded that the overall thrust of the message had been endorsed by both the President and the Secretary of State. *Le Figaro*, on April 30, reported that, following implementation of the Soviet economic blockade, Landsbergis had asked Western leaders to provide him with an exit from the impasse so that he could renew the dialogue with Gorbachev.[20]

Pressure continued to mount on the beleaguered Lithuanian capital as, at the end of April, Russian truck drivers blocked roads there to demonstrate against the republic's moves toward independence. Moscow also cut off coal shipments to Lithuania. The republic's government announced limited food rationing, suspended some publications because of newsprint shortages, and broadcast appeals for scarce medicine, especially insulin and antibiotics, as well as baby food. About 40 of the 138 members of the Lithuanian Parliament formed a centrist group quietly pushing for compromise. The first signs of thaw appeared when Arkady Maslennikov said Moscow was no longer insisting that Lithuania rescind its declaration of independence and Soviet Prime Minister Ryzhkov reportedly ordered a sharp increase in natural gas supplies to the Azot chemical plant in Janava, northwest of Vilnius.

On May 12, 1990, the Presidents of the three Baltic republics met to coordinate their future moves. As a first step, they signed an accord reviving the 1934 treaty which created the Baltic Council, defunct since 1939. The leaders also confirmed their intention to promote the full restoration of the state independence of the three republics. Only two days later, Gorbachev published decrees outlawing the declarations on eventual independence issued by Latvia and Estonia. His proclamation was followed in short order by demonstrations in Tallinn and Riga which marshaled army officers and locally resident Slavs in protest against independence. Workers at a number of the plants in Latvia employing large numbers of Russians joined in the protest by launching a two-hour strike. The Latvian Parliament agreed to set up a commission to examine the implications of the declaration of independence but, in spite of warnings from the Soviet Baltic regional military command, it also pushed ahead with a law to exempt Latvian citizens from serving in the Soviet army,

On May 17, Prime Minister Prunskiene arrived in Moscow bearing a compromise offer approved just the day before by the Lithuanian Parliament. Perhaps still worried that the Lithuanian imbroglio could complicate his coming summit meeting with President Bush, Gorbachev reversed his position on not meeting with the Lithuanian leaders until they agreed to abide by Soviet law, and he met with her at the Kremlin for nearly two hours. While in Moscow, Lithuania's Prime Minister also met with Secretary Baker, who was there to help prepare the forthcoming summit meeting in Washington. Baker spoke of Soviet and Lithuanian needs and of the need "to get a dialogue going."[21]

Prime Minister Prunskiene thus returned to Vilnius under pressure from both superpowers to find a way out of the impasse. However, there was informed speculation that she might have welcomed some prodding from the United States to use in dealing with the adamant anti-compromise faction in the Lithuanian Parliament. But even with the additional weight of American intervention, the Parliament proved unwilling to suspend the declaration, agreeing on May 22 only to suspend some of the implementing legislation. Eager to calm the Baltic waters before his summit meeting, Gorbachev fell back once again on his carrot-and-stick tactics. In a meeting with the Latvian and Estonian Presidents, which President Ruutel described as "unpleasant for both sides," the Soviet leader "confirmed his demand to the three Baltic states to abolish their decisions on independence."[22] But only two days later, Gorbachev invited Lithuanian deputies in the USSR Parliament to his office, where he presented a compromise approach to resolving the dispute. Stressing that Lithuania could be independent in two years if the republic accepted his proposal, Gorbachev pledged that economic sanctions would be lifted immediately and independence negotiations could begin as soon as the declaration act was frozen. During his visit to the United States, however, Gorbachev reverted to his earlier position that at least five years would be necessary to complete the separation process. The question, he reiterated, must be decided by constitutional means, which presupposed a nationwide referendum in each republic.

Returning from Washington with American criticism still ringing in his ears, Gorbachev met on June 13 with the Presidents of all three Baltic republics to lay out a proposal he said could lead to negotiations on independence and an end to economic sanctions against Lithuania. In a subsequent meeting with the Presidents of all the Soviet republics, Gorbachev called for a new Union Treaty which would treat all republics as "sovereign states," with virtually as much control over their own affairs as they wanted. This concession was probably forced by the adoption by the Russian Federation, under the leadership of his rival, Boris Yeltsin, of a declaration of sovereignty asserting that Russian law was to take priority over federal legislation.

President Landsbergis was surprisingly enthusiastic about Gorbachev's ideas for remaking the Soviet Union, indicating that Lithuania might even be willing to participate in working out the details of a new relationship. Lithuanian officials said the meeting had been "concrete, constructive and ... even friendly."[23] On June 16, Prime Minister Prunskiene's government recommended that Parliament consider a moratorium on the declaration of independence during negotiations with Moscow. But it took another two weeks, as well as two more meetings between Gorbachev and Landsbergis, before the parliament agreed. At Gorbachev's *dacha* outside of Moscow, the Soviet president told his Lithuanian counterpart that it did not matter what they put in their declaration as long as it had the words "moratorium" and "March 11th" in it. In return, he would not insist that Lithuania admit to being part of the Soviet Union at the moment.[24]

On June 29, the Supreme Council, at the urging of President Landsbergis and by a vote of sixty-nine to thirty-five, with two abstentions, declared a moratorium on the declaration itself but not on the laws enacted later. Accordingly, the law providing for an alternative to compulsory military service in the Soviet Union was not affected. Nevertheless, Moscow responded quickly by resuming oil supplies to the republic on June 30. Shortly afterward, Prime Minister Nikolai Ryzhkov declared that the entire range of punitive measures affecting natural gas and other items from bearings to pharmaceutical supplies had been ended. The worst of the crisis seemed to be over.

At the end of July, the Presidents of the three Baltic republics administered a telling blow to Gorbachev's fading hopes for a new Union Treaty among the fifteen republics by declining to take part in it. Their clear preference for complete independence received important encouragement from Boris Yeltsin, who reportedly agreed to negotiate treaties on mutual relations between a sovereign Russia and each of the sovereign Baltic states. Later, on November 27, responding to a series of incidents in which nationalists had tried to pressure army troops to leave their republics, Gorbachev sanctioned the "use of arms" against such harassment. "We intend to restore order. If this is not done, our course of reforms will be wrecked."[25]

During a closed-door session of the Central Committee on December 10, General Secretary Gorbachev assured its members they had nothing to fear from his new Union Treaty, the draft of which dropped the word "socialist" from the country's name, replacing it with "sovereign." But six republics, including the three Baltics, had already refused by that time to sign the treaty, and all of them had declared some form of autonomy or independence. Adding to the pressures for devolution, many of the USSR's autonomous regions and even smaller subdivisions were also insisting on their sovereign rights. At the same time, some of the Lithuanian districts populated largely by Poles tried to proclaim Polish National-Territorial Districts within that republic.

The Soviet Defense Ministry announced on January 7, 1991, that it was sending paratroop units to the Baltic republics and other separatist regions to arrest draft resisters and military deserters. In Lithuania, only 12.5 percent of those called up had reported for duty, and figures for the other Baltic republics, although better, were still not satisfactory. Landsbergis termed the military move a "huge provocation," suggesting that the young men who had not answered draft calls lie low, away from their home addresses. "No one here is required to join the army."[26]

On January 10, Gorbachev sent a message to the Lithuanian Government insisting on immediate compliance with the Soviet constitution. Violence flared again as the Communist-led opposition launched a strike which closed the Vilnius airport and threatened to spread to the republic's only nuclear power station. An alliance of twenty-eight strike committees and opposition groups, drawn mostly from Lithuania's Russian and Polish inhabitants, announced the formation of a National Salvation Committee, which would be prepared to run the republic on Gorbachev's behalf. Soviet troops using tanks and live ammunition then stormed the Lithuanian press center and a building occupied by the Lithuanian civilian militia. Later, they extended their control in overnight raids on police, telephone, and railroad installations.

Major General Vladimir N. Uskhopchik, commander of the Soviet military garrison in Vilnius, supposedly carried out the attack at the request of the shadowy National Salvation Committee, the members of which were unknown. General Uskhopchik informed reporters that the military forces were operating in accordance with directives from President Gorbachev. On Sunday, January 13, the Soviet army used tanks and machine guns in an assault on the main television and radio transmitter in Vilnius, leaving a reported thirteen people dead and more than 150 wounded. Much of the night attack was filmed by television cameras and broadcast later in the West. Nevertheless, Soviet military spokesmen maintained that they had not shot anyone and that the only shots fired had been those of Lithuanian snipers. Gorbachev professed ignorance of the events and asserted that he had had no foreknowledge of the Sunday attack.

Thousands of Lithuanians, responding to appeals from President Landsbergis, formed a protective cordon around the Parliament building in Vilnius. Members of Parliament and President Landsbergis continued to work in the barricaded building, encouraged by the vocal support of some 20,000 of their fellow citizens outside. *Sajudis* proclaimed a general strike for Monday, January 14.

Many Lithuanians condemned the United States and President Bush personally for failing to prevent the escalation of violence, and Landsbergis again charged that Bush had sold them out because he was preoccupied by events in the Persian Gulf.[27] In Washington, President Bush issued a statement condemning Soviet military action in Lithuania, which threatened "to set back, or perhaps even reverse, the process of reform" that President Gorbachev undertook when he came to power in 1985. The twelve nations of the European Community also condemned the Soviet actions and warned that, if repression continued, a $500 million technical cooperation accord, as well as a $1 billion food aid package, could be suspended.

Unrest in the other Baltic republics seemed to foreshadow further attempts by pro-Moscow militants to seize power. The central committee of the pro-Moscow Latvian Communist Party on January 14 called for an All-Latvian Public Salvation Committee to take over if the Parliament refused to disband and the government refused to resign. Supporters of Latvian independence barricaded streets in Riga with trucks, buses, and automobiles because, as one of them said, "We didn't want our people under the tanks of the Soviet Union."

Boris Yeltsin again threw his support to the Baltic independence leaders by sending an appeal to the United Nations Security Council to intervene. He also signed mutual defense protocols with the governments of the three republics, including a promise to "render assistance to one another in case of a threat to their sovereignty."[28] Yeltsin said he recognized the independence of Lithuania and hoped to visit it. The National Salvation Committee there responded with a telegram warning that "they could not guarantee his safety."[29]

Meanwhile, President Gorbachev continued to deny responsibility for the deaths in Vilnius, saying that his appeals to Lithuania to rescind its attempt to secede had brought rejection of any form of dialogue. The decision to send the troops into action, he maintained, had been made by the local commandant, Major General Uskhopchik.

In Vilnius, the mood remained somber as the bodies of most of those killed by Soviet troops on January 13 lay in state in the city's Sports Palace. The Red Army tightened its grip on the republic's communications by seizing the Parliament's last radio outlet. But pro-independence broadcasting continued from Kaunas, the second largest Lithuanian city. The faceless National

Salvation Committee declared that if Gorbachev did not impose direct Kremlin rule, violence would continue and spread to other republics. When the Landsbergis government was dissolved, its spokesman said, the committee would also be dissolved and the world would never know their names.

There were some signs of relaxing tensions, however, as Lithuanian officials and Soviet military officers, led by General Valentin I. Varennikov, a Deputy Defense Minister, agreed to an overnight truce. President Landsbergis sent home the huge crowd in front of the Parliament building after receiving assurances that the military would not attack it or other sites in the city. He told reporters that, after an inconclusive telephone conversation with the Soviet president, "I don't know if the responsibility lies with Gorbachev or the top brass. We will learn later, perhaps at a future Nuremberg trial."[30] His criticism of Gorbachev was echoed in the remarks of Mayor Anatoly Sobchak of Leningrad, who demanded that the National Congress of Peoples' Deputies sit in judgment of him.

Terror resurfaced in the Baltics again on January 20, this time in Riga, when a group of the black beret troops known as OMON (Special Purpose Militia Detachment) killed five people, spraying the area near the Ministry of Internal Affairs building with automatic weapons fire. President Bush expressed concern about the latest shootings, and officials said that the United States, together with other Western governments, was considering sanctions against the USSR as a means of underscoring its concerns. The United States also agreed to join other CSCE governments in seeking "an explanation" from the USSR for its actions.

On January 21, senior leaders of all three Baltic republics were warmly welcomed by the Congress in Washington and met later with Secretary of State Baker. The summit meeting projected for February 11-13 in Moscow was described as "up in the air" and was later cancelled. By a vote of ninety-nine to zero, the Senate passed a nonbinding resolution condemning Soviet action in the Baltics and recommending a number of punitive moves against the USSR. At a conference for the foreign press, President Gorbachev finally expressed regret for the civilian deaths inflicted by Soviet military units in the Baltics and promised an investigation. (The investigators' report, some weeks later, blamed the Lithuanian demonstrators for the violence. During an interview in April 1992, Gorbachev accused Landsbergis, alleging that he had only "a couple of weeks left in his political career" and "needed the provocation.")[31]

In a plebiscite of February 9, which Gorbachev had declared "without legal foundation," Lithuanian voters were asked only whether they supported Lithuania's becoming an independent democratic republic. The plebiscite results, as expected, showed a massive nine-to-one landslide in favor of independence. The turnout reached 84 percent of the electorate, ridiculing Communist Party claims that the people were not really behind the March 1990 declaration of independence. In addition, the results appeared to reflect a fair amount of support for independence even among the republic's Russian and Polish residents.

Latvia and Estonia followed suit in March by holding their own polls and boycotting the March 17 referendum sponsored by Moscow. The results in both countries favored independence but by less sweeping margins than in Lithuania. Gorbachev called the results "useful" but repeated his statement that the polls had no juridical force. The slowly improving atmosphere in the Baltics encouraged the European Community Foreign Ministers at their meeting on March 4 to unfreeze the aid package they had put on hold after the crackdown in Lithuania and Latvia.

Throughout 1990 and the first half of 1991, Eastern European leaders trod carefully on the subject of the Baltics to avoid offending what seemed to be an increasingly unstable Soviet Union. Poland's Lech Walesa was particularly circumspect in addressing the issue but began to speak out more freely after November 1990, when the German-Polish treaty affirming Poland's western border was signed. The Polish Government's official caution in dealing with Lithuania contrasted sharply with the enthusiastic public support in Poland for the Lithuanian cause and the substantial aid accorded to the republic by Polish private organizations and citizens. But the government, aware that large numbers of Soviet troops remained in Poland and that its economy was still dependent on good relations with the USSR, was not willing to run substantial risks by adopting too high a profile on Lithuanian independence.

It was left to Czechoslovakia to lead the way in Eastern Europe by opening an "information office" in Lithuania. President Vaclav Havel even implied some kind of quasi-diplomatic status for the office by saying that it would report to the Czechoslovak

Foreign Ministry. In addition, the Hungarian Parliament voted for formal links with the parliaments of all three republics.

The Nordic countries were less reluctant to enmesh themselves in the affairs of their Baltic neighbors. Even Finland was prepared to negotiate cooperative agreements with individual Baltic republics, priority of course being given to Estonia. A joint Nordic information office was opened in Tallinn in January 1991, and the three Baltic republics began to share an office in Copenhagen, financed by the Danes. The Danes and Swedes also let it be known that they would be ready to act as hosts for Baltic governments-in-exile if the need arose. In March, on the first anniversary of Lithuania's declaration of independence, Norway followed up Gorbachev's Nobel Peace Prize by giving a special peace prize of $475,000 to Landsbergis.[32]

Although Iceland is not by any criteria a Baltic nation, it proved to be the most outspoken of the Nordic states on the question of independence for the republics when its Parliament (Althing) announced in February that it intended to open diplomatic relations with Lithuania. Foreign Minister Jon Baldvin Hannibalsson expressed the hope that his country's example would be followed by the other countries of the Nordic Council and the North Atlantic Treaty.

The Soviet Foreign Ministry denounced the Althing's decision as an attempt to interfere with the USSR's internal constitutional process, termed it an unfriendly action, and informed Reykjavik that the Soviet Ambassador was being recalled, pending clarification from the Icelandic side.[33] Iceland responded by withdrawing its Ambassador as well but offered to act as mediator at talks between the Soviet Union and the Baltic states. The Icelandic Government also decided to open a bureau in Tallinn in order to establish closer relations with the Baltic republics.[34]

In the next Nordic gesture, the President of the Danish Folketing, Hans Peter Clausen, told the Lithuanian Parliament on February 12, 1991, that the Danish people were united in their support for the Baltic states and invited a delegation from the Parliament to visit his country.[35] But in speaking to the Folketing on February 27, Foreign Minister Uffe Ellemann-Jensen noted that establishing diplomatic ties with the Baltic republics presupposed Soviet acceptance and that it would be "an empty gesture" to appoint an ambassador who was unable to function in practice. Swedish Foreign Minister Sten Andersson had taken essentially the same line during a foreign policy debate in Stockholm a few days earlier.

News that the Foreign Ministers of the three Baltic republics had been invited to Copenhagen for the February 1991 Nordic Council meeting prompted secret Soviet démarches to all the Nordic capitals. According to *Svenska Dagbladet,* Moscow's notes said: "He who fans the flame of separatism in the USSR does not want good relations with the Soviet Union but wishes instead to undermine them. With such an attitude, we cannot build a new European order and a new type of international relations."[36] Danish Premier Schlüter described the Soviet warning as quite inadmissible and unacceptable, adding that such statements have always been a sign that someone's arguments appear weak. "If we are interfering, we are doing so on totally legitimate grounds," he said, and cited the Paris Charter of November 1990, which gave CSCE member countries the right to call attention to problems in other states.

When the Nordic Council convened, it elected former Danish Prime Minister Anker Jørgensen as chairman. Although some delegations asked that the Baltic representatives be permitted to attend as observers with the right to take part in debates, opposition from Finland and Sweden prevented this. Instead, they were invited simply as "guests" of the council. In what *Komsomolskaya Pravda* described as "a procedural ruse,"[37] Jørgensen then adjourned the meeting temporarily so that the Baltic foreign ministers could address its members during the break. At the Paris CSCE meeting, in contrast, the USSR had been able to invoke that organization's unanimity rule to block participation by Baltic representatives.

After the Nordic Council meeting, the Finnish Government began to take a more hospitable attitude toward parliamentarians from the Baltic republics. Thus, when the Assembly of the Council of Europe met in Helsinki in spring 1991, representatives of all three parliaments were welcomed to the meeting. In what seemed to be an encouraging straw in the wind, USSR parliamentarians were also present, attending an international meeting on the same basis as the Balts for the first time. Once again, the worst of the crisis seemed to be over. Some observers claimed to see a growing willingness in Moscow to accept the secession of the Baltic states if this could be accomplished without too great a loss of face and without undermining the entire Soviet superstructure.

Notes — Chapter XIV

1. T.S. Eliot, "The Love Song of J. Alfred Prufrock," in *100 American Poems* (New York: Penguin, 1948), 138.
2. *New York Times*, January 11, 1990.
3. *Associated Press*, January 28, 1990.
4. *Washington Post*, March 13, 1990.
5. *Washington Post*, March 12, 1990.
6. *New York Times*, March 22, 1990.
7. *Washington Post*, March 21, 1990.
8. *New York Times*, March 29, 1990.
9. *New York Times*, March 31, 1990.
10. *New York Times*, April 1, 1990.
11. *New York Times*, April 3, 1990.
12. *New York Times*, April 6, 1990.
13. *New York Times*, April 8, 1990.
14. *Washington Post*, April 11, 1990.
15. *New York Times*, April 14, 1990.
16. *New York Times*, April 18, 1990.
17. *Le Monde*, April 25, 1990.
18. *Wall Street Journal*, April 22, 1990.
19. *Le Monde*, April 28, 1990.
20. *Le Figaro*, April 30, 1990.
21. *New York Times*, May 19, 1990.
22. *New York Times*, May 23, 1990.
23. *New York Times*, May 25, 1990.
24. *The Economist*, July 7, 1990.
25. *Washington Post*, November 28, 1990.
26. *New York Times*, January 8, 1991.
27. *New York Times*, January 14, 1991.
28. *New York Times*, January 15, 1991.
29. *New York Times*, January 18, 1991.
30. *New York Times*, January 18, 1991
31. *Komsomolskaya Pravda*, April 4, 1992.
32. *New York Times*, March 12, 1992.
33. *Pravda*, February 15, 1991.
34. *Foreign Broadcast Information Service*, February 25, 1991.
35. *Foreign Broadcast Information Service*, February 12, 1991.
36. *Foreign Broadcast Information Service*, February 28, 1991.
37. *Komsomolskaya Pravda*, March 1, 1991.

XV

Nordic Exposure

I t was not until 1948 that the phrase "Cold War" came into popular parlance, following its use by Bernard Baruch in testifying before a committee of the U.S. Senate. But a really cold war had already been underway in the frigid waters of the Arctic for two years, starting long before most Americans became aware of a possible military or naval threat from the USSR. As early as 1946, the U.S. Navy had begun an active program of reconnaissance and research under the Arctic ice, hoping to fill the gaps in its knowledge of the principles and tactics of submarine combat in sea-ice.

By 1954, the United States had launched its first nuclear-powered submarine, the *Nautilus*, which later became the first boat to traverse the North Pole under the ice. Although the U.S.-Soviet agreement of 1972 on avoiding incidents at sea limited the dangers of inadvertent encounters with Soviet vessels, both sides continued to carry on a vigorous game of hide-and-seek in northern waters. The March 20, 1993, collision between the U.S. nuclear-powered attack submarine *Grayling* and a Russian submarine of the Delta class, only a few miles from the Kola Peninsula, demonstrated that the end of the Cold War did not put an end to U.S. Navy probing in the vicinity of the Russian coast.[1] This followed a similar accident on February 11, 1992 and Moscow claimed that these were not the first accidents between superpower ships in this vicinity, alleging another incident in 1981, when a U.S. submarine supposedly rammed the stern section of one of the USSR's strategic missile submarines. On March 26, 1992, the INTERFAX news agency had reported another intrusion by a foreign submarine "practically directly in front of the entrance to the Russian maritime base of Murmansk."[2]

In addition to submarine operations, both NATO and the Warsaw Pact have for many years been carrying out extensive surveillance of their respective potential enemies in the North Atlantic by other means. Satellites are effective in locating surface ships but have limited capabilities against submarines. U.S. surveillance aircraft from Iceland, Norwegian planes from northern Norway, and British Nimrods based in Scotland are also of little use against undersea craft. Their Russian counterparts, modified Bears and Badgers, are even less effective because their basing possibilities are more limited.

The U.S. Navy's Fleet Ocean Surveillance Center in London is reputed to have responsibility for collecting intelligence data on the North Atlantic from all sources. By using a variety of such sources, analysts can determine the type of submarine detected, its country of origin, and, depending on their library of previous recordings of the "signature" sounds of individual vessels, which submarine it is. A principal source of such data is an extensive permanently deployed underwater acoustic system known as

The "GIUK Gap" — The Passages Between
Greenland, Iceland, and the UK.

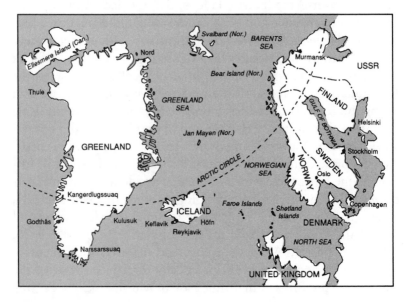

SOSUS, for Sound Surveillance System. Anchored on Greenland, Iceland, and the United Kingdom, with some ganglia perhaps extending as far as Spitsbergen, its hydrophones could pose a serious threat to the survival of Moscow's comparatively noisy submarines which, according to a former Soviet nuclear submarine commander, are six to fifty times noisier than American submarines.[3]

NATO's radar installations on all three of the anchor islands, as well as on smaller islands, plus U.S. LORAN C stations such as the one on Jan Mayen, can also play an important role in monitoring activities in the North. A major NATO objective has been to prevent Soviet submarines from passing undetected through the Greenland-Iceland-United Kingdom Gap to reach a position from which to attack the West's vital sea lines of communication between North America and Europe. Moscow's countervailing effort is believed to include an array of listening devices in the Barents Sea supplemented by the extensive use of electronic intelligence vessels.

For some time, the U.S. has been concerned about the vast military and naval complex located on the Kola Peninsula, just east of northern Norway, which has harbored the greater part of the USSR's submarine-launched ballistic missiles. The coast of the peninsula, which is ice-free throughout the year as far east as Svyatoy Nos, is the only area in the European part of the former USSR to offer direct access to the open sea. The chief base of Moscow's Northern Fleet is located at Polyarniy, and the peninsula is host also to large repair facilities at Rosta and the submarine yards at Severodvinsk as well as facilities for the production of ballistic missiles for submarines at Severomorsk.

Concentration on the problems of combat under the ice grew with the advent of the Reagan Administration in the early 1980s as the U.S. Navy, under the prodding of Secretary John F. Lehman, began to take a more pronounced interest in Nordic waters. But joint Norwegian-American concern about the Soviet naval build-up in the High North preceded Secretary Lehman's vision of a more forward defense at sea. In September 1980, responding to a Norwegian request of several years standing, the Carter administration had agreed to the stocking of heavy materiel in Norway for the use of a U.S. Marine Corps brigade. Designed to deter a possible Soviet attack on Norway, it served to couple U.S. forces more directly with Norwegian defense preparations. In addition, some Norwegian officials argued, the pre-stocking would support the country's position on no foreign bases by making it possible in time of crisis for the government to wait longer before asking for Allied reinforcements.

Given the growth in pacifist and anti-nuclear sentiment in Norway, the pre-stocking decision was bound to be controversial. This was particularly true after U.S. Secretary of Defense Harold Brown commented, in the wake of the Soviet invasion of Afghanistan, that similar moves in the Middle East might trigger repercussions "as far north as Norway." Television coverage of the Vietnam War had damaged the reputation in Norway of the U.S. Marines, and it was argued that some of the heavy artillery to be stockpiled was capable of firing nuclear rounds. In an effort to deflect such domestic criticism, the U.S. stockpiles were not located in the Far North, where they would probably be most useful, but in Trøndelag province, 600 kilometers from Troms, where the main Norwegian defense line is located, some 500 kilometers from the Soviet frontier.

At the same time, consistent with their well-established national policies, there was continued opposition in both Denmark and Norway to the possible deployment of land-based cruise missiles on their territory. In December 1983, when reports appeared that an American think tank had recommended such deployments, both governments quickly rejected them. In fact, U.S. strategic interest in the Far North was by that time much more focused on the seas around the Nordic countries than it was on their land areas. This stemmed logically from technological developments emphasizing the sea-based deterrent and NATO Anti-Submarine Warfare (ASW) capabilities. Climate and geography favor submarine activities in the Arctic Ocean because the ice provides a measure of protection against both surface and airborne ASW, while the mixing of cold water with the Gulf Stream impedes detection.

As part of his campaign for a 600-ship navy, Secretary Lehman became publicly identified with a strategic concept involving the wartime use of U.S. Navy aircraft carrier task forces against Soviet military installations in the north. In an interview in December 1982, Lehman termed the Kola Peninsula "the most valuable piece of real estate on earth."[4] NATO's Supreme Allied Commander Atlantic Headquarters in Norfolk, Virginia, followed suit with the statement that "control of the Norwegian Sea is No. 1 priority" and "the battle of the Atlantic must be fought in the Norwegian Sea."[5]

In fact, because the Soviet Union had put most of its naval eggs in the basket provided by the Kola Peninsula, its adversaries were inevitably drawn to target the area. By the end of the 1980s, some 60 percent of the Soviet Union's strategic submarine fleet, including all of its most modern Typhoon class, was based on the peninsula. Moreover, it had become clear that Soviet planning was based on a bastion strategy, in which its newer ballistic missile subs would remain in Nordic waters during a conflict. From there, they could launch their nuclear-tipped missiles without the risk of running the Greenland-Iceland-United Kingdom Gap or approaching the North American continent.

The U.S. Navy was therefore impelled to seek them out and destroy them in time of war, before they could launch their attacks on the American homeland. As Waldo K. Lyon pointed out in the February 1992 issue of *U.S. Naval Institute Proceedings*, the American Navy prepared to do precisely that. "In the event of a European conflict, the Maritime Strategy explicitly called for sending submarines into ice-covered waters to attack Soviet submarines."[6]

As in the United States and the United Kingdom, the early 1980s showed a pronounced swing toward a more conservative political philosophy throughout Scandinavia and, in fact, nearly everywhere in Western Europe. Although the shift to the right was not nearly so pronounced as that reflected by the Reagan and Thatcher Administrations, Social Democrats found themselves outside of government in Denmark, Norway, Sweden, and Finland. Even in Iceland, a center-right coalition took office in 1983. Freed of their governmental responsibilities, the Social Democrats of Norway and Denmark, like their colleagues in the United Kingdom and West Germany, took pleasure in repudiating the pro-NATO policies they had advanced while in office. Their sometimes frantic search for an "opening to the left" contrasted sharply with the tendency within the governing Socialist Parties of France and Italy, whose devotion to the Alliance seemed to be increasing.

The general European swing to the right was based mainly on domestic political considerations in each of the countries affected. But a good deal of the Scandinavian disenchantment with the peaceful protestations of the Soviet Government during the 1980s stemmed from the Afghanistan war. A few observers called attention to the fact that Afghanistan's Mutual Assistance Treaty with the USSR bore more than a passing resemblance to Finland's 1948 (YYA) pact with that country. The subsequent imposition of martial law in Poland, a country with historical ties to several of the Nordic countries, also undermined Soviet credibility.

This skepticism was spread even further by a series of submarine incursions in Nordic waters. These bizarre episodes, which have still not been explained satisfactorily, were concentrated in Swedish territorial waters, but many incidents also occurred off the coast of Norway. The incursions into Norwegian waters were easier to understand, given Norway's membership in NATO and the significance of Soviet naval installations nearby. "The fjords of northern Norway possess a completely different strategic importance from Swedish territorial waters, and so incursions there are infinitely more worth while and understandable in military terms than incursions into the Swedish archipelagoes."[7] Those incursions were considered a Soviet effort to map Norwegian waters and had become quite routine. From 1971 to 1981, there were 179 reported violations of Norway's territorial waters by Soviet submarines.

The Swedish situation was not so well documented. In the early 1970s, Sweden's coastal defense forces had dismantled their hydrophone systems. Also, as part of the five-year defense plan of 1972, it was decided that the country would no longer have surface vessels devoted solely to antisubmarine warfare. This left only the obsolescent destroyer *Halland* (normally the command ship for torpedo boats) and seven heavy helicopters, which were also tasked for other purposes. The Parliament's decision that "the protection of commercial shipping should take place with other than military means" had left Sweden as the only coastal state in Europe without an effective ASW capability.

There had been occasional reports of foreign submarine activity along Sweden's 2,000-kilometer coastline before 1980, and the submarines of various nations were known to operate in the Baltic. However, the first indication of a new pattern of incursions occurred on March 12, 1980, when a submarine was detected at the entrance to Karlskrona, one of Sweden's two major naval bases. The unidentified submarine was sighted by a minesweeper when the destroyer *Halland* happened to be close by. After warning munitions were dropped, the submarine dived and retreated to the territorial boundary line. Once there, however, it began to use its own active SONAR to track the Swedish ship and soon returned to Swedish waters. Another depth charge was then dropped, but, in accordance with instructions, it was not employed as "effective fire."

As in the past, this inconclusive incident was not brought to public attention. However, another episode six months later, which appeared to signal a new pattern of interaction between the intruding submarines and Swedish ships, generated considerable interest. This time a submarine was discovered quite close to Sweden's main naval base at Haarsfjärden when, according to Swedish naval sources, a portion of its conning tower was observed by a naval tugboat. A submarine hunt then began which lasted two weeks, during which the submarine stayed within Swedish territorial waters, making no attempt to "escape." After ten days, "effective fire" was finally used, but with considerable care so as to avoid the possibility of serious damage to the submarine. Although the Swedish authorities were unwilling to specify the submarine's nationality, it was identified as a Whiskey-class vessel, which could have belonged to either the USSR or Poland.[8]

Reports of similar incursions came with considerable frequency during 1981, causing some skeptics to allege that the Swedish navy was fabricating, or at least exaggerating, the incidents in order to justify an increase in its budget. In fact, however, partly because of serious underemployment in Sweden's shipbuilding industry, the government had already determined on a substantial building program before the submarine incidents occurred.

On October 27, 1981, in a case which drew worldwide attention, a Soviet diesel powered Whiskey-class submarine, designated U-137, ran aground at Torumskär, sixteen nautical miles inside the perimeter of the Karlskrona naval base. When the Soviet captain was questioned, several days later, he claimed that he thought he had been near the Polish coast, some 130 kilometers south of Sweden, when his vessel ran aground. Even if the possibility of such a gross navigational error were conceded, his explanation failed to account for the submarine's successful voyage through a very difficult passage into a restricted security area. Curiously, also, the incursion took place while the Swedish navy was carrying out secret tests of torpedoes, of which there had been no public notice.

Soviet refusal to admit culpability, and a campaign by some Swedish media which argued that the U-137 incursion was in fact an accident, prompted the Swedish defense staff in 1984 and 1985 to make public more definitive evidence. This revealed that the submarine's logbook had been altered and also cited intercepted radio communications from the Soviet Baltic Fleet Commander ordering the captain to claim navigational error.

A particularly damaging side of the incident, given the general Scandinavian allergy to nuclear arms, was the Swedish Government's report that the U-137 was carrying such weapons. The Soviet Government did not attempt to refute this finding. "The Soviet submarine 137 carries, as do all other naval vessels at sea, the necessary weapons and ammunition. However, this has nothing to do with the circumstances surrounding the unintentional intrusion by the submarine into Sweden's territorial waters."[9] After a number of further exchanges and vehement Soviet protests, the Swedish Government released the submarine and its crew. Prime Minister Thorbjörn Fälldin publicly called upon the Soviet Government to prevent "any repetition of these violations of Swedish territorial integrity and of the fundamental principles of international law." The Soviet Government quickly rejected the Swedish protest, noting ominously that the possibility of further "accidents at sea" could not be excluded. More to the point, the number of detected submarine intrusions reportedly jumped during 1982 from the previous average of about ten per year to between forty and fifty.

As Swedish researcher Wilhelm Agrell has pointed out, however, this increase reflected "confirmed" or "probable" reports, not necessarily the number of intrusions. One submarine might therefore have prompted several reports. Moreover, the tendency to make and report observations increased sharply after the U-137 incident. In his opinion, "The major change in the 'alien underwater activity' against Sweden appears to have occurred in the second half of the 1970s, not in the early 1980s, when the activity was gradually discovered."[10]

There had been a relative reduction in the size of the Soviet Baltic Fleet in the 1960s as Moscow chose to emphasize the Northern Fleet. As the Danes were aware, however, Soviet and Warsaw Pact exercises were gradually shifting to the western parts of the Baltic, increasing rather than reducing the threat to their security. "In the summer of 1978, the Baltic Fleet carried out a full-scale amphibious assault exercise, covering all the phases of the operation and all the units concerned, including elements of a motorized infantry division embarked on ro-ro ships."[11] Similar exercises were carried out later, some of which, in 1980 and 1981, were even larger.

In September and October 1982, two submarines and two midget submarines were reportedly operating in Swedish waters in the area of Haarsfjäden, the full-size vessels apparently acting as mother ships for the midget ships. The Swedish navy stepped up its efforts to locate and expel the intruders, while the government established an investigative commission to look into the incidents. In its report of April 26, 1983, the Submarine Defense Commission (SDC) found that "the violations at Haarsfjärden, and other violations during 1982, were by submarines belonging to the Warsaw Pact."[12]

Prime Minister Palme accompanied release of the SDC report with a strong protest note to the Soviet Government and recalled the Swedish Ambassador in Moscow. In comments to the press about Sweden's determination to prevent a repetition of the incursions, the Prime Minister repeatedly used the phrase "with all the means at our disposal," pointing out that "we have previously demonstrated a degree of leniency in our reactions. But this is the last straw. Whoever plans to violate Swedish territory will have to consider that Sweden will now sink submarines."[13]

Palme also apparently attempted to convey his irritation with Soviet policy via a "back channel," through Sweden's UN Ambassador Anders Ferm to retired General Mikhail Milstein and Georgi Arbatov, head of the USSR's Institute of the U.S. and Canada. At the same time, he lashed out at one member of the SDC, Carl Bildt, later to become Sweden's Prime Minister, for visiting officials of the U.S. defense and intelligence agencies just after release of the report. As criticism of government policy mounted in the media and Parliament, Palme countercharged that his critics were endangering the country's neutrality and could therefore be as dangerous as the territorial violations by foreign submarines.

The Soviet response, on May 6, 1983, to the Swedish protest was bleak. "The Soviet Government categorically rejects the Swedish Government's protest as unfounded, and expects the Swedish Government to carry out a new, objective investigation into the case, and to take to task those persons who have given it false material and conclusions."[14] Moscow also proposed a joint Soviet-Swedish commission to review the evidence, a suggestion Stockholm rejected although it turned over several tapes of technical evidence to the Soviet Union. In a more conciliatory vein, Soviet President Yuri Andropov later assured Palme, via Finnish President Koivisto, that no Soviet submarines had violated Swedish waters since the U-137 grounding in 1981.

In January 1984, Foreign Minister Andrei Gromyko came to Stockholm for the opening session of the Conference on Confidence and Security-Building and Disarmament in Europe and met with Palme. After the meeting, the Prime Minister informed the press that "Sweden has, through Andrei Gromyko, now obtained notice from the Soviet Union's highest leadership that Swedish neutrality is respected and that it is understood that submarine intrusions cannot be tolerated."[15]

In reality, as indicated by leaked Foreign Ministry summaries of their conversations, Gromyko did not provide such assurances and, as sometimes happens in such cases, the formulation offered by Palme was his own. Responding to Palme's remark that Sweden desired good relations with the USSR, Gromyko reportedly asked "what kind of dragons the Swedes actually saw out in the Baltic." He concluded with the observation that "the USSR had no cause to be active in Swedish waters, and therefore the question should not be discussed any further."[16]

Less than a month after Palme's meeting with Gromyko, another egregious example of a submarine incursion took place in Karlskrona harbor. This incident, which evidently involved three full-size submarines, some midget submarines, and small, motorized diver vehicles, lasted for more than thirty days. The Swedish forces dropped many depth charges, but still for warning purposes rather than for effect.

The Swedish Government reportedly considered introducing the issue of submarine violations into the proceedings of the Security Conference but in the end did not do so. Sweden's Under Secretary of State made only an oblique reference to territorial integrity and the problems of the Baltic in his June 1984 address to the conference. Moreover, the government's subsequent references to the issue appeared to reflect a clear step back from previous statements. Its foreign policy declaration to Parliament on March 21, 1984, for example, mentioned only "a number of observations in which the responsible authorities could not rule out that there was a question of purposeful penetrations of Swedish territory."

Continued incursions by "unidentified" submarines were the source of many wrangles over the succeeding years, within Sweden as well as between Sweden and the Soviet Union. The Social Democratic government was embarrassed on several occasions when senior military officers commented on the continuing violations. In February 1985, a domestic mini-crisis erupted after Foreign Minister Lennart Bodström said he thought his country's reaction "hysterical" and stated that the Swedish Government "assumes that the USSR behaves rationally ... and could not see any rational explanation as to why the USSR should violate Swedish territorial integrity." Former Prime Minister Fälldin demanded Bodström's resignation, but Palme firmly supported the Foreign Minister. Nevertheless, after the Social Democrats were reelected in September 1985, Palme replaced Bodström with Sten Anderson.

The attempts of Finnish President Koivisto to calm the atmosphere were probably welcomed by both the Soviet and Swedish Governments but, because of abrupt changes in his position, failed to accomplish his objective. In December 1984, he described the submarine stories as science fiction novels and also forwarded Soviet denials of responsibility to Sweden. The following month, however, Koivisto visited Stockholm, where he was briefed by the Swedish Defense Minister, after which he indicated that he now believed the SDC report. Later still, he seemed to retreat to his original skeptical position. A Soviet naval missile, which went astray in late 1984, crossing Norwegian territory and crashing in Finland, kept attention focused on Soviet submarines, albeit this time in the Arctic.[17]

In December 1985, Prime Minister Palme devoted a large part of his foreign policy address to the issue of submarine violations. He cited the SDC judgment that it was Soviet submarines which had violated Swedish territory and noted that, since the April 1983 protest to the USSR, "the Commander-in-Chief has reviewed observations and indications in his quarterly reports and this has led to the conclusion that underwater activities have also been carried out by foreign powers since 1982. The difference is that, despite all our efforts, it has been impossible to identify the nation or nations involved. Thus the prerequisites necessary for diplomatic actions to be taken against a particular state have not existed."[18]

The Prime Minister added that serious violations by Soviet submarines in 1981 and 1982, along with overflights of Gotland in 1984, had created strains in Sweden's relations with the USSR. He implied that the subject would be raised during his official visit to the Soviet Union the following spring.[19] Palme was assassinated on February 28, 1986, however, and the visit to Moscow was carried out by his successor, Ingvar Carlsson, with no evident change in the pattern of reported incursions.

Evidence continued to accumulate that Soviet submarines were regularly violating Swedish territorial waters. A number of theories were advanced as to why the USSR might be continuing such a campaign, even after the radical changes which had occurred in the political and strategic situation in Europe. The explanations seemed to fall into one of two categories: either the incursions were essentially motivated by specific military concerns or they were designed for political intimidation.

Wilhelm Agrell argued the case for military justification, noting that the Soviet Union's shift in emphasis from nuclear to conventional warfare required that NATO forces be denied the use of Scandinavia as a base of operations. Logically, therefore, the arrival of Western reinforcements had to be prevented and the collapse of NATO defenses in the north assured by a Soviet conquest of Sweden. "Against a Soviet attack through Sweden no effective Norwegian or Allied defense could be organized."[20]

Agrell also pointed out that Swedish military planning was based on the assumption that a Soviet attack would have to be preceded by considerable military preparations and that there ought also to be certain political warning signs. In his view, routine underwater operations of sizable and well-coordinated units along the Swedish coast indicated that the USSR might be planning an operation in which important elements of the Swedish covering force would be put out of action at an early stage. If so, "all of the detailed preparations would have to be carried out in advance, all changes in the nature of the targets must continuously be surveyed and all units must be familiar with the specific character of operations along the Swedish coast."[21] Suspension of the incursions could make it impossible for Soviet plans to be carried out without time-consuming preparations. Agrell concluded that this might explain the continued Soviet activity in the face of Swedish awareness of it and the damage done to the Soviet image throughout Scandinavia.

A Swedish diplomat, Örjan Berner, also concluded that military motivations lay behind the Soviet submarine incursions, although he was inclined to see them as impelled more by defensive than offensive requirements. In a book written during 1983–84, while he was on sabbatical at Harvard University and well before his posting to Moscow as the Swedish Ambassador, Berner agreed with Soviet protestations that sending submarines into Scandinavian waters would be contrary to their own political interests. In his view, suggestions that Moscow wanted to demonstrate its superpower status or to dramatize its domination of the Baltic underestimated Soviet self-confidence, not to say arrogance.

> *To fulfill its defensive tasks, the Soviet military in the region must prevent NATO from acquiring bases from which sustained operations can be carried out. If NATO controlled Swedish coastline territory, the Soviet defense of the Northern flank could be threatened.... Soviet military actions to destroy base facilities and early-warning systems or to occupy small parts of the coastline would perhaps be feasible, but they entail the risk of drawing in forces from the opposite side and thus creating the danger that was to be averted.*[22]

Berner went on to say that "the submarines have been discovered in geographical locations that indicate an interest in possible penetration of the Swedish heartland," although he did not believe such an objective would be realistic. He concluded that "whatever military benefits might have been gained from the submarine operations in terms of reconnaissance information or military preparedness, they will probably have been offset by the obvious result of the incursions, which is that the Swedes will have to increase defense spending precisely to meet such contingencies, which hitherto have been given low priority."[23]

The Swedish diplomat pointed out that "military strategists in Moscow and elsewhere of course prepare for a variety of contingencies. Their plans do not necessarily indicate their real intentions but rather are intended to lay out the possible military options they want to have available in any given theoretical situation." He judged that "the submarine intrusions into Swedish waters have principally to do with military contingency planning in the event of a European war. However, in terms of the peacetime situation, there is considerable evidence that Swedish neutrality is not only accepted in Moscow, but is perhaps viewed in a positive light. In any case, it is regarded as not amenable to any radical change."[24]

On the other side of the argument, Steve Lindberg, a Finnish scholar, stressed the possible political motivations behind the USSR's apparently insensitive handling of the incidents. He noted approvingly Agrell's comment that "the Russians have gained a more attentive listener in Sweden." Lindberg recognized also that the Soviet incursions encouraged Sweden to improve its anti-submarine capabilities, as well as to upgrade its defenses generally. A more robust Swedish defense might, in Moscow's view, impede NATO just as much as it did the Soviet Union.[25]

Lindberg also agreed with Agrell's observation that, from a Soviet viewpoint, the Catalina aircraft incident in June 1952 came to be seen as a successful demonstration of power in which Sweden learned its lesson. "This was perhaps not the (original) intention with the Soviet action, but the Soviet authorities, like Sweden's, doubtless drew their own conclusions from the opposite number's action."[26] Similar factors, he believes, might be at play with regard to the submarine incidents.

Lindberg argued that continuation of the submarine violations, once they had become known, were prompted as much by political as by military purposes. In support of this argument, he cited Soviet Admiral Sergei Gorshkov's view that "shows of strength ... off foreign coasts ... have made it possible to achieve political ends without armed activities, simply by exerting pressure with the aid of one's potential power."[27] Lindberg also pointed to Soviet practice as well as theory, referring to the large Soviet naval maneuver off Iceland during the 1973 "cod war" with the United Kingdom.

In 1981 and 1982, Lindberg reasoned, the Soviet leaders were concerned about the new threat from NATO's intermediate-range missiles, which could reverse the success they had recently had in changing the correlation of forces in their favor. Once the "Whiskey on the Rocks" episode became public knowledge, Moscow could have decided to demonstrate its dominance of the Baltic as a way to counter the American deployment of cruise missiles and Pershing II ballistic missiles. This could, at the same time, "show Sweden the difficulty of achieving by military means neutrality in the immediate vicinity of a superpower neighbor to whom neutrality was not ideologically acceptable."[28]

Moreover, in Lindberg's view, "Through submarine incursions in which absolute verification of nationality is only obtainable by forcing the submarine to the surface by the use of arms which may also sink it for good, something which the Swedes and not even the Norwegians in a similar situation have been willing to risk, the Soviet Union can control the course of events and keep the risks always associated with military activities against another country down to a level which they find acceptable."[29]

Steve Lindberg's thesis that continued Soviet submarine incursions in the Baltic were in large part politically motivated, plausible but not entirely convincing when he published it in 1987, became more credible with the passing years as the alternative military rationale became less persuasive. Undoubtedly, Russian military staffs continue to plan for a wide variety of contingencies, including conflict in the Baltic or the High North, but the retreat from Eastern Europe and the former USSR'S internal convulsions must have changed their basic estimate of the situation.

Whereas the Soviet defensive glacis on the southern shore of the Baltic once ranged almost as far as Lübeck to the West, eastern Slavdom had now been pushed back to Kaliningrad. The Baltic States, having declared their independence from Moscow, were agitating for an early withdrawal of all outside military forces. In the light of the USSR's dramatically increased vulnerability on the central front, it seemed doubtful that Moscow's strategists would seriously contemplate a major military operation in the North, where it could not significantly affect the course of events in Eastern Europe. Politically, on the other hand, there might well be some benefit in reminding all the other states around the Baltic that Muscovy is still number one in its self-defined "sea of peace."

Instability within the USSR might serve to justify rather than to discourage a demonstration that "Big Brother" was watching. Because the Nordic governments had been most outspoken in supporting independence for the "captive peoples" of Latvia,

Lithuania, and Estonia, it was those governments which most needed to be reminded of the potential risks of "interference" in Moscow's "internal" affairs.

One more important factor, taking into account both Russia's weakened position in Central Europe and the substantial cut in its land-based intercontinental ballistic missile force under the START agreement, could be summarized as follows: the strategic nuclear missiles aboard the submarines based at Kola can be seen as one of Moscow's few remaining aces in the hole, politically as well as militarily. Keeping open the option of a lightning strike through Sweden to block possible NATO moves in the Arctic might be worth the risk of further irritating their Nordic neighbors. To protect the Kola submarines in wartime, as George Lindsey has speculated, the "USSR could probably neutralize NATO's fixed detection systems off the North Cape by cutting the submarine cables bringing information ashore, thus allowing submarines to pass undetected to the south and west of Svalbard."[30]

The failure of the attempted coup of August 1991 and the ensuing turmoil within the former Soviet Union could have been expected to lead to an early end to the submarine incursions. If they continued, control of Moscow's civilian leaders over their military commanders would appear to be even more suspect than some allege. Bureaucratic momentum might for a time account for the Russian navy's persistence in such activities, but while the former Soviet republics were frantically seeking economic assistance from all the industrialized countries it appeared to make no sense whatever.

It seemed to be no coincidence, as *Pravda* used to say, that the submarine sightings in Swedish waters apparently stopped shortly after the failed putsch in Moscow. Sweden's top military commander, General Bengt Gustafsson, told reporters in February 1992 that the last report of an unexplained intruder came in September 1991. He also said that officers of the Russian Baltic Sea Fleet continued to deny that their submarines were involved in any exercises inside Sweden's territorial waters. When those officers were shown evidence of a 1989 intrusion, they reportedly agreed that it suggested activity by a submarine but insisted that the vessel was not one of theirs. Gustafsson seemed to imply that the intruders might have been under the command of a military intelligence agency operating independently of the Baltic fleet.[31]

General Gustafsson's hopes for an end to the troublesome submarine incidents faded quickly as reports of new sightings began to accumulate and the Russo-Swedish negotiations on the matter bogged down. In September 1992, he termed one violation "the worst in 10 years."[32] Prime Minister Bildt himself supported the General's condemnation, pointing the finger of blame directly at the Russian authorities.[33] In February 1993, Bildt brought up the issue with President Boris Yeltsin, who reportedly acknowledged that intrusions into Swedish waters had been made by "underwater vehicles" but stopped short of admitting that the "vehicles" were Russian.[34]

Some Swedish sources continued to maintain that the reported sightings were "ghosts on the brain" of military leaders hoping to justify additional military expenditures. As detailed above, however, many serious analysts have concluded that something suspicious was going on under the sea in Sweden's territorial waters. Rear Admiral Claes Tornberg of the Royal Swedish Navy, writing in *U.S. Naval Institute Proceedings* in March 1991, summarized the situation as follows: "Of course, many reports are false. But the amount of hard evidence is so high that we have a fairly good picture of what is going on. We have:

- Sightings documented with photos;
- Active high- and low-frequency sonar contacts;
- Passive sonar contacts;
- Magnetic detection;
- Bottom tracks from special vehicles."[35]

The case is not closed, therefore. Meanwhile, the original submarine U-137, the famous "Whiskey on the Rocks," has been sold to a Swedish amusement park, where it will no doubt contribute to the innocent merriment of countless Swedish children.[36]

Notes — Chapter XV

1. *New York Times*, March 23, 1993.
2. *Foreign Broadcast Information Service*, March 26, 1992.
3. "Post Soviet Prospects," *Bulletin of Center for Strategic and International Studies*, Washington, D.C. No. 12, April 1992.

4. *Washington Post*, December 29, 1982.

5. Bjøl, *Nordic Security*, p. 21.

6. "Submarine Combat in the Ice," *U.S. Naval Institute Proceedings*, February 1992.

7. Steve Lindberg, "Submarine Incursions for Political Consumption," *Nordic Journal of Soviet and East European Studies*, 4#(1)(1987), 61.

8. Milton Leitenberg, *Soviet Submarine Operations in Swedish Waters 1980–1986* (New York: Praeger, 1987), 34.

9. Ibid., 43.

10. Wilhelm Agrell, "Soviet Strategy and War Planning in the North," *Nordic Journal of Soviet and East European Studies*, 4#(1)(1987), 83.

11. Ibid., 87.

12. Leitenberg, *Soviet Submarine Operations*, 54.

13. Ibid., 63.

14. Berner, *Soviet Policies Toward the Nordic Countries*, 132.

15. Leitenberg, *Soviet Submarine Operations*, p. 78.

16. Ibid., 79.

17. John Ausland, *Nordic Security and the Great Powers* (Boulder, Col.: Westview Press, 1986), 160.

18. Leitenberg, *Soviet Submarine Operations*, 102-3.

19. Ibid., p. 103.

20. Agrell, "Soviet Strategy and War Planning in the North," 89.

21. Ibid., 90.

22. Berner, *Soviet Policies Toward the Nordic Countries*, 140.

23. Ibid., 145.

24. Ibid.

25. Lindberg, "Submarine Incursions for Political Consumption," 64.

26. Ibid.

27. Ibid.

28. Ibid., 75.

29. Ibid., 76.

30. George Lindsey, *Strategic Stability in the Arctic* (London: IISS Adelphi Paper 241, 1989), 42.

31. *New York Times*, February 13, 1992.

32. *Svenska Dagbladet*, September 1, 1992.

33. *New York Times*, September 24, 1992.

34. *New York Times*, March 8, 1993.

35. *U.S. Naval Institute Proceedings*, March 1991.

36. Pierre Schori, speech at the Woodrow Wilson Center, Washington, D.C., March 3, 1992.

XVI

A New Era Emerges

This book began with Bismarck's dictum that geography is the only permanent element of international relations, a verity dramatically illustrated in Europe during the 1980s and one likely to apply equally well to the post-Cold War era. With the fundamental reorientation of Soviet foreign and domestic policy after 1985, the concomitant collapse of the Soviet Empire, the unification of Germany, and a much weakened central government in Moscow, the relationship of forces as the world knew it during the Cold War has been altered beyond recognition. Geography, however, remains unchanged.

The geography of Northern Europe provides some significant continuity for the new era. Scandinavia's population of about 23 million is spread over some of the most strategically sensitive real estate in the world, extending across the North Atlantic from the Russian border to within a few miles of Canadian territory. Denmark still sits astride the exits from the Baltic, European Russia's direct link with the rest of Europe and to North America. The Danes also continue to control access to Greenland and the Faeroes, while the Norwegians stretch over much of the strategic High North. The Nordic area thus remains the crossroads of Northern Europe for military as well as commercial traffic, and the strategic balance in the North will therefore continue to be of concern to Moscow and Washington, particularly as long as either side retains intercontinental nuclear weapons.

Northern Norway and the Norwegian Sea have generally been seen as the "northern flank" of the Alliance, with the rest of the Arctic as a strategic vacuum, a view that reflects a mercator projection and the perspective of those concerned with the defense of Europe; but as seen from a polar projection by those concerned with intercontinental war — the Strategic Air Command, the North American Aerospace Defense Command, the U.S. Navy, and other Western strategic planners — the Arctic forms a forward and central theater of operations. For aircraft or ballistic missiles, the shortest route between the two contending superpowers has been via the North Pole, and the ocean is deep enough in much of the Arctic region for nuclear submarines to operate under the protection of ice cover. It is not only the sea itself which is sensitive in such a context, of course, because shore stations which provide navigational, communications, and intelligence support are vital to military operations.

Viewed strategically across the top of the world, therefore, Northwestern Europe and the adjacent seas can be seen as NATO's eastern or right flank, rather than the northern flank, while the Pacific theater is the left flank, as George Lindsey has pointed out.[1] Planners in the USSR's Strategic Rocket Forces, Long Range Aviation, and navy naturally came to have a mirror image of this view.

Baltic Exits

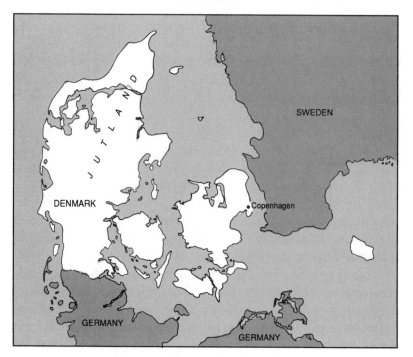

An Intercontinental Perspective — The Polar Projection

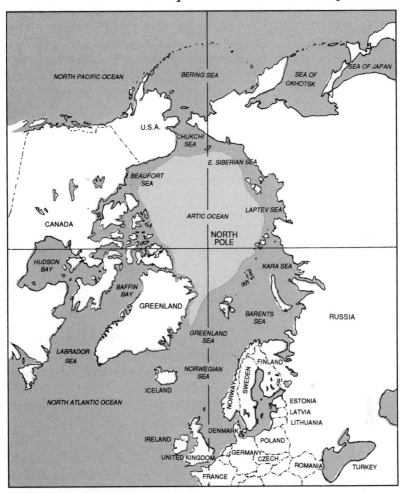

These perceptions on both sides have not changed very much in spite of the liberation of Eastern Europe from the Soviet yoke and the substantial cuts in nuclear forces under way in both East and West. Recognizing that the central front is no longer a primary source of concern, the U.S. has begun to withdraw the bulk of its conventional forces from the continent. The intermediate-range ballistic missiles deployed during the 1970s and 1980s are gone. But substantial cuts in Moscow's land-based multi-warhead ICBMs increase the significance of its submarine-based SLBMs, most of which remain concentrated in the Kola area.

The primary Soviet interest in the Nordic area was described by Johan Jørgen Holst a number of years ago as one of denial, i.e., preventing any of the Nordic states from becoming a base area for a major Western power. He concluded, therefore, "From the Soviet point of view the existing situation is probably tolerable or even satisfactory."[2] American leaders shared Moscow's relative satisfaction with the position of the Nordic states, as well as the desire that a prospective enemy not establish itself in Scandinavia. The "maritime strategy" proposed in the 1980s by U.S. Secretary of the Navy John Lehman would have concentrated U.S. naval forces in the northern seas rather than in support of NATO's continental strategy based on a forward defense in Central Europe, but it was not adopted. However, the unification of Germany and the dissolution of the Warsaw Pact, which has reduced the threat to NATO from central Europe and pushed Russia's defensive lines back to the eastern edge of the Baltic, could provide a new rationale for a maritime strategy. Alternatively, NATO might reconsider a peripheral defense strategy, anchored on bastions along NATO's flanks, as favored by General Eisenhower when he was Supreme Allied Commander in Europe.

The rapid evolution of Russian strategic thinking has also had implications for the Nordic area. Under Gorbachev, the reassessment of Moscow's real options rapidly accelerated and the impact of his "new thinking" on the Soviet army was felt as early as January 1987. As Michael MccGwire has shown, the CPSU Central Committee instructed the Soviet military at that time to develop plans and reformulate doctrine to reflect the assumption that world war could and would be averted by political means, an assumption which was later reflected in a Warsaw Pact statement.[3] The worst case contingency of global war was thus replaced by the more limited contingency of conflict on the Soviet periphery.

Jettisoning the requirement to prepare for global war, coupled with the concept of "military sufficiency," then opened the way to substantial cutbacks in Soviet nuclear and conventional armaments, as reflected in the INF, Conventional Forces in Europe (CFE), and START agreements. MccGwire's conclusion has been confirmed more recently by a number of Soviet military leaders, for example Rear Admiral Yuri Korshunov.[4]

But not all of the USSR's military leaders were prepared to accept the enormous strategic and operational changes imposed on them under Gorbachev's introduction of *perestroika, glasnost,* and "new thinking." Midway through the Gorbachev era, the Baltic states took on a critical dimension as some Soviet leaders became concerned over the dangers involved if the Baltic states were to succeed in breaking away from the USSR. Some senior military figures, along with former Prime Minister Pavlov and KGB chief Kryuchkov, who were later key conspirators in the August 1991 coup attempt, claimed they saw Western plots to undermine the Soviet Union. Viktor Alksnis, an air force officer of Latvian descent, told the USSR Supreme Soviet in November 1990 that Soviet military intelligence had evidence of a CIA plan to create a new confederation comprising the Baltic States, the Ukraine, and Byelorussia, invoking Moscow's persistent fears of a new *cordon sanitaire* sealing Russia off from Western Europe.

Such claims reflected the coming fragmentation of the Soviet Union rather than a new threat from the West. The referendum of March 1991 on Gorbachev's appeal to the republics to stick together in a revised Soviet Union was boycotted entirely by six of the fifteen republics. At the end of April, Gorbachev and representatives of the nine remaining republics, (three Slav and six Muslim) signed what became known as the "Nine Plus One Agreement," which promised substantial powers to the republics. A broader group of thirteen, including all but Estonia and Georgia, agreed in May to work together in the implementation of an emergency plan to steer the country out of its economic crisis. Even Lithuania accepted "observer" status to these talks.

But in April, Soviet military units, in reaction to the perceived threat to Soviet unity from Baltic aspirations for independence, had resumed harassment of the Baltic peoples. Bloody attacks, some of which seemed to be timed to embarrass President Gorbachev, were carried out by the "black berets" of OMON. However, the clearly inopportune nature of the attacks from Gorbachev's point of view lent credence to the Soviet leader's denials of responsibility for the incidents in Vilnius and Riga earlier in the year. In spite of the brutal attempts of the MVD and the Soviet army to throttle nationalist sentiment in the Baltic republics, the Lithuanians, closely followed by the Estonians and

Latvians, continued to demand an early end to their loveless marriage with the USSR.

The formal signing of the Nine Plus One Agreement, scheduled for August 20, 1991, precipitated the abortive putsch on August 19, which led with breathtaking speed to the collapse and dissolution of the USSR. Although rescued temporarily by Boris Yeltsin and his supporters, Gorbachev was forced from office in December. The Baltic states were recognized as independent, and Yeltsin began his struggle to rally together as many as possible of the other republics in a "Commonwealth of Independent States."

Russia and the other former republics of the USSR are now passing through the greatest social upheaval since the Bolshevik Revolution, with occasional echoes of the "Time of Troubles" which followed the death of Boris Godunov in 1605. Nationalist fervor and democratic institutions may not yet be ready to coexist on the Eurasian vastness of the former USSR. Even the Russian Federation may fracture; autonomous regions within the federation, such as Tataria and Yakutia, which possess valuable supplies of energy and other natural resources, may reject Moscow's control over those resources. At the same time, the need for a strong fist to rule Russia is an article of faith throughout the country and a return to frankly authoritarian rule cannot be excluded.

Whatever the course of events in Russia and the former Soviet Union, geography dictates that the Nordic and Baltic peoples will continue, for better or worse, to reside next door to a large and powerful population of Slavs. With the end of the Communist régime, the Nordic countries can expect a fair measure of respect from the Slavic populations: in spite of Moscow's propaganda to keep them ignorant, Soviet citizens were well aware of the gap between their living standards and those of their Nordic neighbors. Unable to migrate to Scandinavia, many of them made their way to the Baltic states, which they considered the best available alternative. Soviet public recognition and appreciation for the Scandinavian system was reflected in a poll of July 1991 in which less than a quarter of those polled favored "a free-market form of capitalism such as found in the U.S. or Germany" and the majority voted instead for "a more democratic type of socialism," especially "a modified form of capitalism such as found in Sweden."[5] This view may exaggerate the differences between the German and Swedish economic systems, but it is indicative of a receptivity on the part of the Soviet public to the Nordic way.

Indeed, despite recent economic stringencies, the Nordic countries remain among the world's most prosperous. Norway and, to a lesser extent, Denmark have benefited from important oil finds in the North Sea; the others are less well endowed with natural resources, but all share an educated and able workforce. The International Human Suffering Index rated Denmark the world's most comfortable country in 1992, and its Nordic neighbors followed closely behind.

The Nordic countries have also played a prominent role in East-West arbitration, elaborating and protecting "the CSCE process" and the "spirit of Helsinki," both before and since the signing of the Helsinki Final Act in 1975. Whether as members of the NATO caucus or as leaders of the neutral and non-aligned countries, the Nordic states have been second to none in their emphasis on human rights as a basic element in preserving international peace. The Charter of Paris, signed by the leaders of all the CSCE participating states on November 21, 1990, with its emphasis on democracy, the rule of law, and friendly relations among states, looms as a monument to Nordic ideals. Together with Sweden and Finland, moreover, the NATO Nordic governments made an important contribution to the successful conclusion in 1986 of the Stockholm Conference on Confidence and Security Building Measures and Disarmament. They have also played a key role in organizing the North Atlantic Cooperation Council as a forum which brings together the members of NATO and the members of the former Warsaw Pact.

Throughout the Cold War, there were recurrent concerns among NATO leaders that the USSR might be able to neutralize the Alliance by exploiting Western fears of nuclear war to support Soviet campaigns for nuclear-free zones and similar actions. Often triggered by periodic demonstrations of Moscow's willingness to use military force to accomplish its objectives, such concerns sometimes led to charges that the Soviet Union was using Western peace movements to "Finlandize" Western Europe, lending the term a pejorative flavor to which Finns objected very strongly. But the Soviet failure in the early 1980s to prevent the deployment of American intermediate range nuclear missiles in Western Europe finally demonstrated the limits on Moscow's ability to affect

Western policy through the manipulation of public opinion. Meanwhile, a similar fatigue from nuclear confrontation, combined with the growing disparity of living standards between Eastern and Western Europe, had lured Warsaw Pact countries away from the Soviet embrace and made Western trade and economic cooperation more important than socialist solidarity. In the end, it was the East — not the West — Europeans that gravitated toward the other camp.

Scandinavia's NATO members now appear to be even more confirmed in their adherence to the Western Alliance than they were during the Cold War years. Earlier hopes for an entirely Scandinavian solution to their security problems expired in the wake of the failed Nordic Defense Pact negotiations in 1948-49, and even the NATO members among the Scandinavian countries are reluctant to leap into a new defense arrangement with Western Europe under the Western European Union, close as their economic and political ties are becoming. NATO's Nordic allies continue to value the link with the United States and do not want to be forced to choose between North America and Europe. Indeed, some Scandinavians still feel that they have more in common with their allies across the Atlantic than with those in Southern Europe.

Meanwhile, an enlarged and further empowered European Community continues to define itself, extending its writ almost to the borders of the Russian republic. Europe's sense of a common identity still grows, if haltingly, dramatized by the projects under way to build physical as well as symbolic bridges between the continent and its periphery. Work is currently proceeding, not only on the "Chunnel" between France and England, but on three large projects bridging Europe to Scandinavia, all of them anchored in Denmark. Despite considerable public skepticism, the Norwegian Government reopened membership negotiations with the EC in April 1993, soon after having received consultative status in the Western European Union, the military bridge between the EC and NATO. But Iceland's unwillingness to give up its exclusive fishing rights within the 200–mile zone around the island and its concern that European investors might take over local land and businesses have limited its interest in EC membership.

As for the non-NATO states, Sweden applied for admission to the EC in June 1991, casting aside its previous doubts about the incompatibility of EC membership with its neutrality. Finland hesitated, however, concerned over the growing military cooperation, via the WEU, in the EC's overall pan-European approach. For a time, the Finns hoped that the projected drawing together of a rump EFTA and the EC would provide an alternative in which to grow as part of a real "European Economic Area." Even after their application to join the EC in March 1992, many Finns, like Icelanders, remained concerned that membership will leave their forests and other natural resources open to exploitation by outsiders.

Helsinki's closer association with Western Europe followed shortly after a basic revision of its relationship with Moscow. President Gorbachev had, in 1989, categorically endorsed Finland's status as a fully neutral state, and the following year, Helsinki unilaterally reinterpreted the Paris Peace Treaty of 1947 to remove the treaty's restrictions on Finland's armed forces and its relations with Germany. Subsequently, Finland exercised its new freedom of action in defense procurement by ordering American F/A-18 fighter aircraft and by purchasing important quantities of arms from Germany — mostly from the stocks of the German Democratic Republic's defunct People's Army.

The revamped Fenno-Russian relationship was formalized in a new treaty which accompanied an exchange of notes on January 20, 1992, declaring that the 1948 Fenno-Soviet Treaty on Friendship, Co-operation and Mutual Assistance ceased to be in force, not only with Russia but also with "all other States which formerly constituted the Union of Soviet Socialist Republics." Finns were probably amused when the new treaty was hailed by the Russia's Deputy Foreign Minister, Boris Kolokolov, as "de facto recognition of Russia as a sovereign independent state."

The new treaty has quite a different tone from that reflected in the 1948 pact, beginning with Article 1 which bases the agreement on the UN Charter and the Final Act of the CSCE, which, in turn, provides for peaceful changes in international frontiers so that the new treaty could provide for a renegotiation of Finland's borders in Karelia and the Petsamo area. The 1948 treaty required Finland, in the event of an armed attack by Germany or any state allied with it, to fight to repel the attack, if necessary with the assistance of, or jointly with, the Soviet Union. It also required the two contracting parties to confer with each other in case of the threat of such an armed attack. The new treaty, in contrast, requires the two parties, in situations where international peace or security is endangered, simply "to contact each other, as necessary, with the purpose of using the means offered by the United Nations and the CSCE in the settlement of the conflict."

Even more striking is Article 6, calling for the promotion of "co-operation between Finland and the adjacent neighboring regions of Murmansk, Karelia and St. Petersburg," an invitation to Finland to extend technical and developmental aid to the troubled economies of adjacent Russian areas. Separate treaties cover such aid as well as trade and economic cooperation between Finland and Russia. Treaty language calling attention to the "rich traditions of the mutual interaction among their peoples" must sound ironic to the Finns and other neighbors of the former USSR; on the other hand, Article 10 could contribute to improved regional relationships by committing both parties to "preservation of the identity of Finns and Finno-Ugric peoples and nationalities in Russia and, correspondingly in Finland, the identity of persons originating in Russia." These pledges on preserving ethnic identities and promoting mutually beneficial economic relations among the neighboring areas have obvious relevance for Russian relations with the Baltic states, which gained large numbers of Russian residents after World War II.

In the case of Northern Europe generally, it appears that the past may in fact be paradigm as well as prologue. Geologists tell us that the Scandinavian peninsula is still rising very gradually toward the level it had before the last ice age, and a similar phenomenon may be taking place in the political sphere with the re-emergence of an age-old relationship among the peoples of the Baltic Sea and the High North. Its peoples — Slav, German, Baltic, and Nordic — have struggled with one another through the centuries for hegemony over the Baltic Sea and the Scandinavian peninsula as well as for national identity and independence.

The Baltic peoples cannot escape the geographic realities that have made their area a contested marchland for 1,000 years, nor can they escape the general trend in the industrialized world toward interdependence. The Baltic countries, like Finland, are well aware of their close economic and personal ties with Russia, whose proximity and resources could, in time, help the Baltic countries to modernize and expand their economic infrastructures to compete on a more equal basis with the advanced countries of Western Europe. The collapse of the Soviet economy underlined the extent to which Finland's prosperity, and the comparative well-being in the Baltic states, had depended on access to the relatively cheap energy and undemanding consumer markets of its giant neighbor. Economic as well as geographic considerations will argue for continued close relationships with their Slavic neighbors and with the other former Soviet republics.

But the Baltic states, with their well-located ports and Hanseatic history, should find no major impediment to comparable links with their Western neighbors as well. Together with such nascent democracies as Poland, Czechoslovakia, and Hungary, the Baltic states could be a new middle-European bridge linking the Germanic lands to the successor states of the USSR. Indeed, Lithuania now separates the Kaliningrad (Königsberg) district and its valuable port from Russia and the rest of the commonwealth. Kaliningrad, which became part of Russia as a consequence of Nazi Germany's defeat in 1945, is ice-free in winter, and of considerable strategic importance as Russia's most westerly naval base in the Baltic. Thus Moscow will believe it must maintain access to Kaliningrad *oblast* by land and air, to supplement links by sea. Königsbergers aspire to more autonomy and the creation of a free port like prewar Danzig might be a solution, but it might also gravely complicate matters. Moscow's interest in using the Lithuanian port of Klaipeda and other ports in the Baltic republics should be much less of a problem. Use of their largely commercial facilities would be to the mutual economic advantage of all parties.

The old equilibrium in the North is now being replaced by a new but not necessarily a more stable one. This new configuration involves a unified Germany and a truncated Russia, at least temporarily in disarray, plus several newly independent but old nationalities which inhabit the territories between them. In this new situation, the Baltic states may come to appreciate the postwar experience of the Nordic peoples, especially the Finns, whose relationship with Russia has some resemblance to their own.

In retrospect, it is clear that Helsinki's prudent regard for Soviet perceptions during the Cold War was only one end of a continuum stretching across all of Scandinavia. The twin facets of this Nordic approach to relations with the USSR were reassurance and deterrence. Finland stressed reassurance while Norway emphasized deterrence; Sweden tried to balance the two as evenly as possible; the more nuanced Danish and Icelandic positions tended to fall in between those of Sweden and Norway. All of them, however, tried to emulate the Norwegian slogan calling for a maximum of deterrence with a minimum of provocation.

In support of such a stance by the Baltic states, Poland could perhaps play a balancing role similar to that formerly played by Sweden between Russia and the West. In the new equilibrium, Germany would constitute a buttress for the Western position, support for which would extend back to the United States and Canada. Continued Western cooperation with Russia and the other former republics of the USSR could help strengthen Baltic independence and prosperity.

Just as justice is often found in the interstices of the law, current strivings for national independence may find their fulfillment in the interstices of a future, less rigid and less polarized international system. The failed August putsch in the USSR revealed that the fissures in the Soviet Union were even wider than anticipated. Just as the Finns in 1917 gained their independence in the streets of Petrograd as well as in Helsinki, the liberty of the Baltic peoples in 1991 was won in the streets of Moscow as well as in Vilnius, Riga, and Tallinn. Lithuanian resistance to the imposition of a National Salvation Committee in January 1991 and their stand in front of the Parliament in Vilnius, in turn, contributed to the anti-coup movement in Moscow. According to the testimony of members of the elite KGB "Alpha" group, the opprobrium heaped on the units participating in the January attacks in Vilnius was one of the factors leading to their refusal to attack the Russian Parliament in August 1991.[6]

The disintegration of the Soviet Union, which Russian Foreign Minister Andrei Kozyrev accurately described as "a tectonic shift" in the world's political landscape,[7] seems to warrant a review of the American position in Scandinavia, as well as in other areas. Whereas the Nordic and Baltic countries were either spoken for or off limits during the Cold War, the new era provides opportunities for new relationships and increased cooperation. The United States could, for example, join the Nordic countries in a common endeavor to facilitate the emergence in the new Eurasia of democratic governments and societies. Some of this cooperation could continue in multilateral fora, such as The World Bank, the United Nations, and the CSCE, but there is ample room for new bilateral and regional initiatives as well, building positively on the long-established relationship of the Scandinavians and the Slavs.

Geography may be the only feature of international relations which does not change, but there are some other aspects which seem worth preserving despite the fundamental changes of recent years. The way the Nordic countries managed to maintain regional equilibrium over the nearly fifty years of international tensions that marked the Cold War may prove the best way to achieve a Baltic equilibrium in the new era as well.

Notes — Chapter XVI

1. Lindsey, *Strategic Stability in the Arctic*, p. 5.
2. Johan Jørgen Holst, ed., *Five Roads to Nordic Security* (Oslo: Universitetsforlaget, 1973), 4.
3. Michael MccGwire, paper presented at World Congress of the ICSEES at Harrowgate, England, July 1990.
4. *Krasnaya Zvesda*. November 14, 1991.
5. *New York Times*, July 15, 1991.
6. *Washington Post*, September 27, 1992.
7. Andrei Kozyrev, "Russia: A Chance for Survival," *Foreign Affairs* (Spring 1992), 1.

Selected Bibliography

Almdahl, Preben. *Aspects of European Integration: a View of the European Community and the Nordic Countries*. Odense, Denmark: Odense University Press, 1966.

Amundsen, Kirsten. *Norway, NATO, and the Forgotten Soviet Challenge*. Berkeley: Institute of International Studies, 1981.

Andrew, Christopher, and Oleg Gordievsky. *KGB*. New York: HarperCollins, 1990.

Ausland, John. *Nordic Security and the Great Powers*. Boulder, Colo.: Westview Press, 1986.

Bayer, James A., and Nils Ørvik. *The Scandinavian Flank as History*. Kingston, Ontario, Canada: Center for International Relations, 1984.

Beloff, Max. *The Foreign Policy of Soviet Russia*. 2 vols. London: Oxford University Press, 1956.

Berner, Örjan. *Soviet Policies Toward the Nordic Countries*. Lanham, Md.: University Press of America, 1986.

Bilmanis, Alfred. *A History of Latvia*. Princeton: Princeton University Press, 1951.

Bjøl, Erling. *Nordic Security*. IISS Adelphi Paper 181, London: Spring 1983.

_____, ed. *Danmark og NATO*. Copenhagen: Gyldendal, 1968.

Bogomolov, O. T. *Sotsialisticheskoe Sodruzhestvo i Problemy Otnosheniy Vostok-Zapada v 80e Gody*. Moscow: Politizdat, 1987.

Calcovoressi, Peter, and Guy Wint. *Total War*. New York: Penguin Books, 1979.

Chernysheva, O. V. *Shvetsia v Gody Vtoroi Mirovoi Voiny*. Moscow: Izdatelstvo Nauka, 1980.

Churchill, Winston S. *The Second World War*. 6 vols. Boston: Houghton Mifflin, 1948.

Clemens, Walter C., Jr. *Baltic Independence and Russian Empire*. New York: St. Martin's Press, 1991.

Craig, Gordon A. *Germany, 1866–1945*. New York: Oxford University Press, 1978.

Croft, Stuart. *The Impact of Strategic Defenses*. IISS Adelphi Paper 238, London: Spring 1989.

De Porte, A. W. *Europe Between the Superpowers*. New Haven: Yale University Press, 1986.

Derry, Thomas K. *A History of Modern Norway, 1814-1972*. Oxford: Clarendon Press, 1973

Ferro, Marc. *The Great War, 1914–1918*. London: Unwin, 1977.

Florinsky, Michael T. *Russia: A History and an Interpretation*. 2 vols. New York: Macmillan, 1955.

Gaddis, John Lewis. *The United States and the Origins of the Cold War, 1941–1947*. New York: Columbia University Press, 1972.

_____. *Strategies of Containment*. New York: Oxford University Press, 1982.

Garthoff, Raymond L. *Detente and Confrontation — American-Soviet Relations From Nixon to Reagan*. Washington: Brookings, 1985.

Gorshkov, Sergei G. *The Sea Power of the State*. Malabar, Fla.: Krieger Publishing Co., 1979.

Hadenius, Stig. *Swedish Politics During the 20th Century*. Stockholm: The Swedish Institute, 1990.

Haagerup, Niels J. *A Brief Introduction to Danish Foreign Policy and Defence*. Copenhagen: Forsvarets Oplysnings-og Velfaerdstjeneste, 1975.

Hart, B. H. Liddell. *History of the Second World War*. London: Pan Books, 1974.

Heclo, Hugh, and Henrik Madsen, eds. *Policy and Politics in Sweden: Principled Pragmatism*. Philadelphia: Temple University Press, 1987.

Heisler, Martin O., ed. *The Nordic Region: Changing Perspectives in International Relations*. Newbury Park, CA.: Annals of the American Academy of Political and Social Science, November 1990.

Holst, Johan Jørgen. *Five Roads to Nordic Security*. Oslo: Universitetsforlaget, 1973.

Holst, Johan Jørgen, Kenneth Hunt, and Anders C. Sjaastad, eds. *Deterrence and Defense in the North*. Oslo: Norwegian University Press, 1985.

Hough. Jerry. *Russia and the West: Gorbachev and the Politics of Reform*. New York: Simon and Schuster, 1988.

Huldt, Bo, and Atis Llejins, eds. *Security in the North — Nordic and Superpower Perceptions*. Stockholm: Swedish Institute of International Affairs, 1984.

Hyland, William. *Mortal Rivals*. New York: Random House, 1987.

Jensen, Bent. *Sovjetunionen og Danmark*. Copenhagen: Det Udenrigspolitiske Selskab, 1987.

_____. *Tryk og Tilpasning: Sovjetunion og Danmark Siden 2 Verdenskrieg.* Copenhagen: Gyldenal, 1987.

Jervell, Sverre, and Kare Nyblom, eds. *The Military Buildup in the High North: American and Nordic Perspectives.* Lanham, Md.: University Press of America, 1986.

Jones, Gwyn. *A History of the Vikings.* New York: Oxford University Press, 1984.

Jutikkala, Eino, and Kauko Pirinen. *A History of Finland.* New York: Dorset Press, 1988.

Kaslas, Bronis J. *The Baltic Nations.* Pittston, Pa.: Euramerica Press, 1976.

Kennedy, Paul M. *The Rise and Fall of British Naval Mastery.* Malabar, Fla.: Robert E. Krieger, 1982.

Kennan, George F. *Russia and the West Under Lenin and Stalin.* Boston: Atlantic Monthly Press, 1960.

Kissinger, Henry. *White House Years.* Boston: Little, Brown & Co., 1979.

_____. *Years of Upheaval.* Boston: Little, Brown & Co., 1982.

Laar, Mart. *War in the Woods: Estonia's Struggle for Survival.* Washington, D.C.: Compass Press, 1992.

Larsen, Karen. *A History of Norway.* Princeton: Princeton University Press, 1948.

Lauring, Palle. *A History of Denmark.* Copenhagen: Höst amd Son, 1960.

Leitenberg, Milton. *Soviet Submarine Operations in Swedish Waters, 1980–1986.* Washington: Center for Strategic and International Studies, 1987.

Lindsey, George. *Strategic Stability in the Arctic.* IISS Adelphi Paper 241. London, Summer 1989.

Misiunas, Romuald J., and Rein Taagepera. *The Baltic States: Years of Dependence, 1940-1980.* Berkeley: University of California Press, 1983.

Moberg, Vilhelm. *A History of the Swedish People.* 2 vols. New York: Dorset Press, 1989.

Möttöla, Kari, O. N. Bykov, and I. S. Korolev. *Finnish-Soviet Economic Relations.* London: Macmillan, 1983.

Nilsson, Gunnar, chairman. *Sweden's Security Policy: Entering the 90s.* Stockholm: Report by the 1984 Defence Committee, 1985.

Ørvik, Nils. *Semialignment and Western Security.* New York: St. Martin's Press, 1986.

Ovinnikov, P.D. *Zigzagi Vneshney Politiki C SH A.* Moscow: Politizdat, 1986.

Penttilä, Risto E. J. *Finland's Search for Security through Defence, 1944–89.* New York: St. Martin's Press, 1991.

Puntila, L.A. *The Political History of Finland, 1809-1966.* London: Heineman, 1975

Riasanovsky, Nicholas V. *A History of Russia.* New York: Oxford University Press, 1984.

Ries, Thomas. *The Nordic Dilemma in the 80s — Maintaining Regional Stability Under New Strategic Conditions.* Geneva: Programme for Strategic and International Security Studies, 1982.

Riste, Olav., ed. *Western Security: The Formative Years.* New York: Columbia University Press, 1985.

Ross, Steven T. *European Diplomatic History, 1989–1815.* Malabar, Fla.: Robert E. Krieger, 1981.

Senn, Alfred Erich. *The Emergence of Modern Lithuania.* New York: Columbia University Press, 1959.

Seton-Watson, Hugh. *The Russian Empire, 1801–1917.* Oxford: Clarendon Press, 1990.

Scott, Franklin D. *Sweden, The Nation's History.* Carbondale: Southern Illinois University Press, 1988.

Singleton, Fred. *A Short History of Finland.* Cambridge: Cambridge University Press, 1989.

Sundelius, Bengt. ed. *Foreign Policies of Northern Europe.* Boulder: Westview Press, 1982.

Tamnes, Rolf. *The United States and the Cold War in the High North.* Cambridge: University Press, 1991.

Taylor, William J., and Paul M. Cole, eds. *Nordic Defense — Comparative Decision Making.* Lexington, Mass.: Lexington Books, 1985.

Thomas, Hugh. *Armed Truce.* New York: Atheneum, 1987.

Tomasson, Richard F. *Iceland, The First New Society.* Minneapolis: University of Minnesota Press, 1980.

Turner, Barr. *The Other European Community — Integration and Cooperation in Nordic Europe.* New York: St. Martin's Press, 1982.

Ulam, Adam B. *The Rivals.* New York: Viking, 1971.

____. *Expansion and Coexistence — Soviet Foreign Policy 1917–73.* New York: Praeger, 1974.

____. *Dangerous Relations.* New York: Oxford University Press, 1983.

Vloyantes, John P. *Silk Glove Hegemony, Finnish-Soviet Relations, 1944-1974.* Kent State University Press, 1975.

Wahlbäck, Krister. *The Roots of Swedish Neutrality.* Stockholm: The Swedish Institute, 1986.

Wendt, Frantz. *Cooperation in the Nordic Countries — Achievements and Obstacles.* Stockholm: Almquist and Wiksell, 1981.

Index